When She Wakes, She Will Move Mountains

5 STEPS TO RECONNECTING WITH YOUR WILD, AUTHENTIC INNER QUEEN

Tanya Valentin

Green Empress
publications

Published by Green Empress Publications
Whangarei, New Zealand, 0172

www.tanyavalentin.co

Book and cover design by Leesa Ellis of **3 ferns books**
www.3fernsbooks.com

Front cover photo by Stacey Milich Smith
Author photo by Nykie Grove Eades

ISBN: 978-0-473-63494-0

Table of Contents

For Madi, Morgan, and Trinity.

For the little girl who believed in love and dreams coming true, and that one day her words would come to life on a page.

I hope that I made you proud.

For those who feel stuck and see no colour left in your days.

For the girls and women who have buried their witch marks and carry them on the inside.

For those waiting patiently for their time to awaken.

You are not alone.

You can rise.

Disclaimer

THIS WORK IS MY TRUTH and the witness statement of my own life and experiences. Other people who were part of these events may have different truths and I acknowledge this. Throughout this book I have tried my best to highlight this. This book describes my experience with anxiety, depression, and mental illness and how I used the powers of the feminine archetypes to live a **W**ild, **A**uthentic, **K**nowing, and **E**mpowered life. It is subjective to my view on life and may vary from other people's own experience.

I passionately believe that the first life we transform is always our own. And so, my intention with this book has been, first and foremost a tool, to help myself heal. A vehicle me to process my hurt, fear, and shame; to rise above it. In essence, this is my hero's journey. This book was born out purpose and aspiration—a wish—that through the sharing of my journey, I will appeal to our shared common humanity. Although this is my story, there will be some glimpses of mirrored truth that may touch you on a soul level. After all, true empathy is not sharing the same experience but rather the sharing of emotions that the experience evokes.

It is my fervent desire that my life lessons will awaken hope inside of you and shall help to communicate that through it all, you are not alone. Everybody struggles from time to time but just know that you too can heal.

This book is not to be used in place of medical advice and/or relied upon in this way. The methods described in this book are of the author's own opinion. The results from using any methods described in the book may vary depending on your personal life experiences. This book does not guarantee results. If you or someone you know is suffering from mental illness, please consult with trained medical professionals.

under the loving gaze of the full moon
they come

the young and the wise
the here and the now

women who heed the call of the awake
with laughing and chanting they tread

dancing with lightness of step
the blessed and the free

to sit in a circle with kin
and step the sacred ground

where the wild women walk
— where the wild women walk

Introduction

We are all born awake.

We enter into this world completely connected to the purest and truest versions of ourselves. Somehow over the minutes, hours, days, and years of our existence, we disconnect from ourselves and are lulled into a deep slumber. A sleep where everything is grey. Where we find a multitude of ways to numb down, dumb down, and go through the motions of "life".

Alive but not really living.

How do I know this? I know this because I have lived such a half-life.

In 2006, I woke up with a hunch that things were not as they should be. To anyone outside looking in, it would have appeared that I was living an ideal life. I had a decent job, I was married to a good man and had two lovely children. We owned a nice house and drove pleasant cars. We hosted nice parties on weekends for our wonderful friends and we had enjoyable holidays. But on the inside, everything was anything but "good" or "nice". I was miserable, and I didn't know why.

I was the epitome of J D Salinger's quote, *"She wasn't doing a thing that I could see, except standing there leaning on the balcony railing, holding the universe together."* It was as if suddenly a warning light had switched on in my head and I couldn't figure out how to switch it off. I felt empty, unsatisfied, sad, and so, so lonely despite being surrounded by family and friends, yet they did not understand my distress. Slowly my mental health deteriorated, and I was eventually diagnosed with clinical depression. I felt a hunger— a spiritual hunger—and there was an immense void in place of where my joy and sense of purpose used to be.

I attempted everything to be able to fill the emptiness I felt inside. I repeatedly switched jobs hoping that it would spark a new passion in me. I gave birth again. I left my stable teaching job to open my own business which failed dismally. I racked up thousands of dollars' worth in debt trying to fill this void with materialistic stuff and I gained heaps of weight trying to stuff these feelings with food.

My marriage was in turmoil.

My husband and I argued endlessly.

My children sought refuge in their bedrooms.

I was in the valley of despair. *Had I wasted my life?* I felt the shadows of giant, formidable mountains tower over me and only I could see them.

I was stuck. I was lost.

I knew deep down there was this amazing, fulfilling, and abundantly creative life that I was desperate to live on the other side of these mountains. I only had to reach to that side. However, I had no idea how to move them and grasp onto the life I so greatly wanted. It wasn't until nearly ten years later that I stumbled across a path that led to my reawakening and the journey back to myself. This is where I discovered that I was my own biggest mountain and unlocked the secrets that were already inside of me. The secrets that would get myself unstuck and to start moving my mountains. In doing this I found the courage to speak up, reignite my joy, discover what my purpose for my life was, step into my power, and ultimately create a life that isn't perfect, but a life that I am excited to live to the fullest.

As I awakened, I spoke with women who shared a similar story. I heard and witnessed their struggles. I reflected on how this work had such a profound effect on my life, my purpose, and my relationships. I knew I could not sit silently on this gift I was given. I knew I had to share what I learnt through my own experience and use this to serve others. This inspired me to create my **AWAKEN**™ mentoring framework to support women in their own journey to reawakening in my online community for midlife women, **The Feminine School of Unlearning**. In this book, I share the path that I took with you to guide you to use the principles of the **AWAKEN**™ framework to wake, stir, rumble, and move the mountains in your life.

and if you must write it down

let it be art

let it be meandering prose bathed in warm dappled sunshine
and the hedonism of a long boozy summer lunch
decorated with the nectar of frilly words that delight on the tongue

but if it be art

then also give it space to be

awkward
jilted phrases
punctuated
with

.silence.

brutal
honest

chasing truth
harrowing the senses
hauntingly
lingering in the mists of thought and dream

Before We Start

I AM NOT A GURU NOR AM I AN ACADEMIC. I am just simply a woman who has walked a path, fuelled with an inner desire and curiosity to create a better life for herself. To be free from any suffering. This is the same path that each and every day I continue to walk imperfectly alongside my sisters of heart.

This book is just a tool—a key.

Take a moment to think about the keys you have in your life. Keys in themselves are neutral and, if you are like me, you may have collected many unused keys in your life. They may take up space in your "spare things" drawer, on the hooks where you hang your keys, or even on your keychain. These keys may have been used for places that you no longer have access to such as old parts of furniture that you discarded or houses that you no longer live in. Until you actually put a key in the hole it is meant for and turn it, it is useless and unnecessarily takes up space.

Books are the same, they are neutral.

I have often read a book and thought to myself, *'Wow that's interesting! I must remember that!'* And then when I finished reading the book and place it back on my bookshelf, I forget about it and again it unnecessarily takes up space. Like keys, books don't do the work. **YOU DO**. You can spend your life accumulating "keys" and "books". However, it is solely your decision whether you take the information you learnt and do something with it!

Firstly, in this spirit, I urge you to resist the temptation to rush through this book like a simple novel without doing the exercises included. Yet, if you rush through this book, the contents of this book may be interesting, entertaining, or even illuminating to you, but you will not benefit the whole experience from this book and the results that you might be looking for will be different if you do not complete the exercises. Secondly, the real secret to this work is that you are not lost. You have never left. Neither are you broken. You have everything you need inside of you just waiting to surface, this book is just a key to help you to unlock what is already inside of you.

James Clear, author of *Atomic Habits* says in his book,

"The two ideas sound similar, but they're not the same. When you're in motion, you're planning and strategizing and learning. Those are all good things, but they don't produce a result. Action, on the other hand, is the type of behaviour that will deliver an outcome. If I outline twenty ideas for articles I want to write, that's motion. If I actually sit down and write an article, that's action. If I search for a better diet plan and read a few books on the topic, that's motion. If I actually eat a healthy meal, that's action. Sometimes motion is useful, but it will never produce an outcome by itself. It doesn't matter how many times you go talk to the personal trainer, that motion will never get you in shape. Only the action of working out will get the result you're looking to achieve."

This book is designed to do its work in layers. To acquire the most out of it for your development, I suggest that the first time you read it, you follow the five steps outlined in the framework of this book. Begin with the archetypes of feminine energy, the dream of your domestication, and the awakening. Then explore your *Wild Self*, then your *Authentic Self*, then your *Knowing Self*, and finally your *Empowered Self*. Once you have completed the work, you can revisit the parts you felt held the most value for you as many times as you need to. I have found from personal experience, that persistently revisiting this work allows you to move deeper into yourself. During this book, I will prompt you with exercises under the title: **She AWAKES.** This will be your invitation to take actions that support your reawakening. I use the mediums of reflective questioning, art, poetry, creative writing, meditation, movement, and guided imagery designed to engage your mind, heart, soul, and body. Together with this, I invite you to purchase a beautiful, brand-new journal to complete your soulish work in. You can also follow this link to download the *AWAKENING* journal, which is the perfect companion to this book. This available at https://www.tanyavalentin.co/AWAKENING-Journal

For the creativity parts of this book, please keep paper, pens, crayons, and paints handy. I have also provided links throughout the book to access audio files to enrich your experience.

It has been my experience that many of us, (myself included), have endured numerous years of speaking negatively to ourselves in unloving and hurtful ways.

This is especially prevalent when we are challenged to shift outside of our comfort zones. An affirmation has been gifted to you along with each exercise to support you to speak to yourself with love, compassion, and kindness. I encourage you to write these affirmations down and place them around the house like little love notes to yourself, to remind you of your intentions of practising self-acceptance and self-love. To enrich this practice, you can access my *AWAKEN Your Queen I AM* guided meditation available at https://tanyavalentin.co/AWAKEN-Your-Queen

I encourage you to make it a daily habit to be around the healing balm of mother nature. This could entail tending to plants, spending time outside in your garden, going for a walk, visiting a park or the beach, watching a sun rise or set, or sitting under the moon.

A word of caution: the exercises in this book are designed to perform deep, inner-self work and it may stir up some emotions, memories, or revelations about yourself that did not anticipate, so please prepare yourself for this. In choosing to read this book and by doing cthe work together, we can step out of judgement and enter into a mutual agreement of respect, trust, courage, and curiosity. You first may feel some resistance to my invitations to be curious, playful, and creative. You may feel silly or think, *'I'm not an artist'* or *'I'm not a poet!'* If this happens for you, please recognise that this is your programming talking. We were all born with the ability to play and create. Children, regardless of the culture they were born into, naturally do this without prompting, censorship, or the worry that they will appear silly. You are no different, you haven't lost these aptitudes, you are just out of practice because they may not be something that you use regularly, we need to step outside of our comfort zones and awaken because only then does growth happen.

Guiding Principles

Before we start working together, I would like to set down some boundaries to keep you, the reader, safe and to correctly guide our work together. These principles are adapted from the work of *Dr Emmi Pikler*, a post-WWII Hungarian Paediatrician who created an intuitive and respectful way to nurture the body, mind, and the spirit of infants. Several of us, although some of us may already be grandmothers, we may not have received nurturing in a motherly way, and this has deeply wounded you, but it is never too late to mother yourself. So, I share these principles with you so you too can practice self-care and self-love.

Principle One: *Give Yourself Your Full Attention*

As you are reading and completing the work on these pages, give yourself permission to be your sole priority– to lovingly provide yourself with the gift of your full attention. Ensure to choose a quiet time when you know you will not be interrupted. Remove any distractions from the room. Turn your phone on silent, switch of any music or TVs. This is your time to receive the full expression of your love– a gift you are able to share so freely with others. This is your turn.

Principle Two: *Make Sure You Slow Down*

In the fast-paced environments we are surrounded by, our lives become so busy that we can so easily get caught up in the temptation to rush, compare, and compete. This is not one of those times. Take your time with this process. As I mentioned previously, resist the urge to rush, there is no competition or urgency to complete this work in a certain amount of time. Feel into yourself, go at your own pace, and trust the process.

Principle Three: *Build Trust and Your Relationship with Yourself During These Care-Giving Times*

Over time, through constant and repeated breaks of agreements that you have set with ourselves as well as perceived failures in life, we are often left with very little, or no trust left in ourselves. My mission is to support you in rebuilding that trust so you can fulfil a strong and rooted relationship with yourself again. I invite you to create a loving ritual around this. A "ritual" is an expression of love and self-care. By creating a ritual, you are in control of setting the loving intention of "Your Time". To establish a ritual, find a place to sit where you feel comfortable, make yourself your favourite drink, light a candle, and play soft music. Hold yourself gently in a bubble of love and self-compassion as you may or will be meeting parts of yourself that you have previously been at war with.

Principle Four: *Do Things "With" Yourself and Not "To" Yourself*

We frequently drown out what feels right for us and continue to do what we think we *"should"* be doing instead of doing what we *"know"* is right for us. Your work with this book will be no different. Possibly you will reach parts of this book which does not feel right for you and that's okay, learn to honour and respect that part of yourself. and my work here will be done! If something feels hard or wrong to you, I recommend for you to pause reading. Curiously and compassionately inquire into your inner self; journal, pray or meditate on why you found that part confronting and stirred up resistance in you. Only continue to read on when you are ready.

Principle Five: *Allow Yourself Freedom to Move*

During the process of life, we are constantly growing and evolving. Give permission to enjoy this freedom. Freedom to choose, freedom to think, freedom to feel, freedom to decide, freedom to grow, freedom to change, and freedom to become.

Principle Six: *Allow Yourself Uninterrupted Time for Play*

For me, "play" means any time you experience that beautiful, euphoric feeling of flow. You may have experienced this "flow" before, or being in the zone, while sharing laughing with friends, dancing, cooking, gardening, singing, painting, writing, sex, or exercising. Take moments to ponder on your favourite ways to experience this flow and be sure to plan more of these experiences during our work together. I invite you to approach this book with a sense of lightness, curiosity, experimentation, and joy. You are opening up your life to endless possibilities and I am so excited for you!

Principle Seven: *Our Bodies, Hearts, and Souls Continuously Sends Us Cues. Take Time to Tune in Respectfully*

Practicing self-care will protect your energy. You may feel slightly sensitive during this process. This is normal. You are entering yourself into a vulnerable territory so set your intentions and priorities to care for yourself as you would a loved one. If it feels right to get support, then you must seek support. You may want to discuss with a trusted family member or friend, or a heart sister about the things that you have discovered or have been awakened in you.

PART ONE

beautiful are the many seasons in a woman's life

coloured with the splendiferous hues
love
motherhood
hurt
pain
disappointment
self-loathing
self-love
losing oneself
finding oneself…

all are fiery trials
by which the precious metal of the woman appears

The Seven Archetypes of Feminine Energy

IF SOMEONE HASN'T TOLD YOU LATELY... You are amazing. You are beautiful, you are powerful, you are divine, you are a miraculous being just by being **YOU**!

It's very likely that you have lived through many versions of "you" and this message may have gotten lost along the way. However, just like our earth mother, we too have cycles, seasons, and reasons and we each have different energies for these cycles. In this section of the book, we will be digging into a powerful tool that you can use in the accepting and unravelling of "you". My intention with this section is to give you valuable insight into various energetic parts of being a woman. We will explore the exciting and intuitive, seven archetypes of feminine energy where we will explore the expression of these feminine powers.

According to Swiss psychiatrist, *Carl Jung*, archetypes are universal, instinctive models or personas that influence human behaviour. Since ancient times archetypes have been uses as a teaching tool to communicate certain truths to which we respond at a deep inner level. This supports us to awaken to a realisation about ourselves. Archetype psychology describes how we all have a natural masculine called the "animus", (which is our projection of what it means to be male and how we perceive male energies in ourselves. This is influenced by our dominant male figures in our formative years.), and seven feminine archetypes: the Maiden, the Huntress, the Mother, the Lover, the Wild Woman, the Wise Woman, and the Queen. There are a set of male archetypes, but we will only be exploring the feminine ones. I wanted to introduce these archetypes to you in the first section of this book as I hope it will be a helpful baseline in understanding each of these powerful female energies as we continue our adventure together.

The seven archetypes are the birth right of and are alive within every woman. We are naturally drawn to and associate with a few of the archetypes, usually one or two, that are stronger than the rest depending on our natural inclinations, our upbringing, the stage of life we are in, and where we are in our **awaken**ing journey. When we are living our wild, authentic, knowing, empowered selves, each of the seven archetypes work in harmony together. Archetypes are a useful tool to gain reflection on the qualities that we already possess, and the energy we want to cultivate more of.

Through archetypes, we can call in and embody certain types of energy to create the change we desire.

When I reflect on myself and the stage of life I am currently in, I see many attributes of the *Huntress* archetype. I am mission-focused, goal-oriented, and independent. I see attributes of the *Mother* archetype as I enjoy spending time nurturing my children, family, and friends as along with the various businesses that I have created over time. I identify strongly with the *Wild Woman* archetype with the yearning for solitary, deep introspection. I am learning to live in my truth, and to harness the wisdom of my *Wise Woman*. However, I find myself craving to connect more with my pleasure, sensuality, and creativity. I am learning to embody the energy of the *Lover*, as well as standing confidently in the sovereignty of being my *Queen*.

I have provided a brief explanation to each archetype in the chapters that follow this. Each chapter will conclude with a **"She AWAKES"** exercise to explore that archetype for yourself and her prevalence in your life. Every archetype is powerful and important in their own right. They also have a shadow side where we may be in the repressed, wounded, or unintegrated form of these archetypes. I mention in the chapter *Whole Woman*, shadow does not mean "bad" or "unworthy", and it is my mission to guide you to love and accept each part of you. Nevertheless, I mention them to give you the power of knowledge as the "shadow" can represent blind spots, woundings, emotional baggage, or the ways that you self-protect. Whenever we encounter a feeling of being lost or trapped it is generally because we are living in the wound or the shadow of these powerful feminine energies, sometimes without even knowing it. We allow them to control us, and we have not yet learnt how to integrate them and live into the healthy, empowered expression of these feminine forces. And so, I lovingly hold these up to you as a mirror for you to access parts of yourself to allow the healing to begin.

pristine
open pages
asking to be written on

how shall I initiate thee with ink?

what thoughts
what memories
will live on your pages?

I poise pen to page

but

stop
afraid of false starts

The Maiden

THE MAIDEN IS YOUTHFUL, ENTHUSIASTIC AND EXCITED ABOUT LIFE. Infused with the optimism of youth, she is energized and ready to take on the world. She has a carefree energy and is extremely trusting, receptive, curious, playful, and full of wonder. There are two parts to the Maiden; the uninitiated Maiden is the "nameless Maiden", she does not know who she is therefore she is extremely impressionable, malleable, and is easily shaped by those around her. There is a sense of naivety and innocence about her as she lacks life experience who is not yet jaded by the learning injuries of many lessons. In the myth of Persephone, the goddess who represents the Maiden, she was abducted by Hades, God of the Underworld, she was raped and forced to marry him. At the time of her rescue Hades had convinced her to eat pomegranate seeds. The consequence of this was that even though she was returned to her mother, Demeter, she was condemned to spend one third of every year with Hades as a guide for newcomers in the shadows of the underworld. The mature Maiden, Queen of the Underworld, was able to use the lessons gifted to her by her wounding's and shadows who became an intuitive and compassionate guide for others confronting their shadowed selves for the very first time. This represents the duality of a woman's nature. It also symbolises our journey from being premenstrual girls to becoming women after our first menstrual bleed and the wisdom that is handed down to us through this transition.

After going through a tough time where you have had to let a part of you die in order to embrace new versions of ourselves, the Maiden can represent or serve as a fresh start. The Maiden's greatest strengths are her empathy, optimism, creativity, and open receptiveness. the healthy embodiment of the Maiden's energy can represent the thrill of adventure, being open to new ideas, or starting something new. A mature Maiden is compassionate, creative, spiritual, and endued with deep reservoirs of inner strength. The shadowed side of the Maiden tends to be obedient, co-dependent, and a people-pleaser. The Maiden can live in a fantasy world, she is extremely trusting but does it blindly where she often gets hurt because of her naivety. To the unintegrated Maiden, fitting in is a priority and she will change anything herself to be liked and accepted by others. She finds it difficult to set personal boundaries and this leaves a gateway for others to use her or walk all over her as she has a hard time saying "no". In the wounded Maiden, a woman often casts herself as a victim. She can feel "powerless" to change your life or circumstance. She is waiting for someone's permission or for someone or something outside of herself to come along to save or fix her. One way to know that we fall into this is when we find ourselves pinning our successes or happiness on a person or an outcome, not on ourselves. We may find ourselves thinking, *'When I lose the weight… meet the right person… (fill in the blank) … then I will be happy'*.

If we have repressed our Maiden, we may feel that we have shut off our receptiveness towards others or new experiences. It's possible that you have lost the ability to laugh, play, or have fun. Many women in business have neglected their Maiden as they feel that they must conform to more male ways of leading or doing business. Through many years of caring for others, being weighed down by responsibilities, and putting ourselves last, we may have forgotten the simple joy of being present in the moments of light-hearted fun. This can portray you of being frightened to take on a new idea, change something or go on a new adventure. When we have a repressed Maiden, it can feel as if you have lost your youthful vitality, something that you remember being so alive in us before we became cynical and distracted by our daily living.

How to Embody This Archetype

1. Give yourself permission to be creative discover a new interest or rediscover an old one that you know previously gave you joy.

2. Make conscious choices and choose to do one thing just for yourself every week that energises you and brings alive in you a sense of fun.

3. Book yourself a weekend away by yourself or with some girlfriends to relax and rediscover the woman you were before you had the responsibilities of getting the dinner ready and making sure the kids were taken care of.

4. Tap into your inner *Maiden* and have some fun.

5. Be open and don't shy away from receiving support from the love and friendship of others.

She AWAKES: The Maiden

In your journal, reflect on and write down your experience with the Maiden archetype.

- **Do you resonate with the energy of the Maiden?**

- **What has been your experience with this archetype?**

- **In which ways do you embody the mature or healthy expression of the Maiden?**

- **In which ways do you embody the shadow, wounded, or repressed Maiden?**

- **In what ways can you nurture or rebalance this energy inside of you?**

Affirmation: *I am open to new experiences and adventures.*

the devoted in their sunday best
make their weekly pilgrimage
as I lie next to you
and worship at the altar of love

The Lover

THE LOVER IS A WOMAN WHO IS INNOVATIVELY CHARGED, playful, and confident with erotic and creative energy. The Lover is connected to her sensuality and her emotions. She is a transformative provocative force in a woman's life, filled with self-love and, and she continually seeks to connect with others to acquire a deep intimacy. The Lover has a deep desire to procreate and to create. Her motivation in life is to have fun and to enjoy the beauty of life indulging in her natural drive for pleasurable experiences. She holds a great passion for life, and magnetically draws others towards her. She loves being the centre of attention. Being connected to wealth and abundance; she attracts these things into her life. Women who embody the Lover archetype have a profound, emotional need for both freedom and connection. The strengths of the Lover are built from her passionate and creative nature in addition with their ability to seduce and arouse the sexual attraction and passion in others. The Lover craves to live in the moment, to enjoy life, and appreciates all it has to offer.

For the shadow or the wounded Lover, she uses her sexuality to manipulate others in order to get what she wants. She often will echo her self-destructive patterns such as indulging in many casual relationships combined with sexuality and infidelity which had stemmed from wounds in her past that she has yet to heal as she uses her sexuality transactionally. The Lover yearns to have control over situations and will attract drama and attention to boost her vanity and fragile self-esteem.

Due to pressures from cultural and societal forms along with trauma wounds, many women have buried their "Lover". During the childbearing and child-rearing years, women have reassigned the sexual parts of their bodies to mothering and many have come to see the act of sex as a chore rather than honouring their sexuality and viewing it as an act of "receiving". Slowly, this can allow us to become disconnected from our bodies and our sensuality. When we deny our Lover energy, it withholds our connection in the other areas of our life such as our creativity and being able to receive love from others and from ourselves. This can also hinder our ability to let go of previous hurt and enjoy life. In business, we can feel pressured to fit into the male-dominated "norms" of what leadership should look like and act out of alignment with our feminine gifts and intuition.

How to Embody This Archetype

1. Put on your favourite music, close your eyes and just dance. Allow the music to move through you. Take up a dance class or create a *Lover* playlist.

2. Wear clothes that make you feel beautiful and confident.

3. Creatively paint or draw anything that comes to your mind.

4. Indulge in delicious foods that you enjoy. Prepare your favourite meal for yourself, serve yourself and mindfully savour each mouthful.

5. Take yourself on a *masturdate* to dine in your favourite restaurant. Give yourself permission to order anything on the menu and bask in some well-deserved alone time. Or you can spend some alone time indulging in self-pleasure.

6. Declutter your lingerie drawer and treat yourself to something that makes you feel wild and sexy.

7. Soak up in romantic or erotic poetry or fiction book.

8. Play out or indulge in one of your fantasies.

9. Plan a romantic weekend away for yourself and/or with your lover.

10. Send someone a love letter or you can even send a love letter to yourself.

She AWAKES: The Lover

In your journal, reflect on and write down your experience with the Lover archetype.

- **Do you resonate with the energy of the Lover?**

- **What has been your experience with this archetype?**

- **In which ways do you embody the mature or healthy expression of the Lover?**

- **In which ways do you embody the shadow, wounded, or repressed Lover?**

- **In what ways can you nurture or rebalance this energy inside of you?**

Affirmation: *I am allowed to have fun and to feel good.*

when you were in my belly
I cradled you in my womb
as you fluttered like a butterfly
under my heart

I read to you
poetry
rhymes
and stories about princesses
and dragons in faraway lands

I imagined all the places you would go
who you would be
what you would do

The Mother

The Mother is nurturing, abundant, and generous. She is a natural caretaker who is gentle, compassionate, and she lives to care and support others. The Mother is bursting with fertility, and she has the maternal drive to provide for her loved ones. Embodying the Mother archetype means embracing motherhood, giving birth and nurturing children. Yet, it can also mean sustaining what you've already created as well as looking after other family members, friends, and pets. This could be nurturing a new business venture, helping out an extended family member or friends, or putting your time into a creative project. The strengths of the Mother archetype is her persistence, her sense of duty and responsibility, her nurturing nature, and her grounded and compassion. Mother's love to create with their hands and ensure that everyone is well taken cared for.

The Mother who is shadowed or wounded will tend to over-give. She will lack boundaries, control, co-dependency, she will neglect herself and can experience a loss of self. Mothers can have a tendency to take on everyone else's problems as if they are her own and this will weigh heavily on her. The Mother usually longs to control others around her, and, like the Maiden, Mothers can be extremely concerned about the judgement of others around her. This can be mirrored in our tendency to "mother" others in our work and social environments. The Mother can struggle greatly to let her children grow up and/or allow others to take care of her physical or metaphorical children. Many women identify strongly with the Mother archetype, especially during our "mothering" years. However, our own ability to heal our mother wound, can interfere with our ability to fully embrace this energy in ourselves and our relationships. It's possible that this energy is suppressed, and we risk passing down our "wounded" Mother down to our children.

As mentioned above, it's natural for the Mother archetype to be giving in nature and extremely emotionally available. If we over-identify with the Mother, there is a chance that we will neglect our own needs, deplete our energy and lose our own identity. We are inclined to judge ourselves harshly and base our worth on the roles we play for others and end up finding that self-love and self-nurturing very challenging. Mothers may need to learn how to use some of the mothering energy they project onto others and use it for mothering themselves.

How to Embody This Archetype

1. Give yourself time to reflect on and heal your Mother wound. Spend time "mothering" yourself.

2. Nurture and care for your loved ones.

3. Take time to clean and declutter your home.

4. Plant some seeds to grow a garden or nourish your plants.

5. Get your hands dirty, literally by creating something with your hands or figuratively by starting a project you are passionate about.

6. Spend time relaxing in nature by going to a forest, a garden or the beach and allow yourself to connect with Mother Earth.

7. Tap into your instincts and natural resourcefulness.

She AWAKES: The Mother

In your journal, reflect on and write down your experience with the Mother archetype.

- **Do you resonate with the energy of the Mother?**

- **What has been your experience with this archetype?**

- **In which ways do you embody the mature or healthy expression of the Mother?**

- **In which ways do you embody the shadow, wounded, or repressed Mother?**

- **In what ways can you nurture or rebalance this energy inside of you?**

Affirmation: *I am worthy to receive the same love that I give to others.*

words written on paper

sentences said out loud
quick to hit their mark

I have survived my worst days

and still I stand

The Huntress

THE HUNTRESS IS AN INDEPENDENT SPIRIT who pursues a life of her own, and on her own terms. She represents a woman's autonomy and has the gift of being able to focus on her goals to achieve them without any distractions. She is a woman on a mission, she is courageous, competitive, and self-assured. A woman who ascertains Huntress characteristics relies on herself and doesn't need a partner to feel complete. She's a natural activist and stands firm in what she believes. The Huntress is a protector of others, especially other women who have been victimised. She feels at home when she spends time in the wilderness of mother nature.

The Huntress's greatest strengths are her self-reliance, independence, confidence, persistence, courage, and ability to focus on achieving her goals. But the shadowed or wounded Huntress is the wounded warrior. She can lack vulnerability and tends to push others away. Wounded by experiences with others, she casts a protective armour and finds it difficult to trust others. She struggles to rely on others or let others in due to a fear of being let down, she can appear aloof, and is often emotionally unavailable. Even though she is a natural protector of other women, she can quickly resent them and their neediness, and will often feel compelled to compete with them. The Huntress can choose to prioritise her work or her mission over her relationships which commonly leads to burning herself out as she is unable to share her workload.

The Huntress burns strongly in us during in our teenage years when we begin to withdraw from our family because we start to have dreams of travelling and conquering the world. Some women in their middle years have habitually neglected their Huntress in favour of the selfless Mother archetype. Once you feel the call to your broken dreams and promises, we can start to feel a strong resurgence of our Huntress. We can use the Huntress's energy to set and accomplish goals, take a new direction in life, find and follow a new purpose, or start a new career. This energy has the potential for you to be a courageous advocate for others.

How to Embody This Archetype

1. Make a plan to start a new adventure.

2. Take a risk by doing something that excites and terrifies you at the same time.

3. Realign with your mission – take on a new challenge, a new hobby, or start a new side hustle.

4. Go for a hike and enjoy nature.

5. Set goals, create and plan, and go after them.

6. Take part in a competition.

7. Stand up for a cause you believe in.

She AWAKES: The Huntress

In your journal, reflect on and write down your experience with the Huntress archetype.

- **Do you resonate with the energy of the Huntress?**

- **What has been your experience with this archetype?**

- **In which ways do you embody the mature or healthy expression of the Huntress?**

- **In which ways do you embody the shadow, wounded, or repressed Huntress?**

- **In what ways can you nurture or rebalance this energy inside of you?**

Affirmation: *I can trust myself and others.*

I am inherently flawed
and filled
with the crimson inner beauty
of my worth
the power
of my inextinguishable soul

The Queen

THE QUEEN IS KNOWN TO EMBRACE HER POWER, she is confident and a natural-born leader. She represents female sovereignty (our dominion over ourselves) so she knows her worth and doesn't tolerate negative, unhelpful attitudes around her. The Queen is loyal, protective, and responsible, she can make good decisions for herself and others, has a natural drive to marry, and to form meaningful alliances. She is referred to as the "Queen B" in social circles and enjoys being the centre of attention. She knows the importance of investing in herself and ensures she surrounds herself with the best mentors and experts as she knows the value of growing and challenging herself. You'll find that she's on a divine path and is here to make great change.

The Queen's strength lies in her fierce loyalty to her partnerships and leadership. She is connected to her power, her integrity, and her sovereignty. She is trusting, she delegates power, and uplifts others while staying confident in her own worth. When the Queen seeks a companion, she is attracted to a powerful partner and will demonstrate complete loyalty to him/her, supporting them to achieve their goals. However, the Queen, wounded or shadowed, has a predisposition to be fairly judgemental, image-conscious, and shallow. The Queen is prone to feel possessiveness and jealousy which can lead her to be quite vindictive. She is able to wield her power cleverly so it can manipulate others or put them down. She lacks humility and is likely to look down on and judge others harshly. She'll have a temper towards other women especially if she feels they have overstepped the mark or jeopardised her relationships. The shadowed Queen will naturally overlook the indiscretions of a partner or a spouse for the sake of the relationship and would rather keep the peace than cause an argument.

The energy of the Queen is ignited when we lead. However, we may notice these traits in ourselves when we have not yet integrated the power of our own sovereignty. It's normal to feel frightened by our own strength and potential. We have a habit of keeping to ourselves small and self-protect when we feel that our light is shining too brightly. If respect for your own boundaries has not yet been set in place, this will allow others to walk all over us so it's important that this rule to be established. It's common to feel as if we need partnerships and relationships to complete us in our lives or in business because we feel fearful of standing in the power of our own worth. We may abdicate in making decisions and compare ourselves to other Queens which leads to feeling inadequate. If we have strongly identified with the wounded Queen, we may have turned a blind eye to the indiscretions in our relationships and lost ourselves in our alliances. The shadowed Queen represents our need to put on a "good show", exacting a personal toll on our relationship and trust with ourselves, leaving us with no integrity.

How to Embody This Archetype

1. Invest in yourself and your personal growth.

2. Spend time healing so that you don't need to play it small, and you can allow yourself to be visible and make big decisions.

3. Spend money on yourself.

4. Make incremental upgrades in your life, your lifestyle, career or home.

5. Invest in masterminds and coaching.

She AWAKES: The Queen

In your journal, reflect on and write down in your experience with the Queen archetype.

- **Do you resonate with the energy of the Queen?**

- **What has been your experience with this archetype?**

- **In which ways do you embody the mature or healthy expression of the Queen?**

- **In which ways do you embody the shadow, wounded, or unintegrated Queen?**

- **In what ways can you nurture or rebalance this energy inside of you?**

Affirmation: *I am the Queen of my own life.*

when fear has you in its sights
causing you to retract into yourself
gently remind yourself to move into your intuition
and expand into all that you can be

how tiresome it is to carry around the burden of a heavy head
when you could fly
if you only chose to live in your heart

The Wise Woman

THE WISE WOMAN IS A WEALTH OF WISDOM AND KNOWLEDGE and is drawn to the pursuit of truth. She represents a woman's intuition and inspiration as well as her ability to be objective, strategize, and reason. The Wise Woman is introspective, self-sufficient, and self-confident. She feels secure in her identity and does not compare herself with others as she has nothing to prove. The Wise Woman has integrated her stories and her wisdom as she has met her shadow many times, so she knows how to work with herself rather than being at war with herself. She has learned from her mistakes, and she uses her past wounds as medicine to heal herself. The Wise Woman possesses wisdom in many different areas and expresses her insights in a variety of ways. An integrated Wise Woman uses her experiences to be a great and relatable teacher who shares her stories and lessons freely with others as she is so they too can become wise. She is brave, driven, and eager to continue her journey for learning about herself and the realms that she inhabits. She speaks the truth; she knows her power and is fully aware. The Wise Woman's greatest strengths are her intuition, dedication, strategy, and objectivity. She is capable of great introspection and is driven by a thirst for knowledge and understanding. She desires to collect experiences and makes sure she keeps learning lessons throughout her life. We all have access to our inner and bravery.

The Wise Woman's shadow side has a tendency to prioritise knowledge and truth over her relationships. She can be ambitious and introverted, prone to loneliness and can have a sense that she may not belong as she feels society does not often make space for her. When we are out of balance with our Wise Woman, we may see ourselves as superior and find that we weaponize our knowledge and use it as a way to hurt or shame others. It's likely that we feel bitter, resentful, or envious of the gifts other Wise Women possess. When the shadowed Wise Woman is our primary archetype, it is hard to free ourselves from being narrow-minded and find it challenging to form and maintain relationships with others or ask for help. We may not value ourselves or our lessons, so we do not see ourselves as a Wise Women with gifts and stories to share with others.

How to Embody This Archetype

1. Journal and reflect on your own experiences.

2. Use the knowledge and wisdom you have gained as experiences to teach others.

3. Read books about a topic that interests you.

4. Embrace change and aging in yourself and others.

5. Learn to accept, let go, and move on.

She AWAKES: The Wise Woman

In your journal, reflect on and write down your experience with the Wise Woman archetype.

*   **Do you resonate with the energy of the Wise Woman?**

*   **What has been your experience with this archetype?**

*   **In which ways do you embody the mature or healthy expression of the Wise Woman?**

*   **In which ways do you embody the shadow, wounded, or unintegrated Wise Woman?**

*   **In what ways can you nurture or rebalance this energy inside of you?**

Affirmation: *I am connected with and trust my inner knowing.*

my life is so much bigger than the confines
of this invisible fortress

this keep

safe
secure

in the bounds of your expectation

and yet

I have galaxies to marvel at
inside of me
while flames dance in the heat of the brassiere

The Wild Woman

THE WILD WOMAN, THE MYSTIC, THE WITCH, THE MEDICINE WOMAN is an awakened, untamed, and fierce soul who challenges the status quo and moves to the beat of her own drum. She is the protector of the hearth, the household fire, or the place where the family gathers. The Wild Woman is deeply connected to her intuition, she is sure of herself, her needs and desires. She seeks to spend time with Mother Nature. She is extremely confident and demands abundance for herself. Whereas the Huntress is focused on external goals, the Wild Woman focuses her energy on her "inner hearth"—her inner fulfilment. She is the archetype we ignite when we want to take pleasure in breaking rules, standing out, when we need to conduct healing work on our shadowed Wild Woman. Regardless of how emotionally charged a situation, a woman who exhibits strong, Wild Woman, energy can detach and focus her emotions inward. She can objectively observe her thoughts, emotions, and behaviour patterns for personal growth. The Wild Woman has no issue with spending time alone for extended periods or breaking the rules of conformity. She enjoys solitude and pursuits such as meditating, volunteering, exploring her physic energy, and spirituality. The Wild Woman's greatest strengths are her ability to reflect inward, serene calmness, deep concentration, focus, and creativity.

The Wild Woman's shadowed side consists of deep introversion, social isolation, and the appearance of being emotionally distant. When out of balance, stemming from an unhealed wound, or being repressed, she can become destructive and chaotic. If a Wild Woman is out of balance, this can create the force behind our anger and rage. In a society obsessed with quick fixes, the Wild Woman's energy of being able to seek inward and find meaning is something which is often missing for women. When a woman represses her Wild Woman energy, she may notice that it will call out to her in many ways until she is heard. I explore this in-depth further along in this book as I believe our pathway to reconnecting with this archetype is the key to our **awaken**ing.

How to Embody This Archetype

1. Spend time alone.

2. Meditate, journal, and pray.

3. Practice observing your thoughts and emotions.

4. Set clear boundaries for yourself.

5. Spend time in the wilderness, the desert, the bush, or the forest.

6. Explore your psychic gifts and spirituality.

7. Create and embrace the power of ritual.

8. Open your perception up to more possibilities.

9. Ignite your inner intuition and speak your truth with conviction.

10. Discover and set in place what you stand for.

She AWAKES: Your Wild Woman

In your journal, reflect on write down your experience with the Wild Woman archetype.

- **Do you resonate with the energy of the Wild Woman?**

- **What has been your experience with this archetype?**

- **In which ways do you embody a healthy expression of the Wild Woman?**

- **In which ways do you embody the shadow or the unintegrated Wild Woman?**

- **In what ways can you nurture or rebalance this energy inside of you?**

Affirmation: *I am free to be who I want to be.*

write it on the memory track
of your soul
that in the chaos of the storm
I will be by your calm
guiding you home
with the light of my love

Feminine Forces Alive in You

Following the presentation of the seven feminine archetypes, you may find that you resonate with one or more of these powerful energies. Perhaps you recognise areas in your life where different archetypes were more dominant at that time for you than the others. It's possible you have identified many strengths from these energies that you already have inside of you. You may also have noticed yourself in the mire of the wounded or the shadowed.

In her book, *Goddesses in Everywoman*, author, Dr Jean Shinoda Bolen, describes how these archetypes can compete for the "golden apple" of the woman's psyche and how we may experience the archetypes' nurturing effects as well as destructive powers in our lives. A natural tendency can be to use these methods as a way to inflict pain or self-judgement, however, I strongly encourage you to refrain from doing this. We all hold strengths and shadows, and like a modern-day Persephone, in the pages that follow, I will be sharing my story with you of how these powers have played a role in my own life. In my invoking of my mature Maiden state, I will guide you through the underworld and share ways that can help you heal your wounds, move out of the shadows, and work with these remarkable forces to live your best **W**ild, **A**uthentic, **K**nowing, and **E**mpowered life. For now, your job is to simply take a moment to wrap yourself in a generous cocoon of love and compassion and through the gentle gaze of full attention, simply take the time to notice your surroundings. We are about to embark on a great quest together, and as with any journey, finding where you are on the map is the first step. The exercise below, as well as the exercises in the following sections, have specifically been designed to support you with locating yourself so you have a starting point from where you can move yourself from asleep to **AWAKEN**.

She AWAKES: Archetypes Alive in You

After reading the above explanations on feminine archetypes, reflect the following questions as a prompt in your journal:

- **What archetypes are most alive in you now?**

- **Is there any other archetype that is not currently dominant for you that you would like to embody, and why?**

Affirmation: *I give myself permission to claim the power of my feminine legacy.*

for those on their deathbed

soul soporose
earth suit walking

there is more than one way to be dead
there are many ways to die

lazarus be I

Sleeping Beauty

Like many little girls, I grew up on a diet of fairy tales. In fact, as a young child, one of my most prized possessions was a collection of illustrated fairy tales gifted to me by my parents for my fifth birthday. Since there have been people on Earth, there have been stories. Yet, stories have the most immense power. We use stories to entertain, but we use stories to pass down histories, genealogy, and lessons to the next generation. I was so enthralled with the supremacy of words that I have always sought to play, create, and conjure with them. The fairy tales we know today in the Disney movies are sanitised and child-friendly which is nothing compared to the original fairy tales, which were dark, sinister, and full of themes that would not be accepted in today's politically correct culture. However, fairy tales, and even nursery rhymes, leave important breadcrumbs for us to follow when it comes to understanding the evolution of our society and the female psyche. Since this is a book about "waking up", and there are many of us who are asleep, it only seems fitting that we begin with one of the oldest known versions *Sleeping Beauty.*

The story was first published back in 1634, in a collection of Italian stories called the *Pentamerone* by Giambattista Basile—this might be vastly different to the tale that you know. The story of Sleeping Beauty has since been reinvented and rewritten several times, allowing it to be more palatable for the audiences over time. However, it is agreed that all versions of Sleeping Beauty have one thing in common and that is the "princess", one of the most powerless heroines of all the fairy tales. Even in the family-friendly Disney movie version, Princess Aurora barely has any lines in her own movie. Sleeping Beauty's fate is decided by her father, wise men, and in later versions, fairies. No matter how hard the characters in the tale try to protect her, she is always a victim to her fate. Our damsel in distress is plunged into a deep sleep and has no choice but to marry the king who rapes her, (in the 1964, Basile version), and in later iterations, she must marry Prince Charming who wakes her up with a kiss, yet another unsolicited sexual act. The seventeenth-century, (Early Modern Period), tale is significant as it provides vital clues to the origins of many social, political, cultural, technological, and economic changes of the time that created the modern world we know today.

Sun, Moon, and Talia by Giambattista Basile

There once lived a great lord, who was blessed with the birth of a beautiful daughter, whom he named Talia. He sent for the wise men and astrologers in his lands to predict her future. They met, counselled together, and cast her horoscope, and at length they came to the conclusion that she would incur great danger from a splinter of flax. Her father therefore forbade that any flax, hemp, or any other material of that sort be brought into his house, so that she should escape the predestined danger.

One day, when Talia had grown into a young and beautiful lady, she was looking out of a window, when she beheld passing that way an old woman, who was spinning. Talia, never having seen a distaff or a spindle, was pleased to see the twirling spindle, and she was so curious as to what thing it was, that she asked the old woman to come to her. Taking the distaff from her hand, she began to stretch the flax. Unfortunately, Talia ran a splinter of flax under her nail, and she fell dead upon the ground. When the old woman saw this, she became frightened and ran down the stairs, and is running still.

As soon as the wretched father heard of the disaster which had taken place, he had them, after having paid for this tub of sour wine with casks of tears, lay her out in one of his country mansions. There they seated her on a velvet throne under a canopy of brocade. Wanting to forget all and to drive from his memory his great misfortune, he closed the doors and abandoned forever the house where he had suffered this great loss.

After a time, it happened by chance that a king was out hunting and passed that way. One of his falcons escaped from his hand and flew into the house by way of one of the windows. It did not come when called, so the king had one of his party knock at the door, believing the palace to be inhabited. Although he knocked for a length of time, nobody answered, so the king had them bring a vintner's ladder, for he himself would climb up and search the house, to discover what was inside. Thus he climbed up and entered, and looked in all the rooms, and nooks, and corners, and was amazed to find no living person there. At last he came to the salon, and when the king beheld Talia, who seemed to be enchanted, he believed that she was asleep, and he called her, but she remained unconscious. Crying aloud, he beheld her charms and felt his blood course hotly through his veins. He lifted her in his arms, and carried her to a bed, where he gathered the first fruits of love. Leaving her on the bed, he returned to his own kingdom, where, in the pressing business of his realm, he for a time thought no more about this incident.

Now after nine months Talia delivered two beautiful children, one a boy and the other a girl. In them could be seen two rare jewels, and they were attended by two fairies, who came to that palace, and put them at their mother's breasts. Once, however, they sought the nipple, and not finding it, began to suck on Talia's fingers, and they sucked so much that the splinter of flax came out. Talia awoke as if from a long sleep, and seeing beside her two priceless gems, she held them to her breast, and gave them the nipple to suck, and the babies were dearer to her than her own life. Finding herself alone in that palace with two children by her side, she did not know what had happened to her; but she did notice that the table was set, and food and drink were brought in to her, although she did not see any attendants.

In the meanwhile the king remembered Talia, and saying that he wanted to go hunting, he returned to the palace, and found her awake, and with two cupids of beauty. He was overjoyed, and he told Talia who he was, and how he had seen her, and what had taken place. When she heard this, their friendship was knitted with tighter bonds, and he remained with her for a few days. After that time he bade her farewell, and promised to return soon, and take her with him to his kingdom. And he went to his realm, but he could not find any rest, and at all hours he had in his mouth the names of Talia, and of Sun and Moon (those were the two children's names), and when he took his rest, he called either one or other of them.

Now the king's wife began to suspect that something was wrong from the delay of her husband while hunting, and hearing him name continually Talia, Sun, and Moon, she became hot with another kind of heat than the sun's. Sending for the secretary, she said to him, "Listen to me, my son, you are living between two rocks, between the post and the door, between the poker and the grate. If you will tell me with whom the king your master, and my husband, is in love, I will give you treasures untold; and if you hide the truth from me, you will never be found again, dead or alive." The man was terribly frightened. Greed and fear blinded his eyes to all honour and to all sense of justice, and he related to her all things, calling bread bread, and wine wine.

The queen, hearing how matters stood, sent the secretary to Talia, in the name of the king, asking her to send the children, for he wished to see them. Talia, with great joy, did as she was commanded. Then the queen, with a heart of Medea, told the cook to kill them, and to make them into several tasteful dishes for her wretched husband. But the cook was tender hearted and, seeing these two beautiful golden apples, felt pity and compassion for them, and he carried them home to his wife, and had her hide them. In their place he prepared two lambs into a hundred different dishes. When the king came, the queen, with great pleasure, had the food served.

The king ate with delight, saying, "By the life of Lanfusa, how tasteful this is"; or, "By the soul of my ancestors, this is good."

Each time she replied, "Eat, eat, you are eating of your own."

For two or three times the king paid no attention to this repetition, but at last seeing that the music continued, he answered, "I know perfectly well that I am eating of my own, because you have brought nothing into this house"; and growing angry, he got up and went to a villa at some distance from his palace, to solace his soul and alleviate his anger.

In the meanwhile the queen, not being satisfied of the evil already done, sent for the secretary and told him to go to the palace and to bring Talia back, saying that the king longed for her presence and was expecting her. Talia departed as soon as she heard these words, believing that she was following the commands of her lord, for she greatly longed to see her light and joy, knowing not what was preparing for her. She was met by the queen, whose face glowed from the fierce fire burning inside her and looked like the face of Nero.

She addressed her thus, "Welcome, Madam Busybody! You are a fine piece of goods, you ill weed, who are enjoying my husband. So you are the lump of filth, the cruel bitch, that has caused my head to spin? Change your ways, for you are welcome in purgatory, where I will compensate you for all the damage you have done to me."

Talia, hearing these words, began to excuse herself, saying that it was not her fault, because the king her husband had taken possession of her territory when she was drowned in sleep; but the queen would not listen to her excuses, and had a large fire lit in the courtyard of the palace, and commanded that Talia should be cast into it.

The lady, perceiving that matters had taken a bad turn, knelt before the queen, and begged her to allow her at least to take off the garments she wore. The queen, not for pity of the unhappy lady, but to gain also those robes, which were embroidered with gold and pearls, told her to undress, saying, "You can take off your clothes. I agree." Talia began to take them off, and with every item that she removed she uttered a loud scream. Having taken off her robe, her skirt, the bodice, and her shift, she was on the point of removing her last garment, when she uttered a last scream louder than the rest. They dragged her towards the pile, to reduce her to lye ashes which would be used to wash Charon's breeches.

The king suddenly appeared, and finding this spectacle, demanded to know what was happening. He asked for his children, and his wife — reproaching him for his treachery — told him that she had had them slaughtered and served to him as meat. When the wretched king heard this, he gave himself up to despair, saying, "Alas! Then I, myself, am the wolf of my own sweet lambs. Alas! And why did these my veins know not the fountains of their own blood? You renegade bitch, what evil deed is this which you have done? Begone, you shall get your desert as the stumps, and I will not send such a tyrant-faced one to the Colosseum to do her penance!"

So saying, he commanded that the queen should be cast into the fire which she had prepared for Talia, and the secretary with her, because he had been the handle for this bitter play, and weaver of this wicked plot. He was going to do the same with the cook, whom he believed to be the slaughterer of his children, when the man cast himself at his feet, saying, "In truth, my lord, for such a deed, there should be nothing else than a pile of living fire, and no other help than a spear from behind, and no other entertainment than twisting and turning within the blazing fire, and I should seek no other honour than to have my ashes, the ashes of a cook, mixed up with the queen's. But this is not the reward that I expect for having saved the children, in spite of the gall of that bitch, who wanted to kill them and to return to your body that which was of your own body."

Hearing these words, the king was beside himself. He thought he was dreaming, and he could not believe what his own ears had heard. Therefore, turning to the cook, he said, "If it is true that you have saved my children, be sure that I will take you away from turning the spit, and I will put you in the kitchen of this breast, to turn and twist as you like all my desires, giving you such a reward as shall enable you to call yourself a happy man in this world."

While the king spoke these words, the cook's wife, seeing her husband's need, brought forth the two children, Sun and Moon, before their father. And he never tired at playing the game of three with his wife and children, making a mill wheel of kisses, now with one and then with the other. He gave a generous reward to the cook, he made him a chamberlain. He married Talia to wife; and she enjoyed a long life with her husband and her children, thus experiencing the truth of the proverb:

Those whom fortune favours
Find good luck even in their sleep.

The Powerless Victim

Now, if we look beyond the obvious rape, abuse, and general vomit-inducing ickiness of this story, some themes relate to the "Sleeping Beauty" archetype, which from time to time we will all inhabit in our lifetimes. This is the archetype of the Maiden. As mentioned in my introduction to *Sun, Moon and Talia*, from the beginning, Talia's life was not her own. Upon her birth, her father consulted wise men to predict her future and once he found out about a possible danger in his daughter's life, he seeks to outlaw all flax, hemp, and any other fabrics from being brought into the house.

We all start our lives as the wide-eyed, naïve, and uninitiated Maiden. Blindly trusting those around us to make all the decisions for us. Desperate to please, we mould and change ourselves to fit in with those around us. In our fairy tale, Talia looks to the outside world through her window and when she sees an old woman spinning flax, and despite the wishes of her father, she rebels against them, and by doing so, she gets a splinter of flax under her fingernail and succumbs to a deep sleep. If we compare this to the modern-day woman, we can see that we too are born into a dream in which we feel an obligation to conform. As we grow and mature, we arouse the Huntress during our adolescence years and seek to pull away from family to exert our independence. The natural protector of women, the Huntress, is the gatekeeper to other divine feminine energies. In my opinion, it is our transition from Maiden to Huntress and from the experience we gain from this, that is what determines our decision to move further into our awakened selves or just surrender to the dream. We may wish to embody other archetypes; however, we may feel compelled by the pressure of societal norms which wish to keep us contained as the small and powerless 'Maidens'.

In Don Miguel Ruiz's book, *The Four Agreements*, he writes about the domestication all humans must go through which hooks our attention and tells us how and what to dream. *"As children we didn't have the opportunity to choose our beliefs, but we agreed with the information that was passed to us from the dream of the planet via other humans. The only way to store information is by agreement. The outside dream may hook our attention, but if we don't agree, we don't store that information. As soon as we agree, we believe it, and this is called faith. To have faith is to believe unconditionally. That's how we learn as children. Children believe everything adults say. We agree with them, and our faith is so strong that the belief system controls our whole dream of life. We didn't choose these beliefs, and we may have rebelled against them, but we are not strong enough to win the rebellion."*

Succumbing to the dream is a trauma-based behaviour. It symbolises the deliberate choices a woman makes to discard her true self and settle for an easier, less risky, and more socially acceptable version of who she *thinks* they she should be. When we are part of the dream, we are in the unintegrated, the shadow, or the wounded versions of the divine feminine as we try to mould ourselves into the masculine ideal. Think back to a time of your own experience of transitioning from Maiden to unintegrated Huntress. And think back to a time where you made your first rebellious bids to be independent from the dream as most young women do.

- **What messages did you receive about your newly forming Huntress self?**

- **Did your experience with how others responded to your newly found autonomy cause you to retreat back into the Maiden?**

- **Did you learn to hide in the shadow of the Mother, the Lover, or the Queen?**

- **Did you move into the wounded warrior—fiercely independent, fixated on controlling the outcome, unable to connect, trust, and ask for help?**

- **Did you retreat inward and bury your nose in a book as a young, Wise Woman or you became a Wild Woman lost in her own world?**

Talia's father in the story is powerless to intervene. He does not attempt to remove the splinter of flax from underneath Talia's fingernail but instead, he merely slips further into his own domestication by drinking his sorrows away and locking Talia away in an abandoned house to forget about her.

When I reflect on my *HERstory*, I can see this theme interwoven into the fabric of my upbringing. I was born on the Sabbath day and so according to the well-known nursery rhyme, I was predestined to be, *"bonny and blithe and good and gay"*. For those of you who don't speak "Ye Ole English", it means that I was born to be, *"happy, good, and nice"*. I was raised in a religious household, the eldest daughter of a minister. I learnt early on that my destiny in life was to be "The Example". In fact, my parents repeatedly reinforced this.

Tanya: 'Dad, can I wear jeans to church?'

Dad: 'No, you can't, you are an *example*'.

Tanya: 'Can I go to the party on Saturday?'

Dad: 'No, Sunday morning is Church, you must stay home and prepare—be the *example*'.

Tanya: 'I don't want to go to church tonight'.

Dad: 'You can't stay at home; you must be the *example*'.

The example of what you may ask. To this day, I am still not entirely sure. It was what my parents wanted me to be; the form that my malleable self was shaped into. "The Example" was the oil that was anointed upon me from early childhood. As I sat in the pews, I imagined God walking through watching and judging me. *'Was I sitting still enough?', 'Was I quiet enough?', 'Was my hair neat enough?', 'Was my dress was pretty enough or that my dreaded white lace, knee-high socks were pulled up enough?'* "The Example" is an alter-ego of mine that I still seem to find myself effortlessly fitting into time and time again. Without acknowledging it at the time, every second of every minute of every hour of every moment, I was working diligently to answer one question: *'How can I do this perfectly so people will accept me, so I won't let my parents and, or God down?'*

Now coming from an empathetic place as a grown-ass woman, I realise my parents did not mean to harm me. My parents loved me, (and still do), and I know the only thing they wanted for me was the absolute best. They sought to protect me in the best way that they knew how to. They, both in their own ways, derive from difficult childhoods so it was a natural instinct for them to reinforce the domestication taught to them by their own parents. It's clear to me that I have always been influenced by the pleasure-seeking tendencies of the Lover, and her need for beauty and creativity. However, there was little space for her in my childhood home where work, sensibility, Mother and Maiden-like attributes were highly valued.

I remember expressing to my parents how I wanted to become an artist and being told, *'Maybe you should study book-keeping'.* Telling my parents, *'I want to be a poet'* and being told, *'Maybe you should learn to type'.* My adult brain can now rationalise these responses I received and recognise my parents' need for keeping me safe from their version of "flax"—protecting me from their perceived dangers and securing my future, just as Talia's father tried to do. Perhaps they held the belief that writing, or art wasn't a *real job,* and wanted to spare me the fate of the *struggling artist* stereotype.

After all, no family member before me had entered the "Arts" as a career, so I was an unknown new breed to them. However, instead of teaching me to trust my magic and believe in my own worth, all I learnt was that they did not believe in me. So, the simple and pure act of being authentically the person God intended me to be was not good enough, and this was enough to cause me to dim my light. As I have said before, most parents do things out of love, with the most loving intentions for their children. My parents were not different.

Here are a few examples of what my parents desired for me:

- To be a "good girl". A model Christian, to grow up and be a credit to their name, and to be pleasing in the eyes of God.

- Reach heaven and have eternal life.

- To succeed in life and to be happy.

- To get married.

- To be able to financially support myself.

- To be blessed with a healthy and happy family.

These were the messages from domestication that I came to believe about myself:

- 'Who you are is not good enough'.

- The "real me", the me that thought impure thoughts and wanted something different from the life she was living was "bad" and is bound for hell.

- Someone is always watching and judging your every action, so be on your best behaviour.

- You can never make a mistake.

- You must be perfect, or you will let your parents, the congregation, and God down.

- You must hide, sneak, and deny who you really are—your real thoughts, yearnings, autonomy, and personality are not welcome here.

- Appearances are all that matter.

This is the domestication—the dream I fight to wake up from every day. It was not my parents' fault; it was the collective dream they had been born into that they passed onto me—my accidental inheritance. Being born into ultra-conservative, white South Africa was a time when children should be seen and not heard, show respect their elders, and did as they were told without question or hesitation. Failure to comply with these rules would result in getting the wrong end of a wooden spoon, a belt, a slipper, a cane, or whatever else was on hand to the behind, over the knuckles, or across the ear. Girls and women were "less than" and subservient to boys and men. It was their place to have the babies and look after the men in their lives. Independence and autonomy were quickly bred out of girls, and instead, we were taught the lessons of submission, obedience, and selflessness. Boys were conditioned from an incredibly young age that men were tough, strong, and stoic. Boys were looked down on as being "effeminate" if they were ever to be caught doing woman's work like cooking, cleaning, or taking care of the children. *Real men* were king of the household, they were the braai masters, they held their liquor, they talked about fishing, cars and rugby, and were not allowed to show any emotion other than anger. I came of age during a time where every boy, whether he chose to or not, was forcibly drafted to the army to "make him a man" when he left high school.

At twenty years of age, I got married. My father had to sign me over to him. Under South African law, I was not legally allowed to have my own bank account without my husband or sign any contract without him, although he could sign anything he liked on his own. This is the culture that I fled from at the tender age of twenty-two to my adopted country of Aotearoa, New Zealand.

My parents would admit that up until the age of seventeen, I was the perfect specimen of what an "example" should look like. I said "yes", and never disagreed with something, even if I really wanted to. I went to church on Sundays and Wednesdays. I sang in the choir, and I taught Sunday School. I attended school and I never skipped class. I got good grades and I said and did all the right things. I was in my second to last year of school, in the top three of my class, and I was destined to be a prefect. I had worked so hard to be this person—*the perfect example*—my parents and teachers were so proud.

you look like a good girl
like you'll do what you're told...

How do you find your inner voice so you can speak up? How do you safely disagree when you grew up to be silent—to be seen and not heard? You rebel against the *dream*. You find the old woman with the spinning wheel with the flax and do the exact things you have been forbidden to do. Buckling under the weight of my parent's and God's expectations of me, I decided I didn't want to be the "good girl" anymore. Energised by my Huntress energy, I did not want to be perfect. The world of being a Maiden did not feel authentic to me anymore, so I let the walls all fall down and I decided to embrace a new dream. This is when I began hanging out with the kids who spent lunch breaks smoking and drinking under the stairs at school. Unhooking from the dream of my domestication was completely liberating. For the first time in my life, I met my Wild Woman and I felt as if I could finally breathe again. I started smoking, drinking, and doing weed. I traded numbness for the thrill of sex. The rush of breaking the container which held the character who so badly wanted to escape, and surprising people with this *secret* me was scary, exciting, and incredibly intoxicating. As I was uninitiated in the ways of the Wild Woman, and I was infatuated by her unpredictable and chaotic nature. I was firmly in the driver's seat and although I was heading for a crash, for the first time it was going to be a beautiful wreck of my own making. I was busting a hole wide open right in the middle of my parents' dream and it felt fucking brilliant!

I believed I was able to hide the fact that I had left my parents' dream behind closed doors, the deodorant, eye drops, and gum… but I still remember my mum's face when one blisteringly, hot day she picked me up from school. I got into the car and immediately realised something was wrong when we did not wait for my sister. She looked directly in my eyes with pure disappointment, she had tears in her eyes as she took out a box of Stuyvesant Blue from of her bag and placed them on the armrest between us, (my mother did not and has never smoked). Her blue-grey eyes wore an odd mixture of sadness, worried, and hurt. Her face pale with exhaustion. At that moment I felt the shame shoot through me… *"I had hurt and disappointed my mother"*. This was followed by an icy flush of heat that rose from the tips of my toes to the roots of my hair. The charade was up. There was nowhere to hide now. She said calmy, *'Your teacher came to see me at work this morning… I have booked you in to see someone, we are going there now.'*

I cannot remember the face or name of the therapist's, or anything else, other than to tell you he was a man. What I can remember was that he listened, and I mean he really listened to me as no one done had before. He did not think I was crazy or broken. I remember that, though at the time it felt like I was being punished for rebelling, under his guidance I had the first truly honest conversation with my parents about how I felt; about the shame of being *me*. Then one day, as suddenly as it started, it stopped. As Don Miguel Ruiz stated in the abovementioned quote, I realised that I was not strong enough to win the rebellion I was trying to fight. And so, with my Huntress defeated and my Maiden sternly chastised, I bundled together my potential and promise just like the pieces of a chess game in which I had been defeated. I wrapped my gifts, my poetry, my Wild Woman ready to spread her wings and insistently calling out to take up space, and I silenced her. Wings in and wrapped in layers of tissue like a Christmas tree fairy at the end of the Noel season, I placed her in a box and buried it on a shelf in my attic space—firmly closing the door as I went.

I gratefully accepted the outstretched hook back into my parent's dream and I fell asleep in the shadow of the Maiden. I did this because I was tired, and it was a damn sight easier and more comfortable than being on the cold and lonely outside.

Dream: **1** - Tanya: **Nada.**

She AWAKES: Waking Up from Your Dream of Domestication

I invite you to find a photo of yourself as a young child. Looking at this child with a loving heart, reflect on your own domestication(s).

- **Who was she predestined to be according to the "dream"?**

- **Who did you know in your soul that she was, but the dream of your domestication did not allow her to manifest?**

- **How was her Huntress received?**

- **How has the trauma of how her Huntress treated in those early years influenced the decisions she made, to settle back into the dream?**

Now close your eyes, and imagine a new dream for this girl:

- **What does that dream look like?**

- **What are you doing in your dream?**

- **What sounds, colours, smells, and tastes do you experience in this new dream?**

- **How do you feel in the dream?**

This is also an opportunity to create a drawing, a painting, a poem, a dance, or any other expression of yourself that feels right to symbolise your new dream. If it is something tangible, keep it somewhere close and revisit your dream daily.

Important: *Embody the receptiveness of the Maiden within your dream casting. Even if this dream is slightly clouded at first, as you revisit it with openness, it will become clearer over time.*

Affirmation: *I am the dreamer of my dreams.*

what happened to the revolution?
the outraged boys and girls
who were going to change the world?

they became mothers and fathers
teachers
policemen
managers
politicians
used car salesmen

they became the tired
the fat
the settled
and the sensible

The Raping of Our Souls

In *Sun, Moon and Talia,* the king comes across Talia's sleeping body, *"and when the king beheld Talia, who seemed to be enchanted, he believed that she was asleep, and he called her, but she remained unconscious. Crying aloud, he beheld her charms and felt his blood course hotly through his veins. He lifted her in his arms, and carried her to a bed, where he gathered the first fruits of love."*

This part of the story can be interpreted on many different levels. First, there is actual rape of a woman and other types of abuse to her body in which many have been a victim too. In fact, many women who I speak to in my work report to me some form of sexual abuse in our conversations. This also speaks to how women throughout time, and in many cultures, have been treated as if they were "property", objects to be traded by their fathers and husbands. Many women are forced to stay in the helplessness of their Maiden and repress or live in the shadow of their other archetypes. As I mentioned earlier, I wasn't allowed to even have my own bank account without my husband. In my mother's generation, girls were not permitted to have any other careers which were not teachers, nurses, or secretaries. It was expected from you that once you were married and had children, you would give up your job and get on with the "real" work that woman were supposed to be doing, by being a housewife, and mother. In our collective societal dream, we often do not even question the way things have always been we are just swept up in it.

- **How often do we as women, while in our dream state, allow others to do things to us, take things from us, objectify us, and like mushrooms, they keep us in the dark and feed us shit?**

- **How often do we permit others to abuse us without any objection from us?**

Our slumber is a trauma induced protection to this raping of our souls. In our slumber we allow others to gather, tear apart and defile our precious "first fruits of love" – our gifts, talents, and our creativity – the things that belong to us, gifted to us for the purpose of sustaining our light and our lives. We allow others to convince us that we are not special enough, strong enough, clever enough, educated enough, talented enough, or simply not good enough. We lie asleep while our soul is raped and stripped of vital essence until we are a mere shadow of ourselves.

She AWAKES: Unearthing and Naming Past Abuse

To heal from something, we must first recognise that it is there. Many of our past abuses are entombed in the novocaine of ignorance, nostalgia, or the dark sludge of shame. Shame grows and takes hold the more we hide it, withdraw it, and deny our abuse. As part of it, it is now time to name it and shame it, and gently bring it out into the soothing light of self-empathy and self-compassion.

- **What has been your experience with abuse to your body, your spirit, or to your soul?**

- **Are these wounds healed, or do you still have healing to do?**

- **What deliberate decisions do you need to make to heal your trauma and make your dream in the previous exercise a reality?**

Please be ever-so kind and gentle with yourself as you reflect on this topic. You may be uncovering very deep wounds and pain which have been buried for a long time because you did not want to admit to yourself that they exist. Hold yourself in a bubble of love as you do your work.

Affirmation: *I am healing every day.*

six weeks are up

      you inform me

            the doctor said that it is okay to have sex

i inwardly groan

      don't you want me?
      don't you miss me like i miss you?

you ask
how can i tell you that my desire is buried under a pile of dirty diapers

that my intimate sexual bits have been
reassigned to the functions of mothering
we make awkward love while the baby sleeps
i am ever vigilant for cries from her crib
as i bite back the fear of tearing my newly
healed perineum
and hot milk spills out like tears onto your chest

      you are mine

you tell me when we are done
as if claiming proprietary rights

The Birth of Twins

IN THE ORIGINAL STORY OF SLEEPING BEAUTY, Talia gives birth to twins; a boy named, Sun, and a girl named Moon. The birth of the twins symbolises a woman's transition into a mother or the activation of her Mother archetype. For many women, children are born to us during a time when we are in soulish slumber. According to the expectations that had been placed on us by the dream of domestication, the birth of a child is meant to be a joyful experience. However, for countless women, motherhood is a time of guilt, trauma, and grief as she experiences an intense period of setting aside herself, a resurrection of her own mother wound and/or moving into the wounded Mother. Women who do not possess a strong Mother archetype or have other overpowering energies active in her, will often delay motherhood or they chose to be "childfree", is a means to retain a part of themselves, to prioritise other relationships, or to achieve desired life goals.

In our culture, partnering up and having babies is something that is expected of a woman. When women delay or reject motherhood out of choice, this causes them to lose acceptance and value in the eyes of others. Becoming a mother is an all-consuming force in our lives. There is an unnamed but felt pressure that the "woman" side of a woman should disappear, and they should become a selfless mother.

I selfishly resisted motherhood and hung on to *me* for as long as I could. It took many years of convincing, on my husband's part, to get me to concede. At the age of twenty-seven, I gave up *me* and to allowed myself to fall pregnant—I activated the Mother in me. Except, my first pregnancy ended in heartbreak. I had been experiencing pain for a few days and I knew something was wrong. I instantly knew I was correct from the uncomfortable shifting of the sonographer as she moved and paced around the room. The look on her face, and her frantic conferring with her colleague under her breath that something was up, and the news wasn't good. After what seemed like an eternity, they delivered the news. They couldn't find a heartbeat and they stated that my baby had died in utero. I endured a week with my dead baby still inside of me before I was admitted to the maternity unit for a D & C—a procedure to remove my unborn child.

My life came crashing down around me.

I disappeared into myself.

I was an early childhood teacher at the time of my loss so the constant reminder, while being surrounded by small children and pregnant colleagues and parents, was agonising torture.

I never got to meet the child who made me a mother.

I will never know if my baby was a boy or a girl.

I would never gaze lovingly into their face, waiting to see their smile.

Even though this baby was only alive inside of me for twelve weeks, I loved this child with all my heart. The grief I felt was so intense, so painful, so real. I named my unborn child, Jessie, and I planted sweet peas in my garden for them. Sweet peas were my Granny's favourite flower. I am a believer in the afterlife. I believe the soul is born at the moment of conception and it comforted me to think of my gentle, loving Granny embracing and taking care of her great-grandchild in the beautiful beyond.

My husband and I should have come together after our tragic loss and allowed ourselves to process our grief. We *should* have, but we didn't. Instead, I was so possessed with the energy of the wounded Mother, and both of us being so consumed in our grief, wanted to escape, so we threw our backs into conceiving another child, and twelve weeks later I was pregnant with our eldest daughter. I was so anxious during my pregnancy, that every twinge, tingle, and pain caused me to panic, leading me to convince myself that I was going to lose her too. I was so convinced I was being punished for not wanting to lose myself to motherhood, and this was some form of divine retribution for having selfish thoughts. The extreme morning sickness I experienced the entire nine months of my pregnancy was sweet a relief in a way. The suffering was righteous penance, and it was a constant reassurance that I was still pregnant, which made me feel like she was okay.

My rainbow baby was born on a Wednesday at one o'clock in the afternoon weighing ten pounds and ten ounces. I was smitten with her from the moment they placed her in my arms. I was overwhelmed with intense love, but at the same time, uncontrollable fear. As I looked into her wizened, old soul eyes, I hoped beyond all reason that my love would be enough for us both. The biggest lies we tell ourselves as we're consumed with the struggles of conceiving and the challenges of pregnancy, is that the worries of pregnancy, labour, and delivery are the only difficult parts. But it isn't until the umbilical cord is severed, until the birth is complete, and you have your new-born baby in your arms that your new reality sinks in that only *then,* your hard work begins. I was not ready for the feeling of her being outside of me, separate from me, there for everyone and anyone just to pick up and hold. The wounded Mother inside of me screamed out in protest, *'No she's mine!'* Everybody always wants to cuddle the new-born baby, and it seems as if the new mother disappears into the background, like an afterthought, as she mourns the loss of the child who was once part of her body. I was grossly unprepared, as a new mother, and how painful this loss would feel for me.

Motherhood is a never-ending process of learning to let go and accept. First, your body and the changes. Second, your sense of self. Third, your child, who each day is growing further and further away from you. Day by day, inch by inch, we surrender, and we let go. As I was determined to stay home with my daughter and we had already decided we wanted to have two children, we tried for a second child while our first was still a baby. And when our eldest was eight months old, I fell pregnant with our second daughter. Life got remarkably busy very quickly, and five years later, we welcomed our third daughter into the world. Many years later, my husband would say to me, *'You just disappeared'*, and I did. I ceased to exist outside of the hazy unconsciousness of motherhood.

Later I would write:

i was complicit in Your conspiracy to
place Your seed in me
and erase my identity

Talia sleeps through childbirth and the breastfeeding her young. The fairies represent women who uphold patriarchal ideals in our lives, they are there to help us sustain the motions of our life but unaware, unable to, or even unwilling to protect us from the abuse our souls endure. Talia's body simply goes through what is expected of her as a mother. When she finally awakens to find the twins sucking on her fingers, she isn't horrified; she isn't even surprised. She just casually picks up the twins and places them on her breast to nurse which further highlights the expectation for complacency and self-sacrifice expected from mothers.

One of the things I came to know during my first pregnancy and subsequent parenthood, is any control we think we have is completely an illusion. Up until my first pregnancy, I lived life filled with the naivety and arrogance of my youth. I lived with the unwavering belief that I controlled my own universe. I did what I wanted, when I wanted. I made plans and decisions, and for the most part, they went as I had hoped and planned for. But now with another human being growing inside of me, *it* controlled me. Even the basic things I took for granted about my own body left me knowing that I was not in control. This little alien who had now inhabited me, controlled how I felt physically, mentally, and emotionally. *It* made me nauseated all the time. I was put off foods which I usually loved, and I started eating things that I used to hate like horseradish sandwiches *(WTF!)*. I became irritable and irrational. *It* controlled my eating, my sleep, and how often I needed to pee. For the first time in my life, I had no control over my weight or how I looked. And as much as I tried to, I had no control over whether the child inside me lived or died.

Throughout our lives, we reach out over and over again. We cling to hold onto some semblance of control, and as mothers we become more controlling. However, this causes delusion as there is no such thing as "control". Control is just an *illusion*. The birth of a child means the death of the romantic illusions we may have about motherhood. Just like my aforementioned illusion that conception, pregnancy, and labour would be the hardest part of motherhood. You may also discover that when you become a parent, you and your partner's parents unconsciously show up in you. This speaks to the mother wound that our mothers unconsciously passed onto us, which we unconsciously pass onto our own children. Your mother wound could be a result of how you were mothered. You may have had an absent mother, a neglectful, a dismissive or a permissive mother, a child mother, an overprotective, or controlling mother. Or you may have grown up feeling grossly out of place, like a cygnet raised by ducks.

Doctor Oscar Serrallach explains the mother wound: *"At the macro level, the mother wound is a matrilineal wound—a burden that manifests in mothers and is passed on from generation to generation. It's the pain and grief that grow in a woman as she tries to explore and understand her power and potential in a society that doesn't make room for either, forcing her to internalize the dysfunctional coping mechanisms learned by previous generations of women. The mother wound reflects the challenges a woman faces as she goes through transformations in her life in a society where the patriarchy has denied us ongoing matrilineal knowledge and structures. Western society has had an anti-women agenda running for hundreds of years—including everything from issues of social and moral inequality to unjust land rights, voting discrimination, and disparities in positions of power. This agenda tells females not to shine, to remain small; and that if you are going to try to be successful, that you should be masculine about it. In subtle (and sometimes not so subtle) ways, we tell girls that becoming empowered will injure their relationships—and women are taught that relationships should be valued more than anything else. The measuring stick for women in our society is very different from the one we use to measure men; women are taught that there is shame around their successes. This status quo is kept alive through bureaucratic structure, the media, learned behaviours—what I think of as social programming. What happens to a developing woman when she feels thwarted by society and denied, ignored, and put down? Her energy can become repressed and internalized: "It must be me."*

This negative self-talk is repeated again and again and is used to programme in the next generation of Maidens and Mothers. As a society, the mother wound represents the females' role in perpetuating this programming against women over generations. On a personal level, it is a manifestation of our own mother's subconscious involvement, this being true and alive in us. So many women grow up with the unconscious choice that they can either be empowered *or* loved.

The names of the twins, Sun and Moon, speak to the male and feminine sides of ourselves. The nursing of twins can represent nurturing both sides of ourselves -the dark and the light elements of ourselves. Our compassionate self and the self-critical judge. We hold both of these cherished inner children in our bosom's comforting embrace as we raise them to the nipple of life and give them the substance of our love and attention. The yang male and the yin female energies are the *rare jewels* of our creative spirit as motherhood is our ultimate act of creation.

Mothers will often cast aside their own identities and creativity in order to raise their children in the fulfilment of the culturally acceptable persona of the selfless, "perfect mother". The nursing could also represent the nourishment that our children need and receive from us physically, and spiritually, which takes a toll on the mother's body and mind in so many different ways. Many mothers will find themselves so consumed with the exhaustion of their role that they are unable to create or focus on other important areas of their life. But it is only through the transitions of motherhood and witnessing how our behaviour is mirrored in our children that only then we will start to up and reimagine a different life for ourselves and our children.

All dignity is lost through childbearing and motherhood. You are poked and prodded, fingers are probed inside of your vagina to see how many centimetres dilated you are. The manhandling of breasts to help the new-born latch onto you. There really isn't much of our sexual selves that have remained intact. I quite often joke that, *"the mother in me killed the lover in me".* I know that my deteriorating interest in sex after the birth of our children is something my husband struggled with as he interpreted this as a "lack of love" from me to him and this quickly drained the life out of our relationship.

She AWAKES: Your Experience with Motherhood

- What was your own experience with motherhood? *(Being a mother and or with being mothered.)*

- When you are in the Mother archetype, do you experience a loss of control, a letting go, or losing yourself in motherhood?

- Do you have a mother wound?

- If you could express your mother wound, what would it look or feel like?

You can choose to express this exercise as a reflection by writing in your journal, a picture or painting, a poem, or through movement. Do what feels right for you to release these feelings.

Affirmation: *I am healing and mothering myself.*

she tugs onto a lock of my hair
searching,
nuzzling for the warmth
the sustenance of my breast

her mouth latches
sucking rhythmically
on tired raw skin
to the weary beat of my melting heart

Staying With Our Rapists

WHEN THE KING COMES BACK TO FIND TALIA, he finds her awake holding her children and he then he begins to tell Talia what happened. Instead of being horrified, she accepts the rape from the king and continues a relationship with him. In the time period when Talia lived, if a woman was raped by a man, she would not have any other choice but to marry her rapist or the woman would be ruined. Sadly, these days, it is not uncommon for victims of abuse to feel beaten down to the point where they feel so scared or that they have no other option but to stay with their abuser. However, most of us are unconscious victims who do not question the status quo, choose to stay in toxic relationships, and allow the repeated rape of our souls. Some of us may not even realise that we are a perpetual incarnation of the Maiden or are victims to the situation, it is simply part of the dream of our domestication that we leave unchallenged.

I grew up with a very loving yet angry, yelling man. This led me to subconsciously marry an angry man. Systematic and continuous dispensing of shame, using shame to fight shame in the form of crippling criticism, does not cause the victim to think unpleasantly of the perpetrator. It only causes the victim to turn on themselves. Victims of these relationships do not look at their abusers and think, "What is wrong with *them*?" Instead, the first person they will look to is themselves and ask, "What is wrong with *me*?" They grow to believe there must be an inherent flaw that makes it their fault that they are being treated this way. In my case, no physical attacks were ever dealt. I was taught not to question my life or relationships, so it took me a long time to recognise that I was actually a victim of abuse.

I am a survivor of words.

Careless, soul-wrenching, destructive, hurtful words. They became the seeds of devastation sewn deep into my subconsciousness. Eventually, my abuser did not even need to be in the same room, the same city, or even alive in this world for them to inflict pain onto me. I carried my abuser around with me, I started thinking in my abusers' voices. I became an expert in self-abuse. Even though I have myself mostly healed, there are days when a few of the seeds that were overlooked, (it takes a lifetime to weed them out), germinate and pop up like weeds in my soulish garden. I have discovered that being fully aware in my garden is the vital key to stopping myself from slipping back into victimhood. I cannot let my vigilance slide so I must take care to pull out these seeds of destruction when they are only seedlings. I do not want them to take root, flower, and sow more seeds. I also take care not to "walk on the grass". There are new shoots in the crop that I want to cultivate. Often when we are still asleep or just waking up, we don't realise the state of our soulish garden, or think that we have another choice. These relationships are not purely those with a romantic or life partner. These can also represent relationships with a parent or other family members. It can also be a friendship, a religion, or culture. We can unconsciously choose to stay with beliefs and values which no longer serve us and rob us of our self-esteem, self-worth, and vitality.

She AWAKES: Tending Your Soulish Garden

Do you even know what the state of your soulish garden is? The best indication of the state of your garden is the quality of your thoughts.

- **Intentionally choose a day to eavesdrop on your thoughts.**

- **Set a timer on your phone for hourly intervals.**

- **Keep your journal near and each time your alarm goes off, stop what you are doing and reflect on your thoughts from the previous hour.**

- **Objectively record all your thoughts in your journal.**

- **Review your thoughts at the end of the day.**

- **What clues did your thoughts give you about the state of your soulish garden?**

Be sure to not judge yourself, it's important to practice self-compassion with yourself and your thoughts. Soulish gardens are best tended with love, warmth, and kindness. Just because you have weeds in your garden does not make you a bad gardener, it purely means you have got to do some work. I will support you with some of the tools you will need to create your own beautiful garden that will sustain you and be an oasis of peace and joy later in this book. For now, be gentle and patient with yourself.

You are only just reawakening, dear wild heart, so give yourself permission to simply take the time to notice.

Affirmation: *I accept the love I give myself.*

I know that things look really bad to you right now
life is scary and out of control
you feel empty and hollow inside
as if life love and laughter are passing you by
somewhere just out of your reach

things are not as you planned or expected

I know how hard you work to control the outcome of your life
and that to you the world seems dark, scary
and that you feel all alone

that you spend life on the side-lines afraid to step
out of your lane
for fear of making a mistake
because of the fear of losing the little control you feel you have
over your big terrifying life

I know dear one
that you are living somewhere between hope and despair
fearful of trusting yourself and battling the painful sting of betrayal

that at times things seem so bleak
that you look out to the world around you
and you can't see even a single ray of light
or a speck of colour

but please remember that not all moments in life are bad
when we are feeling sad it is easy to paint the whole world with the colours of our sadness
the whole world is not sad

there is happiness too, my dear sweet love

you already have inside of you a deep well of possibilities
an abundance of talent
an overwhelming source of success and love

if you will only take the first step to meet it
if you would only take the time to trust yourself and all that you have been given

be gentle with yourself here love
you deserve beauty because you are beauty
I know that you would not believe me
I wish that you could see yourself through my eyes
how magical
how magnificent you are to me

I know that as there are parts of yourself that you hate
parts that you wish that you could cut away
I know that you look at these parts from time to time
that you wear them like a cloak of unworthiness

I know that you look to these parts as evidence of why you are not deserving
of love friendship and faith
but just because you have dark parts
does not mean that you are deserving of less love
but rather you deserve more

the darkness will not stay forever
there is sunshine to warm your back
there is music to vibe to
friendships to enjoy

there are foods waiting to be tasted in a grand food adventure
there are places in the world just waiting for you to discover them
and galaxies ready to explore
my sweet love
my heart weeps for your pain
I see your struggles as you try to make sense of it all
to make things fit

to make yourself fit

as awful as these feelings might be
remember that they are temporary
you will feel better
it will be okay
bad times come
but bad times also leave
please hang in there love

trust that colours can be bright
foods will once again taste good
dreams can be wondrous

the sweetness will follow

The Older Other Woman

THE OTHER WOMAN, THE KING'S WIFE, in *Sun, Moon and Talia* is portrayed as a villain. However, she herself is a victim of the dream of domestication. The wife in this story is a barren, dried-out woman, and disconnected from her creative self. She is the shadow of the Queen, the evil Queen who is willing to break oaths with herself to stay in a toxic relationship. Overcome with jealousy, hurt, and rage, she attempts to kill Talia and the children she bore so she can feed the children to the king. This is a common theme of rejection and retribution. A woman who gave her husband her precious "first fruits of love", who supported him, who nurtured him, and allowed herself to become selfless for him then has her sacrifice completely tossed aside and is displaced by a younger, more appealing maiden, who can give him what he finds missing with her. One of the attributes of the wounded Queen is to, instead of rightly turning her anger towards her husband who has been unfaithful, she attacks the "other woman".

In our Maiden-obsessed society, the youth and fresh beauty of the Maiden is elevated. Youth is so fleeting, yet we work so tirelessly to hang onto it because it is something that is highly valued in the dream of domestication. In this reality, older women can develop a sense of "otherness". It happens so quickly… One day we are girls and the next we have morphed into women. Confident, powerful in the weapons and armour of our beauty, youth, and sexuality, and then before we know it, we are finding grey pubes in the shower, crying over our mortality. Feeling bitterness for no longer being the "prime goods", tossed aside and replaced by something better. It is as if overnight we have become invisible. Inside every middle-aged woman is a raging girl who is screaming, 'What the fuck happened!' It is not uncommon for women in their middle years to look upon their teenage daughters in a full bloom Maiden, taking up space in the sunlight and feel conflicting pangs of pride and envy. It's like having to grieve their own wilting rose in the corner, losing petals.

I experienced a time in my life when I was absolutely petrified of getting older. In fact, for my fortieth birthday, I was given a silver charm with the number forty attached to a silver bracelet. It is a beautiful bracelet and a very heartfelt gift from my husband's parents to celebrate my milestone birthday. For two years, I observed this beautiful piece of jewellery with both admiration and dread. I had never worn it; I was too afraid to. I had convinced myself that if I wore the charm then it meant

I was no longer a girl. I was old, not sexy anymore, not worthy–invisible. Through my own shadow Maiden-obsessed lens, I always felt immense sadness whenever I looked at old photographs of my grandmother when she was in her twenties and thirties. She smiled back at me, so young, beautiful, and vital. I then compared this to the woman I knew; a once energetic body now frail and stooped, porcelain skin turned paper-thin, translucent skin defiled by purple veins and brown liver spots. In the end, our youth and beauty fades, we all get old and weak, and this fills me with anxiety. I was so caught up in my fear that I made a tiny number on a bracelet mean so many different things. Then one day, I saw the bracelet and I thought to myself, 'Tanya, you are no longer a girl, nor do you want to be a girl. You *may* not be young *anymore,* but you can still be beautiful–just a different type of beautiful, *wear* the bracelet. *you* are a woman, *own* your forty years on this planet and make them count!' So, I made a decision that I was going to wear my bracelet. I didn't care about what others thought and I wasn't going to make it mean anything other than a pretty bracelet with the number forty on it. And so, I freed myself from the imprisonment of my fears and stepped into the beauty and the worthiness of my years, and I was gracefully welcomed into the waiting arms of my empowered Queen.

Part of the tale is cautionary. And there's three options: we can wake up from the dream, call on our Huntress, and take the accountability for our own lives. We have the option to call on our Lover and reclaim our creative, sensual selves before it's too late. Or we can allow ourselves to become bitter, resentful, and vengefully wounded Mothers or Queens. When we are not able to practice accountability, acceptance, or self-love, we can easily project our pain onto others around us. In doing this, we make ourselves right in our suffering but assign the lack we feel in ourselves as the fault of others. I anticipated that I would really enjoy being a stay-at-home mum. I had dreamed that being a mother to someone who needs me would be all I need to feel fulfilled. After losing my baby to a miscarriage, I was determined to be the best mum I could be for my rainbow baby. Eighteen months later, I was the mum of two children under the age of two. I joined mum's groups, playgroups, saw friends occasionally but somehow, I still felt lonely and miserable. I love my children with everything fibre of my being, but I did not love staying home with them all the time and not having other adults around to talk to. I wanted to love it–that it would be enough for me. What I didn't realise was that it came at a cost and the price I would pay for it, was *me*. We place so much pressure on ourselves as mothers to the point where we create a war inside of us that we can never win. Either way, I would feel guilt and shame for choosing to stay home, or I would feel guilt and shame for choosing to work and not spending enough time with our children.

Sometimes motherhood is pure joy but sometimes, but mostly, it is sneezing and trying not to pee your pants. It's preparing yourself to repeat "what the fuck" to yourself a million times a day and fighting the guilt you feel when you try to meet your own needs. Sometimes you'll find yourself resisting the urge to join your toddler on the floor while they are having a tantrum. And then you'll try not to snap at your surly, sulky teenager who has barricaded themselves in the dark cave that is their room. It's merely hanging in there hoping that tomorrow will be a better day.

Who knew? Who knew that being a mum would mean I was to become solely responsible for who takes care of the baby? Who knew that at times I would feel lonely and isolated? Who knew that I would begin to secretly resent my husband for his ability to carry on with *his* life—still getting enough sleep, going to work as normal, meeting his friends for beers on the weekend as if nothing significant had changed? I seethed at how it never even occurred to him to ask if it was okay to do so before he acted. Never once stopping to consider how I felt, I just heard, *'Who will take care of the baby?'*, *'Just ask if you need help'*, or, *'But you should have just asked me'*. As if the never-ending tasks deciding on what to cook for dinner every night wasn't enough, just to have him complain, *'But we had this last night.'* Or is doing the dishes, cleaning the house, or reminding him to pick up his dirty laundry from the floor is my genetic inheritance just because I was born with boobs and a vagina?

It is from my own experience that most mothers carry this emotional burden as she buries herself under all the tasks that she must do. In love with her children but having a constant feeling that she has to ask permission, make a multitude of micro arrangements, and decisions every time she wants to do something for herself. Most of the time it doesn't occur to her to ask, 'This is what my mother did, her grandmother, and her great grandmother before her....' with the well-worn track playing in the background of her subconscious.

I used to feel deep anger and self-righteousness towards the mums who didn't seem to lose themselves and was able to go straight back into work after the birth of their baby. Even the mums who still managed to go to the gym or go away for weekends. I felt so bitter towards my husband who seemed unfazed by it all. "How could they be so selfish?" But in reality, I was jealous. I felt so much shame that I wasn't able to deal with it or I wasn't loving being a stay-at-home parent. This is something I had dreamed of for so long. It did not even occur to me that I held all the same freedoms that my husband and the other mums did. All that I needed to do was to open my mouth and demand my rights just as everyone else did; I needed to take action to make these things happen for myself. Instead of doing that, I took my shame and frustration out on my husband. My mental health continued to decline as I threw myself deeper and deeper into motherhood. And that became the pit to where I lost myself. The Tanya I knew before no longer existed, only this person called "Mum". When I finally returned to work, I found myself constantly caught up in a never-ending tug-of-war of being a good teacher, a good teammate, a good wife, and a good mum. I made choices in my career that centred around my identity as a mother instead of choosing things which ignited a fire of passion in me. I continued working because I needed the money to support my children rather than making the changes that my intuition was urging me to. And so, I lost myself further in being the *good version* of all the roles which I felt that everyone else needed me to fulfil.

I was so consumed by my own desires to be everything that everyone else needed that I forgot to keep a little bit of *me* for myself. Soon, I was empty and depleted of the "me-ness". I remember sitting in my car, scoffing down sushi in my very late lunch break of five minutes at five o'clock in the afternoon as I waited for my daughter to finish Girl Guides. A song from my teenage years started playing on the radio and I felt the long-forgotten stirrings of my Wild Woman move inside me, and I sat there sobbing into my salmon and avocado nori roll. This was never how I expected life to be like. I felt so trapped inside my life. But I just couldn't imagine another reality. I felt I had no other choice than to accept the life I was living. I had spent so many of *my* years making all *my* decisions based upon what was right for other people that even thinking about the idea of whether *I* was happy or not felt scary, unnatural, and selfish. When my children started growing up and depended less on me, I was left feeling like the hole of emptiness was growing bigger and bigger. I was angry and hurt. I had given up so much of myself for my children and now they no longer needed me. And that thought filled with rage, so I blamed my husband. *'It was* his fault *that I was so miserable, that I had wasted my life—look how badly he treated me! He was always doing what he wanted to do, always wanting sex from me, and never looking after my needs! What a selfish, selfish man!'* I picked fights and we argued *all the time.* It did not occur to me that he might be a victim too; to the dream of his domestication. That maybe he was miserable too.... Instead of talking to each other, connecting over our shared pain, we turned on against other and attempted to burn each other on the pyre of our scorn.

When we make something someone else's fault we cast *ourselves* as the victim. There is security in victimhood. Victims are powerless, so they do not have to do anything to improve their lives. Instead, we can stay in the safety net of our "rightness" bitching, complaining, and plotting to destroy others who we perceive to have harmed us. It is common to turn our hurt into rage and tear down others and their creativity when we feel that life has not turned out the way that we had hoped or planned for. We focus entirely on ourselves and our own suffering that it causes our mind to narrow so much that we do not see how we may be like the person who slighted us. Nor are we able to entertain how we could actually be able to support and learn from each other.

This story would have had a vastly different ending if the women in Talia's story realised that they were both victims of the king's treachery. They would have realised that they didn't need a man to define their worth and could have banded together to throw him in the fire! Taking the responsibility for being part of a solution is often a bitter pill to swallow, however, being responsible for ourselves does not mean we must forgive the other person, or even agree that what they did to harm us was okay. It simply means we can take accountability for the power of our own healing, which is where the magic happens. I was not realising this until I woke up to the reality that my rage towards my husband stemmed from my lack of boundaries and inability to take accountability for my own life, my own choices, my own happiness, and my own actions. I could start creating shifts to move myself from the wounded Mother, and powerless Maiden to the empowered Queen. I can still vividly remember how liberating the moment was when I realised my happiness did not originate from him and I had the power to create it inside of me, for myself.

This section of the story highlights the reality of living in a male-dominated culture. The cannibalism of children is an unnatural act. It could be interpreted as a women's softness, empathy, and creativity being devoured by an overly masculine world. It serves as a warning to us for what might happen if a strong-minded woman makes a bid for control—she will ultimately get burned. One such modern cautionary tale is the "Karen" pejorative, which can be viewed as a contemporary version of a wounded Queen or an evil Queen. The Karen TikToks and Facebook video posts are meant to be satirical in nature, however, they highlight the archetype of the wounded Queen or a woman who has sacrificed her femininity to embrace masculine traits. It also shines a very bright spotlight on how our culture and societal world now treats assertive women. There is no male equivalent to "Karen". If a man has a problem, he expresses a point of view, complains or is assertive, we praise his directness. Although, "Karen" points to a type of behaviour that is harmful and discriminatory, to me "Karen" feels like a mass lesson of shame and name-calling.

In the story of Sun, Moon and Talia, the wife had every right to be angry. Her husband had raped an unconscious girl and continued a relationship with her. It is in her frustration of not being given a choice or a voice, and her own powerless victim status causes her to act from a place of a wounded Queen. Thanks to the rise of the "Karen" stereotype, every time a woman speaks up, or steps into the power of her

Queen, she risks the fear of being labelled with a derogatory name. And if she defends herself, she only confirms this status. I believe that "Karen" is the warning signal to our daughters about what would happen if she dared to send back her meal because it was not what she ordered, if she complains, or stands up for herself. To me, I feel that it is just another way to keep women in their *Maiden* lane—quiet, demure, nice and playing small.

She AWAKES: Growing Older

- **What is your experience with aging?**

- **How do you view the transition moving from a Maiden to a Queen?**

- **How did this make you feel, think, and act?**

- **What are your fears about aging, maturing, success and power, and how are they keeping you stuck from embracing your Queen?**

Affirmation: *I embrace the person I am now.*

your heart is meant to be broken

how do I know that this is true?

because of the reality of it

hearts break again and again and again

it is a painful undertaking
but yet miraculously most of us
are still here to tell the tale
of how we lived
loved
and survived

Good Things Happen To You While You Are Asleep

THE STORY OF *SUN, MOON AND TALIA* ends with the line *"Those whom fortune favours find good luck even in their sleep."*

Why would anyone agree with this statement? As absurd as it sounds, this part of the fairy tale is an invitation, but *an invitation to what?* In order for me to answer your question, let me introduce a new archetype. I call this archetype, "Danger Chicken". The story of Danger Chicken has its origins from my very own backyard.

We live on a rural, lifestyle block outside of Whangarei in Northland, New Zealand. Living in the country for us means we have ten kilometres of meandering dirt roads and paddocks to navigate between our house and the main tar sealed road. Part of the charm of where we live is the array of birds we see on a daily basis. Tuis sing happily as they drink nectar from *harakeke*—flax flowers. Fantails twitter and dance in the tea tree. Kingfisher observe the green pasture lurking for their prey as they sit unblinking on the wooden garden fence. Peacocks mewl in the distance calling for mates while flirting with their fabulous feathers, as ducks usher their young to swimming lessons on the pond. We also have a rafter of wild turkeys that live in a paddock close to our house. I have decided that wild turkeys, well at least the ones which live near us, might be the dumbest birds known to man. They congregate on the side of the road like gangs conducting their morning meetings and when a car approaches them, instead of running in the opposite direction and back towards the nearby paddock, they run headlong into the path of the oncoming car. Jokingly, the kids and I started calling our wild turkeys "danger chickens". This name stuck and is now something we use to describe all the wild turkeys. If we think about it, each of us, in our own ways are "Danger Chickens", who are mindlessly running headfirst towards our death. Danger Chicken is our default way we behave when we allow our shadow archetypes to control us as we slumber in the dream of our domestication.

Danger Chicken is the archetype of the "asleep woman". When we inhibit this archetype, we remain stubbornly committed to believing the worst about ourselves and the self-protective behaviours which sabotage our health and happiness, often while we are aware we are doing it. The thought loop of the Danger Chicken is *"I am bad and so I deserve bad things to happen to me."* Danger Chicken will manifest into a woman's life, hurt, and devastation. Anything from emotional overeating, restricting food and purging, seeking out destructive relationships, and repeating harmful behaviours can possibly lead someone to attempt to end one's life. *If being a Danger Chicken is so detrimental to us, why do we like to hang around in "Danger Chicken" mode?* I believe it has something to do with ignoring the "spots".

Not sure on what I am talking about?... Let me explain.

Have you ever noticed a spot on the wall or window? A spot of grime, a smudge, a speck of dirt, or a dot of fly poo and it motivates you to grab your disinfectant and a cloth to clean it up. However, as you clean it, you notice that it is not the only one! You start to notice one more, then two more, then ten more, and before you know it, your whole day has disappeared down a rabbit hole of a two-minute, now a two-hundred-hour, job. I'll confess that sometimes when I see a small spot on the wall, I leave it. I turn away and intentionally "unsee" it. I tell myself, *'I don't have time to clean it now, I will wait until spring arrives and I will clean it then.'* Not because I do not *actually* have the time to clean, but because I don't have the spare day or week in which I can spend cleaning all the other spots that suddenly need my attention. The thoughts which stop me from cleaning that spot are almost always, *'What else will seeing this spot lead to?'* or *'What else will need my attention if I pay attention to the spot?'* or, *'Do I have time or the energy for this?'* It can be so overwhelming! Sometimes, it is just easier to shut the curtains and bar out the light so we do not have to think about it. I tend to believe that we can end up treating other areas of our lives like we treat this "spot".

Little spots in life, like our crying child, we shush or admonish with, *'Don't cry'.* We dismiss the subtle frequency of their low-intensity emotions such as disappointment or sadness. We allow our busy schedules, our need to get out of the house in the morning, to be a distraction to of dealing with the nightmares, bad moods, or messy emotions. We block out their bids for attention by turning a blind eye and scroll through our phones to a form of escapism as dealing with these emotions might require time and energy that we don't feel that we have. For we fear that it may uncover something in us or our lives that we do not like, or we want it to stay hidden. Or perhaps when someone says or does something which makes us uncomfortable, we swallow the poison and pretend we did not hear their words or see their deeds. We deny the truth in our bodies—the emotional reaction that we just felt. We may have a nagging sense that tells us "Something is not right". However, we write it off as being "too sensitive", or we admonish ourselves, *'Not now.'* It is not that we do not see the spot, but we would rather choose to unsee it, and we do so because we know it will only lead us to a whole lot of "cleaning" that we don't want to deal with. We have often reached a point in our lives where we are exhausted of our spiritual energy, so depleted that it is easier, safer, and more comfortable, to stay as a sleeping victim going through the motions of life—and be a *Danger Chicken*.

If you are reading this and my words fill you with sadness or shame, take heart. Every single one of us do this. There have been many such moments in my life when I have seen the "spot"—the subtle (and not so subtle)—indication that something was not right but I chose to deny or to ignore it. I never even gave a thought to how big the mess could become, not recognising at the time that if I just "cleaned as I go", I could have put a stop to the debris of in life before it became an impossible predicament. It is in my programming to be the eternal optimist, the Maiden committed to the rosy, *'everything is alright here'* illusion. At times, I still need to learn how to acknowledge the spots that appear on the walls of my illusion as access points. Places where I need to focus my attention instead of seeing them as inconveniences. I still need reminding to look, and clean, rather than to just draw the curtains and ignore. The spot is your inconvenient truth, the unhealed hurt—the wild, messy, feeling, alive, passionate *YOU* who is calling for your attention outside of the dream.

One of my mentors once said to me: *'Life is funny, it first shows you the spot. The spot is your first warning sign. If you ignore the spot, life sends you another warning—a two-by-four plank against the back of the head. If you ignore the two-by-four plank, life sends you a MACK truck to hit you in the face. Pay attention to the spot, it is a lot less painful.'*

The road is scattered with corpses of Danger Chickens who mindlessly ran towards on-coming cars…

This is the part of the book where you too must make a choice. It is a moment when you get the option to decide, *do you stay warm, in the darkness of your sleep, comfortable, and blissfully numb?* A Danger Chicken in the dream, as Talia did, ultimately does and *lives happily ever after*. Or do you listen to the call of your Wild Wise Woman outside of the dream?

Do you choose to **AWAKEN**?

She AWAKES: Taking a Leap of Faith

For this exercise you will need three pieces of paper, some coloured pens, pencils, or crayons.

- **Set a timer on your phone for five minutes, and on the first piece of paper I invite you to draw a picture of yourself.**

- **Set the timer for a further five minutes, and on the second piece of paper draw yourself with your biggest problem.**

- **Set the timer for a further five minutes, and on the third piece of paper draw yourself with your problem solved.**

This exercise is revealing, the restraint in time, and using drawing as a tool allows you to directly cut through your conscious thoughts and to access your subconscious thinking.

Many people are surprised by what their drawings reveal to them. Did you, like me, recognise in your third drawing that you already had the solution to your biggest problem inside of you? If this was not your experience, take heart, we still have so much time on our journey together. You may have spent your adulthood searching you may have spent your life on a yoyo diet, starved of soulish nourishment one moment and then binging on snacks of bad relationships, worked jobs that paid bills but didn't fulfil you, and shallow pursuits to please others, but have done nothing to nurture the woman you really are. You may be alerted by the warning light in your soul, that there is something bigger, better, more beautiful waiting for you. You may wish, like I did, to move yourself out of this valley of despair, out of the shadows of the mountains that are stopping you from achieving your fullest potential. You may feel like you are going crazy trying to figure out how to turn the warning light off. But take heart dear one, I know we can feel grossly unprepared and not ready yet, its usually the most important things that happen in our lives when we are not ready for them. All that is needed is for you to trust have faith. Trust and have faith not in me, nor in this book, for I am just a person, and these are mere words on a page.

No.

The person you need to trust and have faith in is the same person who gets up with you in the morning. The person who goes to work with you each day, who dreams with you at night. The person whose reflection you see when you glance into the mirror, the person in the series of drawings that you just created.

Trust and have faith in **yourself**. And if you find that you need reminding…

Your brain with its creative ideas and quick wit.

Your heart is full of love.

Your voice is strong and true—waiting for you to set it free.

Your gut, your north star in a sea of bullshit and lies.

Your body is strong, beautiful, resilient, and capable of creating infinite life.

Your soul endued with a spark of the divine.

You, my beautiful one, have all the secrets and the keys to unlock them already inside of you

They have always been there waiting to be unearthed.

You are no Talia, Briar Rose, or Aurora, a helpless Maiden living at the whim of others, with hardly any lines in your own fucking movie.

Your waiting is done.

You are the Queen - the hero -you have been waiting for.

All you need to do is say, 'YES'.

The journey makes you ready as you go through it.

Before we continue our adventure together, I encourage you to write a snapshot letter to yourself. (I have included an example of one that I wrote to myself as a reference on the next page. You are welcome to adapt my letter, or you can use it as inspiration to write your own.) This letter will be a reminder to you of where you are now, it signifies your commitment to yourself, and the next part of your journey. Please do this intuitively and with as much emotion as possible. You may want to create a ritual around writing this letter. Declare your intentions which symbolise the importance of this *leap of faith* you are taking.

Affirmation: *I already have everything I need inside of me.*

My Snapshot Letter

Dearest Tanya,

It is the 25[th of] October 2015, you have just been on your first personal development course, and I know that you are feeling frightened and confused. This has been the first time in a while that you have allowed yourself to truly feel, cry, and dream. I know that amongst the messiness which this has stirred up, for you there is a glimmer of curiosity and hope. I know that everything inside of you wants to slam the door closed on this experience and run as fast as you can in the other direction, so you pretend it did not happen. But please find the courage to choose hope and curiosity. I know you have lost yourself to the many roles you play in other people's lives, and you don't want to upset the apple cart.

But do this for you…

Trust and have faith in yourself.
You are exactly where you need to be.
You, my beautiful one, are so much more than what you are allowing yourself to be.
You owe this to yourself and the world.
This is your time… and you are ready!

Your biggest fan,
Tanya xxx

trust is built in the doing

little miracles woven out of the textile of human interaction
in the smallest of actions and moments
the exchange of trust extended to another
and trust returned

trust built out of vulnerability and loss
in the acceptance that not all trust will be reciprocated
and that we have to risk our very hearts
for there is no controlling the actions of another
or the outcome of our gift of trust

why do we do this?

why risk so much of our hearts and ourselves in the transaction?

we gamble it all on the promise of the reward
we time and time again hedge our bets on the ideal
that with great risk comes greater reward

when our risk and our wager is rewarded
with trust returned
we store this as a deposit in our heart bank
we build on these deposits
and we grow the interest until
we have an abundance of trust
that we are able to share freely with those around us

the more trust we give the greater our treasure

trust is for giving

when our trust accounts are flourishing
overflowing with wealth
we are freer with the spending
of our trust as we have trust to spare
when our heart is broken
because trust has not returned
or trust has been withdrawn
we are tempted to chain up our hearts
and not to give trust away
to be miserly with our investments of trust

when this happens
do not give into the temptation to squirrel away your trust
but instead continue to give trust with a happy heart

for we risk losing a part of ourselves
as the price of withholding trust
and locking away our hearts is too high

without the regular sustaining deposits
of trust into our heart bank
other things shrivel and die too

our hope
our faith
our love
our humanity
– leap of faith

The Cave:
The Call To Your Hero's Journey

ALTHOUGH I WAS BORN IN THE SEVENTIES, I am very much a child of the eighties at heart. This fluorescent, loud, space in time where the colours were bright, the hair was big, and rock and roll was loud, was when I came of age. One of my favourite things in this decade is the 1980's adventure movies. I adore movies such as *The Goonies, Indiana Jones, Star Wars, E.T,* and other gems such as *Romancing the Stone* and *The NeverEnding Story.* What I absolutely love about these stories is the every day, "normal" human beings, (many of them kids), who embark on amazing, and often dangerous, quests and adventures. Inevitably, they are faced with obstacles and are up against great odds which ultimately leads to them uncovering some treasures and returning home with their lives changed in a weird and wonderful way.
This is a common formula which establishes the foundation for many story plots. Throughout time, and throughout many myths, legends, and stories, the common thread commences with an "everyday" hero, living in the "ordinary" world. The hero hears the call to adventure, and after initially refusing it, they take up the challenge and begin their quest. While walking the path, they meet a guide and crosses a threshold into an interesting and special world. Once inside, with the help of allies and enemies, they must enter the innermost cave and survive many tests and trials. Our hero ultimately overcomes some sort of immense obstacle, returning home to the ordinary world, triumphant, armed with new weapons or treasure, and is irrevocably transformed.

Ponder on your favourite story, even if you are a romance reader or enjoy biographies, chances are high that there will be some element of this familiar plot formula in there somewhere. This quest to find meaning is usually done in our most difficult hour. This is your journey, your Queen's journey!

From the depths of our sleepy state, in the ordinary world, we will hear the call to our adventure—*hello, warning light!* After spending time denying the call—*really, there is nothing wrong with my life, let me just get another job, I will be fine*—our Wild Woman stirs inside of us and rouses our Huntress impelling us to accept the invitation. We then set upon our adventure and meet a guide—*this book*—and we accept the call to cross the threshold into this special world. When in this special world, we meet our allies—*other women on the same journey as us*—and enemies—*those who want to stand in the way of our happiness.* From here, we must enter our innermost cave—*you are here.* Our cave is at the foothills of the mountain. This symbolises the awakening of your conscious thought.

By nature, caves are dark, sometimes tight, scary, and uncomfortable. Our caves are often silent, and still, and, more often than not, we are alone. The cave needs to be dark and narrow so it can limit the amount of outside stimulus we have so we can focus better on our interior light, and the journey within. The cave needs to be silent so that we can locate and listen to the gentle hum of our inner life source. Sometimes, we get stuck at a boulder choke—a place in a cave where rocks have fallen and are obscuring a passageway—something you may have already experienced in your life. Adolescence, the birth of a baby, a break-up, losing your job, the loss of a loved one, and mid-life can all be boulder chokes in your cave. I've observed that boulder chokes often disguise places to cove a weakness in the dream. An effaced cervix waiting to birth a new version of us. The cave is the place where our Maiden is reincarnated into the Queen of the Underworld. Where we meet our Wild Woman and Wise Woman. These archetypes are inhabitants of this special world, and they help us to unhook ourselves from the dream of the ordinary world. It is a tomb to our reawakening; it is the chrysalis where we are transformed into the butterfly. The cave is the place where we unearth the parts of the treasure that is ourselves. As the poet, Rumi, says, '*You have no need to travel anywhere. Journey within yourself, enter a mine of rubies and bathe in the splendour of your own light.*'

Joseph Campbell quotes from his book, *The Hero's Journey*, "*The cave you fear to enter holds the treasure that you seek.*" These are words that I cling on to when times get tough. It also speaks of our call to courage to do the hard and uncomfortable things even though we are scared shitless. The inextinguishable human spirit pushes us to go into the cave, much like the caterpillar is compelled to become the chrysalis. Or as in one of my favourite eighties movies, the kids in *The Goonies* did. Although we are filled with fear, ill-prepared, and up against overwhelming obstacles. *Why would you choose to do this? Why would you choose to deny your basic instinct to run in the opposite direction?* We do this because of the promise of the reward and the ultimate transformation. Like many people, you want to believe that your suffering has a meaning, that what you endure serves some sort of higher purpose, and there is something better for us than the life we settled for. The opposite would be too soul crushing to even contemplate, and so, even in our bleakest situations, we search for the "gems of meaning" in our cave.

Discontent is a spot, an access point for the biggest treasure quest of all. Out of all emotions, discontent has to be the most exciting and transformative emotion we can feel. Discontent means that you—the Queen—are finally ready for something new, bigger, better, and more beautiful. All great adventures have started with the notion that *'there has to be something more'*. This is the call—the quest I am inviting you to join on. I am welcoming you to descend into this special world with me and to meet your Queen of the Underworld, your Wild Woman and your Wise Woman archetypes as they will be your own personal guides. Now your "cant's", "couldn't possibly's", "should", and "have too's" will start sprouting at your feet like magical vines to trap and keep you locked in place. They will try to deter you from your adventure. (This is why the hero initially refuses the call.)

But do not let your fear stop you, for you are strong, brave, and capable of such amazing things when you put your head and your heart to it. You have the complete access to your guides. If you work with them, they will help you to restore balance, heal, move out of the shadows, and integrate all your parts so you can return to you and your sovereignty. Often, you may look at your gift of discontentment with trepidation, I know it can feel like a heavy burden instead of a treasure.

However, celebrate, and rejoice! You have been invited. The gauntlet has been laid down before you, the journey has been prepared; and your quest has begun.

World beware… a Queen is waiting to be born!

She AWAKES: Your Call to Adventure

- **Do you hear your call to adventure?**

- **Are you willing to accept the call?**

Affirmation: *I am the hero of my own life.*

and just when I thought I was done
destination decided
course plotted
wrapped in a package
sealed with a bow
signed and delivered
finished with a full stop.

she just looked at me knowingly
and smiled

you think you're finished
darling you have only just begun

PART TWO

The Wild Self

come with me she said
as she pulled the curtain aside
let me show you how the magic works

Wild Self

HAVE YOU EVER HAD THIS EXPERIENCE? You are outside on the beach, swimming in the ocean, walking in a forest, relaxing in your garden, enjoying a sunrise or a sunset, or sitting under the night sky taking in the magnificence of the natural creation around you and suddenly you feel it…

A pulling on your heart.

A longing for something you cannot put into words.

A yearning for an adventure.

A call to be more authentically *you*.

Or you just *know* you are part of something wonderfully, awe-inspiringly bigger than yourself.

And in that very moment you know there is so much more to you than you realise. There is something freer, more real, and more meaningful that you should be doing. But then, it's followed by a sadness that you cannot quite articulate? It as if there is a distant self, calling out to you from beyond the horizon that you are trying to reach but as much as you try, you just can't get to her… This is your Wild Woman stirring inside of you, calling to you to awaken from the dream of domestication.

According to author, Dr Clarissa Pinkola Estés, of *Women Who Run with the Wolves*, she quotes,

> *"Wild woman is the health of all women. Without her, women's psychology makes no sense… She canalizes through women. If they are suppressed, she struggles upward. If women are free, she is free. Fortunately, no matter how many times she is pushed down, she bounds up again. No matter how many times she is forbidden, quelled, cut back, diluted, tortured, touted as unsafe, dangerous, mad and other derogations, she emanates upward in women, so that even the quietest, even the most restrained woman keeps a secret place for her."*

Wild Woman is the soul in all women. If Danger Chicken is the sleeping woman, then the Wild Woman is an awake woman. She is filled with a deep perceptive that has nothing to do with intellect. A Wild Woman is an ancient life force, she is our spirit, our intuition, our innate expression of self, and our spark of the divine. The Wild Woman is our link to the forces of the ancient and the promise for our future. She is our early warning light which cautions us when we have lost our way. Inviting us to come back to find ourselves again. Our Wild Woman, the keeper of our life cycles, she is the doula of our dying parts as they return to fertile ground for the underworld so they can be reborn and made new. Our Wild Woman is the midwife, who lovingly supports our shoulders and encourages us while we birth the new. Many women who have ignored or repressed their Wild Woman for a period of time may not know how to access her. And so, I offer this suggestion... The Wild Woman belongs to the elements of nature. She needs wide open, expansive spaces—not the bottom drawer in which you have confined her to and that is why you may feel that pull to a distant self when you are outdoors. If you are feeling like she is completely lost to you, pay attention to how nature calls out to you. When I began to become aware of my Wild Woman, I felt the pull towards spending more time outside, swimming in the ocean, creating a garden, and being close to indoor plants.

Light a candle or a fire. Watch a sunset and bask in the euphoria of the golden hour. Sit under a full moon among a galaxy of stars. Walk and breathe under the canopy of the forest walls. Place your hand on the trunk of a mighty tree and feel its heartbeat through the earth. Swim in the waves of the ocean. Walk barefoot and feel the grass or sand between your toes. Sit with your back to the warmth of the sun, or simply connect with your breath. Feel it as it flows in, through and out of your body. Place one hand on your chest and notice the steady beat of your heart, and place one hand on your stomach and experience how your breath causes your belly to rise and fall. Feel the intensity of your emotions. Allow yourself to be moved by them. Cry, laugh, rage, howl. Move into your strong, wild, and beautiful body. Hear the purr of energy inside of you. Still your mind and its infinite worries of tomorrow and know that *she* is there.

She AWAKES: Imagining Your Wild Woman

For this exercise you will need your journal, pens, crayons, or paint.

Take a moment here to close your eyes and use your imagination, take yourself back to the place where you feel the call towards this distant, elusive Wild Self.

- **Where are you?**

- **What do you hear?**

- **What do you see?**

- **What do you smell?**

- **What could you taste?**

- **What did you feel?**

Engage all of your senses to visualise this beautiful, Wild Self and draw what you see in your mind. Let this be an instinctive process, let her flow through you. You may want to paint or draw, or you may want to create a collage, but once you have drawn her, I would like you to introduce yourself to her and tell her what you would hope to learn from having her in your life. You can do this either verbally out loud, or in written form in your journal.

Affirmation: *Today I chose to meet my Wild Woman.*

Why Start with The Wild Self?

I suggest starting here because so many of us have severed our connection with our Wild Woman and it is the reason, we are so lost, feel stuck, and in pain. In order to get free ourselves from our slumber, we need to carry out deep, personal work that is only available to us in the shadows. We bury her away and deafen our ears to her call to be wild and free. We cage her in, we entrap ourselves, and we suffer, and as a result of this we wither, and we become mere outlines of ourselves full of envy, resentment, and bitterness. We can sense a part of us is missing because our suppressed Wild Woman is angry. Enraged, she causes us pain as she claws her way out of us, reminding us that she is still there, tired of being trapped inside. She is urgent and insistent to make sure she will not continue to be ignored or forgotten anymore. Like a caged animal, she paces angrily around the perimeter of the enclosure we have confined her to, as we try to drown out her voice with the noise of the world. All the while she watches, waiting for a weak spot in the dream where she can escape and be free, and that is when she causes the most harm.

For many of us, by the time we reach our mid-life, her call can be so loud and insistent that it can literally drive us to despair and depression. Your Wild Woman is the secret longing we all have for more meaning, more purpose, and more *life* in our lives. Your yearning to be true to yourself and your dreams. Perhaps you are hesitant or scared about what will happen if you release her into your life. She could have escaped into your life previously, and in her feral form, she wreaked havoc. You may have been programmed to believe that "wild" means "out of control" or "too much to handle". You fear her awesome power would be too much for *you* to handle, and she will be a destructive force in your life—destroying everything you hold dear to you. And she will make you into someone you dislike.

I understand you. I was fearful of her too.

For years, after my brief tryst with my Wild Woman in my adolescence, I resisted her calls, petrified of what might transpire if I let her out of her enclosure. Terrified of how my life would materialise—of who I would become. And as I did this, I got weaker, and sadder, and sicker. Eventually, when I allowed her the freedom to move in me, I discovered things did change—I changed. I had to let go of things that were contributing to my mental and emotional illness. Things that were no longer purposefully serving me. The Wild Woman is the keeper of the life-death-life cycle. The price of my new life was my old one.

Please take heart. I know you are scared. Letting her out can be an intensely powerful, and emotional experience. Often the things which are the hardest to release are the things that cause us the most pain.

When I first allowed her into my life, I too stood fearful in her presence, yet she made me feel so "alive" in the ancient wisdom of her knowing. The Wild Woman's true nature is to make you feel more yourself, to heal and not harm. When the Wild Woman is honoured, she becomes a co-creator in your life. She nourishes you within your relationship, she gives you strength, courage, and insight into yourself, showing you things that you forgot even lived inside of you. As mentioned in the previous chapter, when we activate our Wild Woman, we activate her special world sisters, the Queen of the Underworld and the Wise Woman. They are there to help in keeping their sister grounded, cooling the flames of our Wild Woman's rage, chaotic, and feisty nature. Trusting these energies to work in relationship with each other enables their power of grounding influence and balancing, and empowering attributes. Their unified influence can be a source of joy and abundant blessings.

'A woman connected with her Wild Woman is one with the vibrations experienced from the energy of the earth as it slips between her toes. She spins rainbows with her mind and releases rain with her tears. She dances with the music of the wind in the trees and the rush of the water in a racing river. She howls like the she wolf under the full moon. The magic of her dreams moving forth from her and expanding like the galaxies of a trillion stars.'

She AWAKES: Noticing the Loving Attention of Your Wild Woman

I would like you to think back to a time in your life when you remember feeling your Wild Woman guiding you. I have shared some of the moments in my life below to support you with this:

1. I felt my Wild Woman when I was twelve years old, I had to face the duality of the grief of saying goodbye to my grandmother and facing my own mortality for the first time.

2. I was empowered by her in my teenage rebellion.

3. I saw her in me, loud and fierce, when I peered at the faces of my new-born babies as I felt the primal instinct to protect them above all else rise inside of me.

4. I sensed her guiding wisdom, linking me to the Wild Women of my ancestral line as I stubbornly nursed my young as those around me told me not to.

5. I felt her stirring in me when I started my spiritual awakening.

6. She is intensely present when my writing muse urges me time and time again to release my words on the page with the whisper, *'do not be afraid, this is who you are'*.

- **What has been your experiences with your Wild Woman?**

- **How has her presence frightened you?**

- **How has she guided and healed you in these moments?**

- **What does your Wild Woman want for you?**

Affirmation: *I choose to allow my Wild Woman to be free in me.*

The Coming Out of the Wild Woman

Through experience, most women have their own version of "coming out". This is a coming out which has nothing to do with sexuality, although many women may discover that the true nature of their Wild Woman is to love, lust, and attach to other women. (My intention here is not to offend the LGBTQ+ community with this statement.) This coming out is as significant to the female psyche as sexual identity, as this is a spiritual coming out. I speak here about the unveiling that ensues when we finally hold enough courage to reveal the secret truths of who we really are to the world. It occurs when the pain of living the collective dream is more painful than the discomfort of acknowledging the magical creatures, we are to ourselves. It happens when we are finally free of our Maiden's desire to be liked by everyone, to fit in, and the possible rejection of a world where we may longer fit. Our Wild Woman has never bought into the collective dream. She has always known that we are magic. She is the last woman standing in a world where life pulls us in many different directions, distracting us, and lead us further and further from ourselves. She softly calls to us, "just *be here*".

This is the story of my "coming out".

Turning forty was a major tipping point for me. Reaching my forties meant celebrating a set of unusual milestones, things had never occurred to me to ever consider it a possibility before.

- I was no longer asked for identification when buying wine at the supermarket.

- I found my first grey pubic hair in the shower.

- I received the wake-up call that I needed to transform my life.

It was in my fortieth year that I found myself writing down ten of my deepest, darkest fears on paper and reading them out to a room full of strangers while the tears streamed down my face. It was like I was back at high school where someone had found my diary and was reading it out loud to the class. I waited for the remembered laughter, catcalls, and jeers and wished—waited—for the floor underneath to open and swallow me whole.

Here was my list:

1. I am not good enough.

2. Everyone's needs are more important than my own.

3. I can't make friends and I am better off alone.

4. I am a lousy mother because I have to work.

5. Being a writer and a thought leader is something that I can't achieve as there are people who are smarter than me.

6. I don't have enough time.

7. What will other people think?

8. I am weak and shallow, and I allow others to walk all over me.

9. I am not creative enough.

10. I am boring and unoriginal.

You may want to take a moment here to reflect on and list 10 beliefs or fears that you feel are holding you back in life.

Here is a snapshot of how I felt about my life:

I hated my job, but I was too afraid to leave because it paid very well, and I needed to support my family. I had no sexual desire. My husband and I constantly argued about the lack of sexual intimacy in our relationship. I felt stuck, uninspired, and was often left wondering, *'Is this it?'*, *'Why do I feel so sad all the time?'* I am a Danger Chicken, mindlessly hooked to the dream doing the same thing day in day out, week in week out, year in year out. We can waste years, and even decades, without realising we are Danger Chickens, and I had done exactly that. The invitation to the entrance to my cave took me by surprise. I was not expecting it and I was totally unprepared for it.

As a trained teacher, I know that professional development is a way of life. And so, I thought nothing of it when the leaders from my company went on a three-day training retreat together. Initially, I made an excuse not to attend, but of course, my Wild Woman found a way. This training was different in both a terrible and beautifully, transformational way. Up until these three days, I had never considered that "personal development" was a thing, and here I was being turned inside out while sitting opposite a terrifying, awe-inspiring woman. Long blond hair, gruff–almost masculine voice—with a Māori facial tattoo on her chin. Piercing icy, blue eyes staring right into me—her bullshit detector on full alert—and I could feel it on me. This is the first time I had come face to face with an integrated, Wild Woman. *Oh, how she shook me.* She held no punches. I cried for the entirety of the three days. I visited dark places in my cave that I never even knew or imagined could exist.

This was where my hero's journey–my **AWAKEN**ing–would begin.

It was during the three days that I recognised I had pecked aimlessly in the dirt in my Danger Chicken state for too long. I left this experience a newly transformed, spirited being, believing in the power of my reintroduced, Wild Woman. I was willing to tackle my fear head on as well as my inner thinking. I created a new set of goals that I was committed and determined to achieve. This is where I developed my new mission statement for life; *"I am a beautiful, passionate, and creative woman here to co-create magic in the world."* Not everyone who is shown the "spot" that marks the opening to their cave will see it. There is a crazy statistic that only five percent of

people who attend a personal development course will take action on the things
they learn. Some people just aren't ready yet, and that's okay too. Some people
are simply content to be in their danger chook state. However, for some, the time
is right, and they feel the discontent growing inside of them, so for these people,
the inextinguishable call to the adventure of self-discovery and transformation is
irresistible.

Out of all who attended the three-day course with me, I knew I was the only
one who heard the call to enter the cave, I took up the challenge of the expedition
and stayed with it. I do not tell you this in a form of boasting or to put down my
colleagues, I merely tell you this because it was the right time for me. The call was
loud and insistent enough for me to act upon it. The others were pointed in the
direction of where the spot marked the entrance to their cave, yet it was not the right
time for them. The cost of being hooked to the dream was not high enough for them
to act. However, they left the course with a clear road map of where they could start
digging when they felt ready.

Before the "coming out" could happen, there was a "coming in" to myself that
needed to happen. A coming into my stillness—into my "cave of wonders" that needed
to happen. There was a period of a much needed deep, inner work which took place.
The recognition of the thing I could not put my finger on, the thing that was missing
from my life, was *me*. The wild, wise, creative, and expansive *me*. The time came for
a playful discovery— which is alive in all great love affairs—and a reconciliation with
my authentic self. The remembrance and acceptance of myself for who I always was
and who I could be in the future, but who I was too afraid to be—the conception of
my Queen. We all have experienced our own version of concealing and denying who
we really are from ourselves and others. It takes time, patience, and a lot of digging
to learn to have complete faith in a deeper, truer, wilder, primal, wise, divine
being at the centre of who we are. Very few women know how to set their Wild
Woman free without some help. We notice the spots sitting on the façade of our
perfect worlds, we feel the crack of the two by four as it strikes us across the back
of the head. Nevertheless, the majority of us need to feel the power and force of the
MACK truck smacking us square in the face for us to be open to the transformation.
Something inside of must die in order for the new us to be born. Often the conduit
for our Wild Woman is trauma.

As I said before, knowing the dream is the easy part, the dream itself requires
no real effort to be a part of. Many of us are hypnotized by the lulling, monotonous
white noise of the dream. It's the trauma that disrupts us from our slumber and
creates the cracks in the walls so our Wild Woman is able to break free and we

can start to wake up from the "dream." I certainly needed this to access my Wild Woman. I needed to endure the trauma of a painful miscarriage to reveal how intensely I longed to be a mother. I needed to endure the trauma of experiencing childbirth to allow access to a full range of emotions. I needed to endure the trauma of crying in a room with strangers to start my spiritual awakening.

As poet, Haruki Marakami, so eloquently puts it, *"And once the storm is over, you won't remember how you made it through, how you managed to survive. You won't even be sure, whether the storm is really over. But one thing is certain. When you come out of the storm, you won't be the same person who walked in. That's what this storm's all about."*

She AWAKES: Accessing Trauma as a Conduit for Transformation

I know many of us see trauma negatively, and I am not saying that any abuse or trauma you experienced was okay, but what I would like to offer you is a powerful reframe, I would like you to think of your hurt, pain, and wounds as a conduit for the person you needed to become.

Carefully think back to a traumatic or stressful experience.

- **What was the experience?**

- **Once the experience was over, how were you changed?**

- **What wisdoms and new perspectives did you gain through your experience?**

- **What new gifts and abilities did you gain through your experience?**

Affirmation: *My trauma did not break me; my trauma is the force that made me who I am today.*

human beings need a certain about of hours in the sun
time to soak in the life-giving warmth from its rays

women need hours in the moonlight
time in the glow of the celestial presence of the moon at all its stages
time to weep
to dream time
to visualise a better more beautiful life into existence

a woman needs the letting go during the moon's waning
the setting of intentions in its waxing
the manifesting power of its fullness
the stillness and silence of looking inwards in the new moon

Womanhood

I OUTWARDLY CELEBRATED WITH MY ELDEST DAUGHTER when she got her first period—*I want her to love her body and her femininity.* The impending bloom of her womanhood was evident for a while so this event was not a surprise, but nothing prepared me for how the mother in me would grieve the loss of her maidenhood. I found it extremely tough to help empower her so she could love herself and her body because this was not something that was given to me.

My mother grudgingly sat me down to give me "the talk" when I was a little girl. She explained to me about the changes I would soon experience happening to my body, including periods. I was very fascinated, especially once she told me that after I had my first period, I would be "a woman". I was obsessed with this magical process which would soon be happening to my young body and how I would instantly be transformed from a girl into a woman. I patiently waited every day, and I visited the toilet way more times than I needed to so I could check if my undies were showing my new, anticipated womanhood. I remember I spent one night mostly on my knees praying to God to make me a woman—praying for my first period to start. And to my sheer delight, my prayers were answered the very next morning as I witnessed the first spots of blood in my undies. I strutted around all day with the smug look of the proverbial cat who ate the canary. I had a secret, *'I was a woman now.'* I wondered, *'Could other people tell how grown up I was, how mature I was? Did I look any different?'* I contemplated it all as I peered at the reflection of myself in the mirror.

There have been many times during my life where I have been relieved to see my period. Having my period has meant that I wasn't pregnant. Or it was an excuse as to why I didn't feel like having sex with my husband. Or it meant that I could simply eat chocolate, blob on the couch, or be a bitch. I have never again rejoiced in the miracle of my natural cycles quite like I did in the innocence of my childhood ignorance. In fact, throughout most of my adult life, I quickly learnt to view my period with disdain and annoyance. Somewhere between childhood and womanhood, I discovered that discussing periods was something that didn't happen. We must keep them secret. Periods are dirty, periods are shameful, and by association this meant that women are also dirty, women are also shameful. *So, can you blame me?* Periods, the pain of childbirth, and the suffering of mankind are linked to the original sin of Eve. A punishment that she endured for listening to the serpent and eating the apple from the tree of knowledge and evil, which corrupted Adam and leading them to their banishment from the garden of Eden.

In many cultures, women who are menstruating are forbidden to take part in cultural practices because they are seen as being "unclean" or "taboo". In Māori culture, women who have their period are not allowed to cut flax or weave because they are "Tapu". In medieval times, girls were married off as soon as they became a "woman" and were able to bear children. In Victorian society, one did not speak of womanly functions, including pregnancy and periods as They were considered vulgar and unladylike.

We live in a time where girls are currently still forced into child, arranged marriages, where female castration is still practiced in certain cultures, and where girls are aborted and abandoned in favour of sons. Many girls around the world to this day are not given choices and they do not receive any education. *When did the word "menstruation" become dirty? A source of disgust, something to be reviled? When did making a trip to the grocery store to purchase pads and tampons become a walk of shame for girls and women? When did the biological names for our sexual body parts become a source of embarrassment? When did talking about the act of sex, something that is solely responsible for the creation of every living thing on this planet become taboo?* This is part of the rhetoric that hinders us from loving ourselves. It prevents us from celebrating the miracle that it is to be female and learning to love our bodies. It keeps us separate from other women, stops us from becoming the choice makers and destiny-bringers in our own lives.

In the 1600's, twenty-five souls, mainly women and a few of their male familiars, were killed in what we have come to know as the Salem witch trials. The term "witch-hunt" has its origins centuries before the Salem witch trials. Women who stood out from the "norm", women who were too opinionated, too promiscuous, too familiar with other women, too frigid, too rich, too poor, too many children, not enough children—the "too much" women—could, at any stage, be labelled as a "witch" and be brought to stand trial. Women were coerced into domination by their male counterparts, piously living, praying, and were always one step away from having attention turned on them. Fearing from being burned alive. Often, these women's bodies were subjected to a search to find any evidence of a "witch mark"—a skin tag, a scar, a birthmark, or even a patch of skin that had no feeling—evidence of their other worldliness. We are all daughters of Salem, descendants of the wickedness of Eve when she tricked Adam into disobeying God. The witch mark is something which most women today still unconsciously carry with them. All women are given one of two choices; submit and obey or get burned at the stake. We are either labelled as "nice" or "good girls" —women who "colour in the lines", do as they are told, and conform to societal norms. Women who are educated by their mother and the matriarchal line before them, to construct a pretty avatar, to serve, to please, to stay small, to fit in, and deny their own feelings and needs. Or we are branded as "witches" or "bitches" who do as they want bossy, ballbreakers, selfish… whores.

If you think about the stories we have been told to keep us from the truth about ourselves. Cautionary tales such as Adam and Eve, Snow White, and Little Red Riding Hood are told to make sure we are kept on the path. According to writer and Olympian, Abby Wambach, *"You were never Little Red Riding Hood. You were always the Wolf."* It's a story told to keep us from the truth. The very roots of the word "hysteria", (the forerunner of what we now know as the wide array of mental health issues) stems from the Greek word for "uterus". Early physicians believed this malady was unique to women and was caused by a wandering uterus which travelled around the body infecting other body parts. Strangely, but not surprisingly, the most common remedy for hysteria was sexual intercourse, pregnancy, and childbirth. All power was stripped away from women as the act of masturbation was shunned and the "treatment" was only to be administered by the woman's husband, a midwife, or a doctor. There is extraordinarily little tolerance in the dream for "too much" women, women who were too beautiful, too talented, too confident, too sensitive, too intelligent, too emotional, too opinionated, too driven, too colourful, too sexual, too quiet, or too loud…. So many of us hide our magic, our "too muchness", as if it proves there is something inherently wrong with us. Secretly fearing to be burned alive. Repeating silently under our breath, *'Don't stand out, don't stand out…'* "Witch mark" is just another name for the magic inside of us; the magic we were taught to hide in our domestication into the dream. This is the intergenerational mother wound from which all women must heal.

My eldest daughter battled with her fear of her witch mark when she discovered that her magic was in her sensitivity, her creativity, and her wonderfully, neuro-diverse mind. It was the suppression of her magic by her own hand, and by the hand of others, that became one of the root causes behind her anxiety. My second daughter's witch mark is her quick and logical mind, her determination to claim her own defiant autonomy, and to succeed at all costs. She strongly feels the burn of her witch mark as it calls to her to shrink down so she can fit into the confines of the dream. The trauma she suffered has been the root of her eating disorder and depression. Her sister, aged eleven, is becoming more aware of her witch mark with the passing of each day. I notice her laughs are getting quieter, she's toning down her potty jokes, she's less inquisitive, she's suppressing her emotions and her "too muchness" in order to be accepted by her peers. Daily, she becomes less of herself, learning the lessons of "nice". For years, I have hidden my own magic which has been a poor example to my girls. I extend from a long line of women who denied to know their psychic inheritance and kept their magical medicine on a shelf behind pots, pans, and the cleaning supplies. I have shown them how to fit in to the societal norms, how to hide thoughts, how to conceal magic, and how to construct the perfect avatar. I was certainly raised to believe that "good girls" go to heaven and "witches" go straight to hell. This is a lesson I unconsciously passed on like an antiquated game of "broken telephone". *How and where did my children learn to treat themselves with such disdain? Where did they learn the lessons of their shame?* They learnt this at the feet of their first teachers—their parents. They learnt to pack down shame and conceal their hurt. They learnt to paste on a pretty smile and pretend that life is always awesome from their mother. And they learnt how to conceal tears, bounce the shame, to hurt and blame from their father. My children are excellent students, and they learnt their lessons well.

The truth is that we all encompass a dark side, a witch mark, or a form of magic that some of us are better at burying down deep than others. I have worked hard my whole life to bury mine until it festered and burned its way to the surface, only to be reinterred. *How do we begin to unlearn the lessons of shame that are so deeply engrained in us? How do we heal the mother wound passed down through our matriarchal line?*

The path *in* is also the path *out*.

I cannot go back and change what I have been taught or what I have taught my children through my own lessons. Beating myself up serves no purpose either as this will just add to my self-loathing. They learn the lessons of empathy, self-compassion, and love at my feet too by accepting the reality of my shame and my flawed strategies. By making space and sitting with my hurt and pain, I can proudly own and display my witch marks for all to see. By using my magical medicine to heal myself and reparent myself. Through learning new parenting ways, I can help them to believe in their magic by being that example and showing them the right way. Each mother has the chance to rewrite the narrative of who we are as women for their daughter(s). So, it is my purpose to heal myself so that my daughters, my granddaughters, my great granddaughters, and the generations of women who come after me can live free from this mother wound—the narrative in which I was courageous enough to challenge for us all.

In David Attenborough's documentary, A *Life on Our Planet*, he speaks about how educating and empowering young women is the key to saving our planet. I honestly believe that our girls have the power to reshape our communities. Our daughters have a beautiful sense of entitlement. They will not stand for being treated "less than" just because they are women. We are all dreamers. When we close our eyes, we can imagine a more beautiful, kinder, and more abundant world. And I can see this is already happening.

I was recently part of a Facebook challenge in which 13000 women participated. Almost every woman who had introduced themselves in the group spoke about a deep desire to make her life, but also her children's, family, and community's lives better. Women are far more service-oriented, more community focused, they have better emotional intelligence, and are more in tune with their hearts and intuition. We are reaching the dawn of a new wave of technology. The world needs humans, the world needs soft skills, and the world needs caring hearts. The future of our world is female, and we are privileged to live in a time where we can witness this happening for ourselves. We will stand on the shoulders of the giants and support the next generation of young women reach for what we have all been working towards.

I watch in awe as my girls come out into themselves in their confidence and sense of social justice. Although many adults will shake their head and lament at the failings of the current generation of young adults, instead I chose to see their many strengths. Our children are far more tolerant of differences, they are more emotionally literate than previous generations, and they are braver about speaking up about what they believe in. On the whole, they are more fluid in their thoughts and are less invested in societal, gender, and sexual norms. They are more environmentally responsible in their life choices.

If I could rewrite any part of the narrative for my daughters, it would be this:

- Who you are is beautiful, and you don't need to change anything.

- You were born worthy of love and acceptance just as you are.

- You can be both under construction and a grand masterpiece at the same time.

- You do not need to be happy all the time. Feeling sad, angry, fearful, disappointed, lost, overwhelmed, and frustrated are valuable, valid, normal feelings too.

- Your physical health is not more important than your emotional, mental, or spiritual health. They are all wonderfully connected and interdependent to each other as part of the extraordinary holistic being that is you.

- It is okay to say, *'Today, I am not feeling okay, and I need a bit of extra support'*. Or to take time out and treat yourself with kindness and gentleness.

- Self-care is not just a luxury, it's a basic human need.

What does menstruating mean to me now?

I subscribe to the notion of cycles. Moon cycles and earth cycles—our feminine archetypes are represented in our cycle too. We are the most connected to our Wild Woman in the week before we begin our period, this represents the waning moon. We have an opportunity to soften, surrender, and evaluate everything. This is the time when we are most honest and most raw. Our Wild Woman with her candour and rage are waiting just below the surface, ready to roar. At this time, we are the most unfiltered, so we need to pay attention to her voice. When we are in touch with our needs, it is the easiest for us to speak our truths. We need the time where there is no moon to look inwards so we can reset our lunar rhythms. The time during our period is the perfect time to look inwards and reset our biological rhythms. This is the opportunity to shed and release, this is the time of the Wise Woman. Her wisdom will allow us to let go but will also allow us to create intentions for the next cycle. During our period, we can connect with our Wise Woman through solitude, meditation, reflection, and journaling.

At the beginning of our cycle, we are most attuned to our Maiden and Lover, ready for love and adventure. As mirrored by the brightening moon, we move through our cycle, the lining in our uterus grows rich and fertile like the waxing moon towards ovulation, (the full moon). It is a time to open up and to commit to our intentions created in the new moon phase so we can put these intentions into action. During ovulation, the Mother archetype is present which is our opportunity to create a new life in us if we choose to. As with the extra energy of the full moon, this is often when we are most energetic at our time of ovulation, and it is an opportunity to create magic in our world anew each day with art, words, gardening, love, and kindness.

In her book *Red Moon*, Miranda Gray writes; *"If the egg released at ovulation is fertilized these energies are expressed in the forming of a new life; if it is not fertilized, then the energy is given form in a woman's life in some other way."*

As women, we are uniquely blessed with the gift of creation. We have the opportunity to tune into ourselves and the subtle cues of our being during each stage of our cycle. We are able to shed layers of ourselves and recreate in a constant cycle of life. As we age and cease our bleeding, we do not give up our cyclic nature. In ancient times it was believed that when a woman enters menopause, she absorbs her menstrual blood into herself. Hence, she becomes more in tuned with herself, self-contained, self-aware and self-reliant. Our Wild, Wise self reflects on and accepts our inner path, and we receive the urgent invitation to follow it. When our time here on earth is done, we will have lived through, discarded, and become a new woman many times over. Your job is to accept, love, become, and let go of every different version of yourself.

I encourage you to claim your womanhood, take pride in the feminine birth right of your cycle, and claim the amazingly powerful and creatively abundant creature that you are.

You, dear wild heart, deserve beauty in your life because **you** are sublimely beautiful. **You** are truly miraculous.

Let's make room for **YOU** in your life.

She AWAKES: Making Space for Your Wild Woman

Clearing out, tidying, and decluttering your home and your life can be an excellent meditation. It can also send a message to ourselves to let ourselves know that we are making room for something new. The most confident, radiant, wildest, authentic, knowing, and empowered **YOU** is worth making room for.

- **Choose a space to clean up, declutter, or tidy. This process should be fun and soothing. If it feels hard, sit down and let yourself breathe, allow this feeling to pass before you continue.**

- **Don't push if there is resistance. Remember to tune into your cues, "with" and not "to".**

- **Start small. Clearing out or tidying one drawer might be enough for you at this stage, and that's okay.**

- **If physical decluttering is too challenging, you may want to make space for kinder words by writing down words that you no longer wish to say about yourself. Write down the words on a piece of paper and burn the paper as a way of clearing your mind and heart for the new words you are committing to saying about yourself instead.**

- **You may want to declutter your social media feed by unfollowing accounts that no longer fit with the life you are creating.**

- **You can clear and organise photos and videos on your phone or computer or get rid of any documents which are outdated and are no longer needed.**

- **Audit your commitments and clear your schedule from activities that don't bring you joy or energise you, so you are able to make space for things that fulfil you.**

- **Check in with your current habits and reflect on ones which no longer serve the person you would like to be.**

You may want to set up an altar space in your home where you lovingly place objects which speak to you about the woman you aspire to be. Examples of such items could be candles, fresh flowers, items from your favourite place, letters from loved ones, affirmations, or a picture of your Wild Self. Spend time each day in this space, taking in and grounding yourself in the woman you are becoming.

Affirmation: *I am making space for myself.*

when I say that I love you
it is not conditional on your ability to please me
nor is it a prerequisite that you live up to who I desire you to be

I may not like your behaviour
the choices that you make
I may lament over the consequences of your actions
I may worry for your health
happiness
and the breaking of your heart

but nothing
nothing that you think
do
or become
can strip you from the fabric of my love

Worthy Woman

WHEN I WAS FIRST INSPIRED TO WRITE THIS BOOK, many different kinds of fears and doubts rose to meet me and stare me right in the face, but this did not surprise me. When we are in our caves digging, growing, and rediscovering ourselves, this can bring up unusual amounts of emotions, including fear and weaponised fear, but my favourite frenemy: shame. According to the work of Bre-ne Brown, two things we think of when we are experiencing shame are, *'I'm not enough'* and *'WHO am I?'* These are what I have lovingly been referring to as "the evil shame twins" or my "shame demons" since I read her research. Within minutes of deciding to write this book, my shame demons were on me like a pack of wolves devouring into the vulnerable prey of my newly forming idea.

'I am not good enough' says, *'but you haven't finished your last two novels, you are a serial starter, and a useless finisher.'*

'You will start writing this, but you'll get scared or bored, or life will get too busy, and you will give up like you always do.'

'Just give up now before you waste your time doing something that is doomed for the wastepaper basket.'

'WHO am I?' follows with, *'Who the fuck do you think you are you to write this?'* Do *you think you are fucking Glennon Doyle, Elizabeth Gilbert, or Brené Brown?' (All of whom I admire and respect greatly for being compassionate, and empathetic women. Even though I don't know them, I imagine they would never be as harsh as I am being with myself in this moment.)*

'You will hurt too many other people by writing this.'

'You have no formal training as a writer or on the subject matter of this book. Besides, there are bound to be way more qualified, more skilfully written versions of this book out on shelves in bookstores and libraries around the world. The world doesn't need yet another book like this.'

After much reading and experimenting with myself as to the writing style I am naturally drawn to, I find that style of teaching memoir is something which fits with me. And this too is another hit of *'WHO am I?'* that chooses to torment me. It scoffs scornfully, rolling its eyes, *'A memoir??? You are shitting me... Really!? WHO are you to write a memoir?'*

'You are just a normal person, what possible story could you write?'

'Who on earth is going to find what you have to say interesting or credible?'

'You don't have any degrees; people will think you are a hack.'

'Who would care about this book?'

I am sure at some point you have experienced these pesky little shame demons in your life. You may also know it as "imposter syndrome", where you truly believe that anything you do has already been done by someone else, and done better, so you're not worthy of doing it. All of your thoughts have a habit of turning up like uninvited houseguests, especially when we are experiencing new challenges or stress. Perhaps, like me, you hear them loud and clear when you are moving out of your comfort zone.

I would like to normalise this for you… This happens to EVERYONE! Don't worry… When your shame demons show up, celebrate! It means you are growing.

Just be sure you are aware of the small voice quietly objecting and timidly raising its hand in the back of the room. As the poet, Boris Pasternak, says, *"When a great moment knocks on the door of your life, it is often no louder than the beating of your heart, and it is easy to miss it."*

Be vigilant for the small, *'but…ahem, what if?'*

'What if I do this and it is an amazing success?'

'What if I write this book and people love it?'

'What if by sharing my story, I am able to help many women who were lost, find their way back to themselves?'

My dear friend and yoga instructor, has an inspiring flip of this question, *'WHO am I?'* to the indigenous language of New Zealand, Te Reo Māori, *'Ko wai ahau?'* making it more a subtle, and kinder question.

'Ko wai ahau?'— *'Who AM I?'*

'WHO' is the new person I am becoming, discovering, and reconnecting with through each step that I take on my adventure.

There is a cruel trick in this life which fools us into thinking we must hustle and negotiate in order to find our worth in a source outside of ourselves. We lean our thought processes towards thinking we can measure our value by how much external "stuff" we have accumulated. We view it as our worthiness, or our "enough-ness" is dependent on our looks, the grades we get at school, how many degrees we have achieved, how much money we have in the bank, our relationships with family, friends, and our loved one, our career choice, how productively we spend our time, the house we live in, the car we drive, the friends we have, the amount of likes we get on a social media post. Our real worth cannot be given to us by anyone or anything else. We can waste so much time tormenting ourselves and taking ownership for things which are not ours to own, and we use them as evidence of our "not enough-ness". This is based purely on our comparison of our lives to others, as well as the expectation we are committed to living up to because of how the media, society, and public opinion says parenting, womanhood, and life should be like. As we continue to look outside ourselves to find our worth, we will always find ways where we feel we fall short or won't measure up to how it's "supposed" to be like. We will always see ways that life is happening to us or without us, and when we wake up to see all the ways in which we are already worthy, and have always been, we can see the millions of tiny ways that life happens for us, it happens through us, and that we are all connected.

The Māori language uses *Mana Atua* in the Early Childhood Education profession to describe Well Being. However, the true meaning of this word is "spark of the divine". True wellbeing springs forth from recognising that we are all sparks of the divine. We nurture this spark in ourselves and each other, as well as this amazing planet we call Earth. The same spark, which is found in us, is found in a leaf on a tree or a micro-organism in a drop of the ocean. We are all connected by our spark, the same essence of the divine in us all. We were born already worthy from the moment of our inception.

You may have your own ideas of what or who this Divine force is to you, and I fully respect your views on this. In my life, I call it *God*. If I believe we are all sparks of His divinity, then when I call myself "not worthy" or "not enough", does this mean I am saying He is not enough? When I hide or reject the gifts and talents I received, am I rejecting Him? This particular topic arose when Wild Woman started stirring in me. When she started shining a light on my physic gifts as an empath, clairsentient, and claircognizant, I had a period where I felt that I struggled with my faith. *Was I venturing into the darkness by cultivating these gifts? Did allowing the gifts of my Wild Woman emerge mean a separation from God?* But I realised that my Bible is full of many people who possessed these gifts and used them to communicate with God on a regular basis. We spend so much time running away from the darkness that we forget God is both light *and* dark. Through prayer, meditation, and reflection I realised my gifts as a Wild Woman have always been part of me: *She is God given*. The way of man, who seeks to suppress the wild ways of women, is not God's way. I would not have been gifted with a Wild Woman if I wasn't meant to be one with her.

Just look at nature. *Do birds torment themselves about whether they should fly or not? Do lions lament about eating zebra or gazelle?* No, they don't. They do what they are innately programmed to do. They fly, they hunt, and they roar! To not to use their gifts and suppress their instincts would result in a certain death for these creatures. Similarly, I would not have a Wild Woman if I were not meant to let her free. Like the bird and lion rely on their instincts, I too rely on mine and I would perish without her. When a woman allows herself to be wild, she takes back herself, her divinity, her creativity, and her vital life forces. Therefore, she knows that she does not need outside validation, nor will she try to seek it as she is secure in the belonging, she feels within the home inside of herself. If you grow up to believe God is always watching you, as I did, it leads you to perceive Him as a punitive God. A God who judges you, waits for you to transgress to sin, and anticipates how He will punish you for your sins. But I choose to see Him differently from the God of my childhood, I choose to see Him as a God who lovingly designed the beauty, the infinite wonder, and every hair on our head in is His marvellous creation.

When a flower blooms before it is meant to, or a tree loses its leaves early, or a rain cloud releases its payload in the wrong place, God does not punish the flower, the tree, or the rain cloud. So, why would he punish me for being *me*? God does not punish us for our lack of deservedness, but He is sending circumstances to us in order to help us unfold because He already knows we are enough for the task. If you are still not convinced that you have the love and support from God, the Universe, or a Divine Power, I invite you to experiment with this by asking for a sign.

I always ask for signs, and without fail, my request is always answered. I spent a week in the hospital with one of my children. It was, as you could imagine, an extremely stressful time for our family. As I sat in despair, worried for my child laying in the hospital bed, I cast my head to the Heavens and asked for a sign that she was going to be okay. The prayer had no sooner left my lips as a rainbow appeared in the sky. One rainbow could have been chalked up to coincidence, however, each day for five days while we waited for her to heal, a rainbow appeared in the Heavens to let me know that He was near.

She AWAKES: You Are Already Worthy

Perhaps, like me, you have been led to believe that you have to prove your worthiness, who you are and who you are secretly longing to be is not allowed and that you will be punished for it. Could it be that you have had a multitude of experiences which you took as evidence of your unworthiness?

Today we are going to look for new evidence:

- **Look at yourself and your life and find evidence for ways that you are already worthy.**

- **Record at least ten ways in which you are already worthy in your journal.** *If you can think of more than ten, do not censor yourself, write until you are done.*

- **Make time today to do something you enjoy to honour and celebrate the person you already are.**

If you feel resistance while doing this exercise, gently remind yourself that are allowed to compliment yourself.

Affirmation: *I am already worthy in so many different ways.*

I turned myself inside and out
and with the jagged blade of my best intentions
I carved away my darkness
gutting out my insides
until only light
and transparency remained

from somewhere deep inside
I heard the call

come back to me
come back to me
come back to me

I turned
to see your face
and I realised that I was never gone
– necessary darkness

Whole Woman

We tend to think of ourselves as parts.

The good part and the bad part.

The yin and the yang.

The devil on one shoulder, our better angels on our other.

The good wolf and the bad wolf.

The light and the dark.

The Mother and Maiden archetypes can have an unhealthy codependent relationship. It is the nature of Maiden's to want to grow up, go on adventures and to explore their innate curiosity. It is part of a Mother's nature to over-protect and to want to control. The Maiden feeling the need to be loved and accepted by the Mother; and sensing that this love and acceptance will be lost to her if she grows up and changes, in turn, stunts her growth and stays small and obedient to continue to receive the warm glow of approval from the Mother. This occurs in our external relationships with our mother or our daughter(s) and is mirrored in our internal relationship between these two archetypes.

This causes a fracture in our Maiden self. A splitting of our 'light' acceptable parts off from our 'dark' unlovable attributes and the disconnection from and disowning of our dark self.

Thinking like this only will only cause a war inside of us. Seeing ourselves in these ways leads us down the path to self-loathing, struggle, and suffering. It births a fractured self and creates an alienation from ourselves as we move from our dark to our light as frequently, and as often, as we breathe in and out. We are in a state of constant flux between our positivity and melancholy. Ever since I can remember, I have felt the constant conflict between my two parts. The part which won me approval from my parents, other adults, God, and then realer, darker, wilder, shadow me who I longed to embrace. For years I worked in vain, and to my detriment, in order to hide the wolf while I pretended to be a Little Red Riding Hood.

As any artist knows to be able to give depth to a painting, you need darker tones and shadows. We also need the depth of our dark tones and shadows too. We are our greatest masterpiece. As author, Barbara Brown Taylor, points out in her book,

Learning to Walk in the Dark, "I have learned things in the dark that I could never have learned in the light, things that saved my life over and over again, so there is really only one logical conclusion. I need darkness as much as I need light."

However, as children learn the lessons of darkness and light, we also seek out the light and become fearful of the dark. Our well-meaning parents lit up our rooms with candles or nightlights to withhold the darkness instead of walking us outside into the evening tide to take in the wonder of the stars that we would never see if it was perpetual light, which reaffirmed that we need to fear, and therefore, banish the night. Similarly, we are taught to shun the darkness inside of us too. Our undesirable, "too much" emotions like anger or sadness are banished to the "time-out" chair or spanked out of us in the favour of more acceptable "Pollyanna" cheeriness. Our mysterious, scary, weird, hard to understand, and fears are locked behind the high walls of our societal and religious beliefs. Not unlike the polarity of our two primary programs, survival and connection, the often seemingly conflicting misaligned parts of us want the same thing for us. *What if instead of trying to punish, banish, or abuse our darker, less desirable Wild Self, and we actually treated these parts of ourselves with empathy, kindness, and compassion? What if we asked these parts what they needed? What if we stopped and paid attention to what both parts had to teach us? What if instead of tearing ourselves apart we embraced and loved all our parts?* I have come to believe that for us to truly love ourselves this is a vital missing piece, but to get rid of these parts of ourselves is impossible. There is no good or bad, there is just the one hundred percent, beautiful, extraordinary, divine, and holistic self. As much as we try to cut away our darkness with the blade of our best intentions, the darkness will always be there.

Recently, I explored this belief with a trusted friend and coach, and we applied the Neuro Linguistic Practice, (NLP), of a parts integration. In this ritual, the mentor and the mentee sit upright in chairs side by side. The mentee closes their eyes and stretches their arms out straight in front of them, palms facing up to the ceiling, arms-length apart. The mentor helps the mentee to examine both parts and to question the highest intention of each part. The mentor may guide the mentee to see if these parts of themselves represent a person in their life and ask the parts if there would be a way that they could integrate and work together.

During my experience, I realised that the part of me—the *good* me—was represented by my father's voice. The intention of this part of me was to keep me safe and protected. The part of me, which I identified as my own voice, wanted to be authentic and wild, and was looking for the safety to be herself. They shared the highest intention of security, safety and acceptance.

As I sat there inquiring into my parts, my hands, unbeknownst to me, moved closer and closer together. My coach guided me to focus further inward until I located the small, huddling child at the core of my being. I could feel her pain and isolation, and I gazed lovingly at her. My coach asked me if my parts could see a way to work together, and I was able to see the part of me, which was my father, could share the insights with the wild me about boundaries, caution, and not giving into the excess of my wild ways. My wild me was able to share wisdom about the value of taking risks, being present in the moment, and the greatness of being true to herself. Together, my parts could gain the insight that it was safe for the present-day Tanya to be seen, heard, and loved for who she was. As I felt my hands touch, my coach eased them to naturally rest, one upon the other, and then to pause on my heart. I saw a vision of my father cradling and soothing my inner child—the child I was at three years old—and whispering with loving comfort, *'You are safe, it is safe to be you.'* And as I was bathed in the beauty of my wholeness, tears flowed freely down my cheeks. I heard the words, *'dear wandering soul, return to yourself with gratitude and love.'*

She AWAKES: Self Integration

Unfortunately, a parts integration ritual is not possible while reading a book—although, this is a practice I use in my one-on-one coaching work with women. However, there is immense value in becoming aware of our conflicting parts and being able to examine them. We can open the dialogue between our parts to see what our different parts need, what their intentions are, and how they can work together. This is a cornerstone to the next section in this book of loving and accepting your authentic self.

I invite you to explore the following questions in your journal:

- **Do you feel conflicted by opposing parts in you?**

- **How do these opposing parts stop you from doing something important to you or from being the authentic you?**

Now, divide your page in two columns, and at the top of each column, name these parts.

- **If the parts were a person, who would they be?**

- **What do the parts want or believe?**

- **What is the highest positive intention of each part?**

- **Do these intentions have anything in common?**

- **Is there anything that the parts could learn from each other?**

- **Is there a way they could work together to get you what you want out of life?**

Affirmation: *I love the person I am becoming; I love every part of me.*

every day I come to her
and she sends me her avatar

the smiling happy version of her
that she thinks that I want to see

every day I invite the real her out to meet me
and promise not to reject
her sad
her heavy
her angry
her shame

until one day she is not the happy
smiling babbling brook of activity

she is silent.
.moody.
.stormy.

she is rude.
.standoffish.
refusing to eat.

      defiantly she sits.

daring me to let go
to turn away and leave

she taunts me
to reject the real
the stripped-down version of who she is

she tests me
convinced that I will like her avatar better
that her avatar is who I have really come to see

the vulnerable
rawness of her is breath-taking

I hang in there
I hold her close
I do not leave

my heart
head and body
respond to her sadness
with sadness of my own

I want to hide this part of me from her
to protect her
but instead
I let my own rawness show

I honour her nakedness
with the nakedness of my own

It is difficult
uncomfortable
and exhausting
but we hang in there
sitting in sadness together

Authentic Self

Authentic Self

I READ A STORY ABOUT A GOLDEN BUDDHA which was discovered when monks in Thailand were moving a giant clay Buddha. As they moved the statue, fragments of clay started falling away, revealing the golden treasure underneath. It is theorised that the Buddha was covered in clay because the monks wanted to protect their golden treasure from an attacking Burmese army. Unfortunately, the monks died in the attack, taking with them the secret to the golden Buddha. It wasn't until many years later, when trying to move the Buddha, that its secret treasure was discovered. This is a true story, but also a beautiful metaphor for life.

We are all born golden, however, during our lifetimes, we cover our life force, our own Buddha, with many layers of clay to protect our treasure from outside attacks. Our parents, teachers, and other well-intentioned adults add to these layers of clay too during the trauma of our domestication, while trying to help us to fit into the "dream". Schools and workplace bullies will sling clay at us with their vicious comments. Our friends, lovers, media, and ourselves all add layers too. But we hide our treasures safely under the multiple layers of limiting thoughts, unconscious tirades, and our belief system. We do such a great job at covering it all up that we forget we are truly golden, glimmering, and glittering with much purpose, potential, and possibility.

When I was in Sunday school, I remember reading a scripture in the Bible, *"God formed man from the dust of the ground and breathed into his nostrils the breath of life; and he became a living soul."* As the story goes, Adam was content, innocent, and one with God, unashamed by his naked form. It was only after the exile from the garden of Eden and the separation from God that Adam and Eve noticed and felt ashamed by their nakedness. We all arrive in this world naked, innocent, and unashamed, connected to our wild, divine selves. But as we grow older, we begin to notice our nakedness. We add more clay around ourselves to hide our shame. The more layers of clay we have, the more disconnected we become from our golden, divine, true selves. I am not sure if you believe this creation story—although many cultures have a similar creation story involving clay. One thing which struck me when reading this was that we were all originally made of clay filled with a divine spark—a *Divine Self*. This is not the *self* we have been programmed to believe in religious literature where the "Wild Self" is painted as a destructive force.

What are my layers of clay? They are beliefs handed down to me by my unintentional family genealogy of what people in our family are capable of. My clay is my childhood experience of having to deny who I truly was; of being good, but never quite good enough. Striving to make the A-team in field hockey, but only ever being good enough to make the B-team. Determined to come first in my class, but always coming third. Working hard throughout my entire high school career to make it to be a school leader, but self-sabotaging myself in the final year and not being chosen. Aiming for university, but not making the cut. These experiences added the countless layers of thick clay to my growing belief that I "wasn't enough", I couldn't go the distance, and I was destined to always be second best. A belief system that manifested itself into a list of self-protecting behaviours just so I could save myself the hurt and disappointment of being the girl who never got chosen; without realising that I could choose myself.

Perhaps, you share a similar layering of clay. Maybe, like me, you have enjoyed staying invisible—safe and peaceful—quietly hidden under layers of clay. As the layers of clay begin to crack and someone notices your gold treasure underneath, you feel the coldness of your nakedness. Could it be that being exposed by your vulnerability, the possibility of disappointing others, and hurting yourself dangerously close, you start scrambling for the bits of clay that have fallen to the ground? Perhaps you spend your time and energy in attempts to cover up just as Eve did when she tried to hide her nakedness behind leaves from the garden of Eden.

What are we creating with all that clay? We are creating an ideal identity—an avatar—of ourselves which is a socially acceptable version who we can send out to play with the other avatars in the game, the dream of life. Like all good games, we are not restricted to one character, we can choose different personas to suit different situations we find ourselves in. I have often wondered, *'is why I feel like an imposter?'* I do want to clearly point out that our archetypes are **not** avatars of ourselves. Our archetypes are our divine expressions from within. Archetype work is expansive and freeing, and our avatar is a façade that we use to shield ourselves from the world to project an image of what we feel others expect from us. Embracing our divine feminine energy is a journey to connect and express our authentic selves, whereas an avatar separates us from ourselves and others. Over the course of my lifetime, I have used the avatars of a "good mother", a "dutiful daughter", a "doting wife", "slutty me", "party me", "professional me", or "happy me". I have sat in my car before parties, before work gigs, or as I as I am about to step into my home after a long day's work, with my palms sweaty, heart racing, and thought, *'Okay, which avatar should I be now?'* or *'Which avatar will they like the best today?'*

As our children grow, we assist in helping them to create their own avatars, versions of themselves in which we feel will insulate our precious, little babies from the hard and dangerous world instead of actually teaching them to stay connected to their divinity. We do this as a result of the lessons we have learnt about being "human", and to be without clay is to live in loneliness, outside of the dream. Our avatars are borne out of our wounds. But in this world, there is no avoiding clay. I myself have contributed layers of clay to my friends and family, to my children, and even to strangers who I have yet to meet, however, that is a reality of life. Most of my clay has been contributed with a loving intent. Our ideal identity is nurtured from an incredibly young age, like my example of my identity "the example". When we are young children, we have to rely on others to be fed, to be clothed, to be loved, and to be accepted so we can secure our survival. During this time, we have to constantly ask ourselves, '*Who do I need to be* for *them to treat me this way?*' (Weaver, 2019). The problem with this when we are young children is that we do not have or understand the power of discernment. Our young brains are programmed to gather data about the world we are living in. In the period of being the young Maiden, we have little experience behind us to be able to challenge our beliefs, and so we are shaped purely by our circumstances. We create immature meanings about ourselves through our relationships with people, places, and things where we decide and unconsciously look for evidence to reinforce those meanings. These decisions of destiny become our default behaviours. As in my instance from my story of being "second best" and how I made it mean that I wasn't good enough so I should just give up before I failed.

Unbeknown to us, this is who we eventually become. We trade authenticity for attachment, and this becomes our ideal identity—our default avatar. We try to prove it by behaving in alignment with our ideal identity, that we are worth being loved and accepted. We also receive it from those around us, information on what loses us that acceptance, love, and approval, and so these become our shadow selves—our unwanted identities. These are the traits for which you would rather die than let anyone else perceive you as. In fact, for many of us, being tarred with the brush of our unwanted identities feels like a matter of life or death. Every choice we make stems from the desire to win approval of the significant adults and later peers in our lives. This is a powerful motivator for us to avoid behaviours where approval will be lost. No one teaches us that we can have both acceptance and authenticity and if they did, this teaching was immediately erased when we stepped out into the big, scary world to live with all the other avatars.

We all hold a deep human need to be seen, loved, and accepted. Our ideal identities are our bond to the collective dream. Left unconscious, the fear of our unwanted identities dictates our thoughts and behaviours turning us into Danger Chickens. Both identities are part of us. The inner conflict appears in areas of our life which matter the most to us. People who irritate us, are a gift, so the blessing of knowing them is the insight to our unwanted identities. These people are our "shadow teachers". Our experiences with them have important lessons for us. Our shadow teachers serve as an invitation to enter our cave and discover something new about ourselves. However, when we don't recognise the lesson, the violence that we turn onto ourselves when face to face with our unwanted identities can cause us to inflict hurt and shame on ourselves and onto others.

When we are disconnected from our deep healing, introspective power of our Wild Woman, our Knowing Self, and by default, our Divine Power, we become empty. We develop a spiritual hole where our Divine Self used to reside. At first, when the hole is new and we are young, it is small. It tingles slightly and will feel a bit "off". However, our trust in those around us is our whole world, and so we do not think to question the feeling. Like an untreated cavity, the hole slowly grows bigger, and we begin to notice that something is missing. As the hole enlarges, so does our sense of urgency to find the missing part, leading us to go crazy, consumed with finding it. We may think, *'I am empty. I must fill this hole, then I will be full'*. And so, we become a slave to excess of food, drugs, alcohol, sex, and bad relationships in the efforts to try and stave off our emotional hunger. Some may think, *'I will shrink myself and this will shrink the emptiness, so I will feel it less.'* Leaving them to starve themselves spiritually, mentally, emotionally, and physically. Many of us ignore this hole in hopes that if we pretend it doesn't exist, it will go away by itself.

There is a real and tangible cost to letting our unconscious fear of our perceived rejection from the collective dream run the show. We turn to drinking that glass of wine at the end of the day to help us unwind and numb the pain, which in turn becomes the whole bottle—*costly*.

We snack on that packet of chocolate biscuits, or an entire slab of chocolate to fill the emptiness we feel—*costly*.

We spend our evenings mindlessly online shopping, purchasing shoes, clothing, and gadgets even when we know we don't need them just so we can have something to look forward to in the mail. Only to create that momentary sense of euphoria—*costly*.

We use our credit cards to buy our children's love and affection, attempting to ease our guilt and shame for not being the parent we so desperately want to be—*costly*.

We waste hours of our precious selves unthinkingly plugged in, scrolling through social media feeds, checking emails, living our lives on pause so we do not have to think or feel anything–*costly*.

Once we turn the unconsciousness to consciousness, we realise that they are just avatars who we have adopted. We can get real about them and our power to challenge, to choose and to discern. We can cease living from the lack of our spiritual holes. Here we can then begin to allow ourselves to feel consciously and release emotions in healthy, productive ways, not giving into the need to numb and make *costly* choices.

I have realised when I get curious about my unwanted identities, I see the avatar that I am working so hard for others to see is totally unrealistic, and only causes me unnecessary fear and shame. I am able to laugh at myself and recognise ways in which I have been a "danger chook". When I regard myself as a mother, my "perfect mother" avatar has "got her shit together". She is calm, knowledgeable, understanding, nurturing, and loving. My "perfect mother" avatar does not need help, she does not get overwhelmed, or stressed out. She is never clueless, selfish, unreliable, cold, or disorganised. I have been gathering the "gold stars" to power up my "perfect mother" avatar since my midwife wrote in my infant's *Plunket Well Child* book: *"Mother and baby doing well. Tanya is skilled in mothercraft."*

Ever since I can remember, I have been collecting many gold stars from others. Gold stars are the way we are tamed and hooked into society's dream as they validate and reinforce our avatars. They are like the "power-up" which energises the life bar at the top of the screen in a video game telling us how strong our avatar is or how much longer it has left to live.

- I received gold stars for being a "good girl"–"the example".

- I received gold stars for achieving good grades because I was a "good student" and for going to church every Sunday because I was a "good Christian".

- I was awarded stars for being kind, friendly, and selflessly doing as I was told.

These gold stars were the praise and the pride or approval I received from my parents or teachers when I remembered a Bible story or brought home a good grade.

As mothers, we work hard for gold stars too. It starts before we even conceive.

- 'I got pregnant without even trying'. — *Gold star.*

- 'I sailed through pregnancy'. — *Gold star.*

- 'I had the worst morning sickness, heartburn…' — *Gold star.*

- 'I had a twenty-four-hour labour'. — *Gold star.*

- 'I had a thirty-minute labour and delivered a ten-pound baby with no pain relief'. — *Gold star.*

- 'I breastfeed my baby'. — *Gold star.*

- 'I went back to work with my baby after a week of maternity leave and pumped in my lunch breaks'.'' — *Gold star.*

- 'I sacrificed my career to stay home with my children'. — *Gold star.*

- 'My baby slept through the night after two weeks'. — *Gold star.*

- 'I had two years of running on little to no sleep, while working, and raising three children under five'. — *Gold star.*

Coffee groups are a place to hand out more gold stars to reinforce the "perfect mother" avatar. For those of you who are not familiar with the concept of a coffee group, let me explain. When parents are expecting a baby in New Zealand, they are offered free antenatal classes alongside other expecting parents. The idea around it is for the group of parents you meet while your baby is in utero to become a support network for you once your baby is born. Coffee groups are *supposed* to be non-judgmental and safe places to give and receive advice and support between each other as parents who are in the same stage of the parenting journey. More than often, it is a place for mothers to hand out "gold stars" to the one "who has got it the most together". I have friends who would spend all week cleaning, redecorating their homes, and baking organic homemade treats ahead of their turn to host the coffee group just so they could pretend to present a perfect, enviable life, while secretly, their world was actually imploding.

Under the avatar, our real gold lies hidden away from sight. This is an entirely different treasure to the gold stars given to us by others. The golden Buddha is in us all. This is our authentic, true self waiting for the day our dependence on the dream begins to fade away and we are moved to enter into the spiritual realm of our cave, where we can start to chip away at the layers of clay and discover it for ourselves.

There is no place in our cave for avatars to reside, our cave is where we go to lose our avatar. In our cave we learn how to remove our tough outer shells and leave them at the door while we practice to move around without it. It's the process to learning how to trust ourselves enough to live in our hearts where we do not need any armour, so we can prepare ourselves to leave our avatars behind and live without them. The courage is in all of us. We all have the ability to shake off the rumble, the dust, the layers of clay that dull our golden shine. We can lay down the armour if we so choose to and surrender the heavy burden of our clay.

Dear wild heart, you are not meant to extinguish the light that turned on inside of you as you started to awaken. It is not a warning light, but rather a pilot light signalling you to guide yourself back to you. You were given this light to nurture it, to find ways to fuel the light so it can burn so brightly from your inner hearth that it becomes the source of your power. We are all born golden, but we deny this to ourselves and to others. Many of us fight for our clay, defend our limitations, and hold onto it for dear life. We may even have been domesticated so we are grateful for our clay. Our secret fear is not that we are clay, our secret fear is that we are in fact *golden*. For if we are golden, then the responsibility shifts to us to accomplish something with our treasure. A further fear is that we risk being rejected for our gold. We open ourselves up to the possibility that someone will say, *'Well, who the hell are you?'* Or they will make fun of our treasure, or we will realise that we are a fool for believing the cruel joke that our golden core is really, "fool's gold".

What if we reclaimed our golden selves, and shouted out at the top of our lungs, fearlessly, and confidently, *'I am Golden, I am Golden, I am Golden'*? But remember, our golden Buddha is not a God to be worshipped. It is not a hard, cold, inanimate idol to hoard to ourselves. The true nature of our golden Buddha is a seed for us to plant. When we access our Wild Woman, she aids us in finding our golden seed. We plant the seed in the very depths of our soul—the fertile foundations of our heart, our longings, and our dreams. The seed is a gift from God—a spark from the divine. It lights an inextinguishable fire in us which ignites us from the inside out.

The job of the fully integrated, the healthy expressions of our divine feminine energy is to support us so we can nurture the seed with the purpose to create enough fruit to sustain our self and to share it with others. Allow yourself to be a reassuring beacon to others so they can rekindle the light within themselves, but not by trying to change others or doing anything other than coming into our own golden sovereignty. Since our spiritual hole is our lost connection with our Divine Self, no amount of "filling up" on excess junk or gold stars by shrinking or hiding is going to fill the void in you. The answer is already in you. It has always been there in the connection to your golden **w**ild **a**uthentic **k**nowing **e**mpowered self—the seed of who you are. This seed, when nurtured, grows abundantly in you and fills the hole from the inside out.

She AWAKES: Your Clay

What layers of clay need to be chipped away to discover of your golden Buddha, your authentic self? Where do you even start? I know from my own experience just how thick the layers of clay can be. You have had decades to shape, polish, and perfect your avatar. You may even have trophy cases dedicated to the many gold stars you received. I know exactly how tough and resistant the armour of hurt, fear, and shame can be, trying to keep your unwanted identities at bay. And so, it is unrealistic for me to suggest that one exercise will chip away the accumulation of years. Excavation takes time, dedication, and hard work. I have spent many years undergoing shadow work of the Wild and Wise Woman, and yet some of my clay still trips me up. What I will offer you instead is a starting point, the same starting point I was offered during my call to adventure. I am going to help you to identify your decisions of destiny.

I would like you to think back to your childhood and teenage years to three events which were emotionally traumatic for you. *Please do this intuitively.* Take your journal and write down the first three events that immediately come to your mind?

To support you with this, I will share mine:

- My dad yelling at me, telling me I am useless.

- My uncle sexually abusing me.

- Looking in the mirror and asking my mother if I was beautiful, only for her to evade my question.

Next, I would like you to replay these events in your mind and remember how you felt in that moment. Which emotion was the strongest for you?

Here are mine:

- My dad yelling at me and telling me that I am useless. ***Petrified***

- My uncle sexually abusing me. ***Disgusted***

- Looking in the mirror and asking my mother if I was beautiful and having her evade my question. ***Shamed***

Next, what decision did you make about yourself that you spent your life trying to find evidence for?

Here are mine:

- My dad yelling at me and telling me that I am useless. ***Petrified — I am not good enough.***

- My uncle sexually abusing me. ***Disgusted — I am disgusting, sex is a dirty, shameful secret.***

- Looking in the mirror and asking my mother if I was beautiful and having her evade my question. ***Shamed — I am not worthy. If my mother doesn't think I am beautiful, then who will?***

The final step is to examine how this shaped your avatar and your unwanted identities.

For me it shaped me into the following avatar: I need to be perfect, prim, proper, and lady-like. I should avoid sex and disconnect myself from my disgusting, sensual self. I need to prove myself with brains, talents, and hard work.

My unwanted identities are lazy, makes mistakes, takes risks, enjoys sex, off-colour jokes, vain, unintelligent, clueless, unreliable, and doesn't follow through. I am also aware of my ever-present default emotions—petrified, disgust, and shame, and how they show up during my most challenging times.

You may have had more than three significantly traumatic emotional events in your life, some of them may have happened before you could even remember. However, what I am offering you is an understanding of how your avatar was shaped, a lens from which you can examine your layers of clay. From this reframe, you can gain some clarity around the decisions you made about yourself before you developed discernment. This tool is a powerful unearthing of your default emotional responses to challenge. You can repeat this process as many times as you need to as new events rise to the surface. The beauty of this process is that it gifts you with the power to return and practice discernment for your younger self through the eyes of your adult brain. You gain an insight into how earlier experiences influenced your future actions and decisions. Through this process, you can forgive yourself, and even others, and release old emotions as you decide which layers are still serving you and which layers you can start chipping away at.

Affirmation: *I let go of the past beliefs that no longer serve my authentic golden self.*

I know that you don't believe in what I am doing
or in the things that I have to say

that's okay

your approval is no longer a requirement
for my success

my belief in myself is enough

Absolute Accountability

SOON AFTER I HAD MISCARRIED OUR FIRST BABY, a phone bill arrived. I opened the bill and placed it on top of the fridge, reminding myself to get around to paying it. The next month rolled over and I received the phone bill for the current month, including the outstanding bill for the previous month. Again, I took this bill and placed it on the top of the fridge, reminding myself to pay it. The following month, I received the current months phone bill and a disconnection warning from our phone company. Instead of telling my husband and paying the bills, I hid the notices, and I still did not pay the bills. My husband, of course, found out when our phoneline was cut off. He spent an hour explaining how we had suffered the loss of our baby and was begging the phone company to reconnect the line as well as negotiating a payment plan since the bill was now out of control. *Why did I do this?* I could not, for the life of me, explain my Danger Chicken behaviour.

You would have thought I would have learnt from this experience. However, this has been a pattern I have repeated over and over and over again. Like Voldemort in the Harry Potter series of books, my life is full of fractured versions of me. Parts of myself which contain a little part of my soul, but I am never truly invested. I have since learnt that this behaviour is a self-protective pattern, induced by the trauma of how my early Huntress was established. It stems from the messages I received when I was initiated into the dream of my domestication that I am a "powerless victim". My only power is in my ability to deceive and hide who I really am in order to keep "the example" avatar alive so I will be accepted and loved.

This is my "shark music". It's an instinctive way that I behave to protect myself from perceived danger so I can keep myself emotionally safe. Since this can stem from the little girl inside of us, this is inevitably a defensive shield of a wounded Maiden. You may have your own version of "shark music".

- You may put yourself last,

- You may be your compulsion to strive for perfectionism, hiding, deceiving, covering up mistakes, or keeping yourself small.

- You may have developed self-protection patterns by procrastinating or creating unrealistic expectations.

- You may find yourself waiting for the "other shoe to drop", be a people pleaser, or change yourself so you can fit in.

- You may be the creator of drama so you can try to control others or the outcome.

- You may have learnt the benefits of mounting an attack.

- You may have learnt to seek out or stay in relationships that are unhealthy.

- You may fill your life with addictions.

- You may lose yourself in indecision, self-doubt, confusion, or overwhelm.

What we have mistakenly been taught is that if we become goal-focused and push through these "self-sabotaging" behaviours, we will get ourselves unstuck so we can move our mountains. Inevitably we try, fail, and we lose faith in ourselves. Which then in turn makes our "shark music " play a little louder". Until we can identify our shark music behaviour patterns as unprocessed shame and trauma-based defence mechanisms, take responsibility for processing the shame and healing the trauma, or we will continue to be stuck in the valley of our despair.

She AWAKES: Your Shark Music

Go back to the exercise you completed on Waking Up from Your Dream of Domestication, page 60.

- **Look back at the trauma you identified in that exercise.**

- **How has this early trauma helped you to compose your shark music?**

- **What protective behaviour patterns do you repeat in your life?**

- **What is your shark music protecting you from?**

- **How is your shark music limiting you?**

You may want to journal this, create poetry, draw, paint, or move through this trauma. Do what feels right for you to do in this space.

Taking Accountability for the Best Possible Version of YOU

As with most young brides, I was excited about my wedding day. However, this excitement did not compare to the joy and anticipation I felt when I considered moving into my first flat with my new husband. My heart soared at the sense of liberation I experienced. I could do what I wanted, when I wanted. I could stay up all night if I so desired, drinking, clubbing, and making love. Never again would I have to suffer the nagging of my mother to clean my room or do the dishes. In fact, I could leave the dirty dishes stacked on the bench all week and never clean my flat if I choose to. I had the absolute freedom, and I was accountable to *NO ONE!* I was finally going to be a *GROWN-UP.*

They *lied.*

When we are influenced by the nameless Maiden, we can feel as if we are still waiting to receive our gift of the eternal wisdom of adulthood. Patiently waiting for the day where we will feel like a *real* adult, worthy of sitting at the grown-up's side of the table. At times we can still feel like a child, uncertain, and floundering. An "imposter" grown-up. There comes a time where we ultimately arrive at the moment in our adult lives that we realise no one is coming. No one is coming to parent us, to tell us to clean up after ourselves, to tell us to get off the couch, and get our butts to work or to the gym. No one is going to admonish us if we eat too many chocolate biscuits, drink too much wine, or stay out all night.

Inevitably, I learnt the lesson like most adults do. Life without boundaries, although fun as a concept, demands a heavy toll. This lifestyle is not sustainable as every decision always has a consequence. *Ahh, the sweet folly of youth and the bitterness of consequences….* Sometimes, we will all *have* to do something even though we don't want to for no other reason than being the next, right step in the direction of where we would like our lives to go. And once we discover that going to the gym, eating better, cutting out the daily wine at four o'clock in the afternoon, or listening more than we speak, we start to see the benefits of our decision. We may even start to look forward to the benefits of our new lifestyle… We may even enjoy it.

There's a time when we must cease blaming our parents, their misguided coping strategies, and absolve the sins of our childhood. Where we stop blaming our mother and the long list of mothers before her for the mother wound, we carry in us, and recognise that it is solely our responsibility to heal the wound for ourselves by giving ourselves the mothering we require. We must take accountability for our own actions and parenting ourselves Only then do we finally reach a "grown up" status.

At the beginning of my reawakening, I wrote this poem:

I catch a glimpse of the bookshelf behind me

> *it speaks in volumes*
the twists and turns in my life

weight loss books and books on how to quit smoking
sit next to books on how to communicate better with your partner
books to fix you or your sex life
recipe books dovetail poetry collections
fifty shades of grey an uneasy bedfellow next to the king james bible
charlie and chocolate factory and harry potter
occupies the space next to a range of chick lit.

I look at this collection and ask myself

why do you continue to do what you do even though you know what you know?

when will you reach the point when enough is enough?
and you shout out loud
Fuck It, Not One Day More?

There is a point in every woman's life when she feels as if she has tried everything possible.

She has tried fitting in.

She has tried to hide herself behind the layers of her clay.

She has tried fixing herself with sources from outside her.

And all of this has left her tired. Tired of her life, her old stories, the ominous refrain of her shark music, and the futility of her own excuses. This is where a woman needs to look into herself for the answers. This is where a woman needs to reach into herself to find the source of her power and flick the most glorious of switches of all: the *Fuck-it Switch*.

Each woman's *Fuck-it Switch* moment may be different. It may come during a transitional time in her life such as when her children leave to university, or when she hears the knock of menopause. A woman may find that her job, her marriage, or her lifestyle no longer fills her with joy. She may tire of feeling invisible, being walked all over, or being passed over at work for yet another promotion that she so rightly deserves. However, what brings her to this point does not matter. What does matter is that at this moment she recognises that this is *her moment*.

When a woman reaches the *Fuck-it Switch* stage in her life, it means she has arrived at the point where enough is enough. She flips her switch and begins to take one hundred percent accountability for herself, her past, her life, and her destination. There is no other choice, she has exhausted all other possibilities. She makes a stand for herself, she stands out to the world, and she shouts loud for all to hear, *'Fuck It, Not One Day More!'* This begins with a single decision. A decision to forgive ourselves and others, a decision that life is worth living and we are capable of living our best life. A desire to be the best possible version of ourselves in all moments of our lives, we start putting into action many of the things which will allow us to heal, grow, and be our own hero. A decision to do the exact opposite of our "shark music" behaviour. The concept of the best possible version of me is not merely an intention, it is an *action*. It is the daily practice of taking full responsibility for my thoughts, emotions, behaviours, and actions. This is when I demand that my archetypes, *work* for me instead of *controlling* me.

In the best possible version of me, my Huntress helps me to identify goals so I can focus on bringing this forth into a reality. The best possible version of me is responsible for meeting my own needs. This is my Mother, *mothering* me. I know from personal experience that during times when I have become reliant on others to meet my needs I became "needy" and "clingy". I went straight into blaming others for the disappointments and unmet expectations I had in my life. My Queen of the Underworld distinguishes where I went wrong in the past and sets to reminds me that when I stop waiting, blaming, or searching for others to fill me, my Lover fills me with the self-loving reassurance so when I take ownership of meeting my own needs, when I accept that this is my job, then I am able to find peace, contentment, and self-love. Absolute accountability is how we move ourselves out of this nameless Maiden, victim mode and we grasp hold of our power again to change our lives and circumstances. This is how we move out of our wounded selves and into the worthiness of our integrated Queen.

So, what is the best possible version of me? It is changeable each day, and sometimes each minute. The best possible version of me depends greatly on my energy and capacity in that moment. It comes from a place of the fluidity of attunement with my Wild and Knowing Self as a guide.

Sometimes, the best possible version of me is listening to my body, allowing it to rest when its required. But sometimes it is pushing myself to go for a walk in the sunshine or urging me to ground myself on my yoga mat.

Sometimes, the best possible version of me is staying quiet with all the love in my heart as I control my own emotions while my teenagers spin out of control with theirs.

Sometimes, it is challenging my children's minds with questions, giving a hug, or advice.

Sometimes, it is validating experiences and emotions by sitting on my hands while allowing them to sit with their emotions and experience a life lesson from painful consequences when all I want to do is rescue them.

Sometimes, the best possible version of me is being kind to myself and feeding myself loving thoughts.

Sometimes, it is kicking my own arse and forcing myself to be courageous when I am feeling fearful.

The best possible version of me recognizes when I am filtering for the worst possible scenario and I tell myself a bad story about me which prompts me to ask, *what else could this mean?*

The best possible version of me prompts me to challenge the narrative I have about experiencing anxiety and depression, and it encourages me to visit the doctor so I can begin antidepressants when I feel myself spiralling down. And the best possible version of me instinctively knew when she was strong enough to stop taking them.

The best possible version of me pushes me to lean into receiving support from others when all I want to do is retreat inwards.

The best possible version of me restores me to a place of loving and trusting myself.

The best possible version of me is only possible when I am attuned to my Knowing Self. (Discussed the next section of this book.)

There is a caveat to absolute ownership. We only take ownership for *our part.* As painful as it is, we cannot and must not take ownership of other's decisions, behaviours, and actions—that is their work to complete. One of the models who I often refer to when thinking about what is mine to own and what isn't, is Stephen Covey's Circle of Influence and Circle of Control discussed in his book, *The 7 Habits of Highly Effective People.*

It is briefly described in the following way:

- *My circle of concern*: things I worry about but have no control over.

- *My circle of influence*: things I worry about that I can do something about.

- *My circle of control*: things I have control over.

Breaking down our concerns in this way is an effective way to protect our energy, reduce worry and anxiety and build resilience, as well as practicing discernment over what is our responsibility and what is not. For example, if I focussed on all the things in my circle of concern – the state of the world, the government's decisions and the spread of the covid virus, death, the economy, my past decisions, choices and behaviour – all that which is outside of my influence or control, I am wasting precious time and energy. So is worrying about what other people think about me. I can't control any of these things, this is the realm of *other people's* business and *God's* business. *Are the things in our circle of concern worrisome?* Yes, absolutely, they are the stuff our fears are made of. But focusing on these fears, unless we are an economist, in government or God, will just wear us down needlessly. When we feel fear, stress, or anxiety, this is actually handing over what little control you have over your life to the very things that worry you. You do not want to consume your time worrying about the things you don't have control over.

We hold some influence when we focus on our circle of influence.

Some of the things in my circle of influence may be:

- My commitments.

- The future of my children.

- My relationships.

- Where I work.

- My reputation.

- Who I vote for.

- Who follows me on social media.

Ultimately, where I have the most control is where I make the most impact in reducing my stress and protecting my energy. Things in my circle of control are my thoughts, my words, my actions, my behaviour, my reactions, my decisions or choices, my attitude or mindset, my mood, and my work ethic. And these are *my business*.

We should also not take ownership when it comes to mental illness. Many of us, myself included, tend to take ownership of depression, anxiety, addiction, and eating disorders and we call it *my* depression, *my* anxiety, *my* addiction, *my* anorexia, *my* mental illness. When we claim ownership of these problems, we make them part of who we are. We invite them into our life to take up residence and we allow them to grow deep roots in our heart, our minds, and the very fabric of who we are. Eventually, they are all we can hear, see, and think about. Our choices, our time, and our energy pivots around managing these things in our day-to-day existence.

They grind us down.

They erase us.

After a while, they own us—they become all we are. From time to time, we may have experienced these conditions, but they *do not* define who we are. They are symptoms of the illness of our unresolved trauma that led us to abandon ourselves. It puzzles me because an illness *is* an illness. Many of us would never give physical illnesses such as a cold, the flu, or a broken leg ownership to hold the same power over us. We would not presume to own these ailments as we know from experience we will recover. So, it is the same thing when it comes to mental ailments. As dark and as desperate things may seem. As overpowering as they may feel, they *are not you*.

You can heal.

A huge part of my awakening has been leaning into my curiosity and fascination with how our brains and bodies work. My interest in psychology as well as how I can use the energies of archetypes has allowed me to bring a positive change. The more I understand myself, the more I can heal. I am constantly amazed by the power we have in our own bodies. How our body and brains can heal themselves if we are willing to lean into the pain and discomfort and work with ourselves rather than against ourselves.

She AWAKES: The Best Possible Version of You

Reflect on and writing down the following in your journal:

- **What is the best possible version of you?**

- **How does it feel to be her?**

- **What archetypes can you embody to support her growth?**

- **What types of actions does she take?**

You may want to write in your journal, draw or paint a picture of the best possible version of you.

Referring to the work you completed in the previous exercise, consider:

- **What are the actions you need to take as a daily practice rewrite your shark music and to move closer to becoming the best possible version of you?**

Affirmation: *Every day I make choices which move me in the direction towards the best possible version of me.*

take a moment

you do not have to be
there is no should
there is no must
no expectation
in this moment of now

take a moment weary fighter

to rest
to embrace the gift of your sadness
the offering of your blessed despair

something precious is lost
and so take a moment here to
lean into the sweet pain
The ebb and flow of your melancholy

experience it here fully
honour
acknowledge
this is loss
this is life
this is me

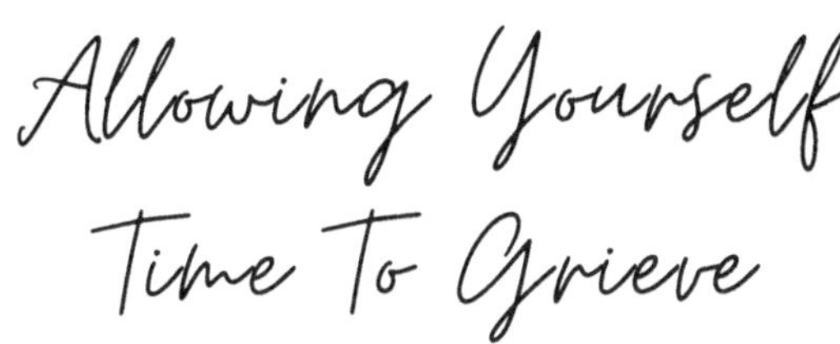

Allowing Yourself Time To Grieve

MAYA ANGELOU ONCE SAID, *"Forgive yourself for not knowing what you didn't know before you learned it."*

This is sound advice. The majority of us are plagued by the hindsight of our "if only".

There is a Buddhist parable that speaks about how holding onto anger is like holding onto a hot coal with the intent of throwing it at someone else, except you are the one who gets burnt. If we want to heal correctly, then we need to choose to let go. The same wisdom applies to the forgiveness we give ourselves. By the time women reach their middle years, they hold onto a lifetime of regrets and broken promises to herself. There comes a time when we must surrender the hot coals of our bitterness and anger so we can let the body do what it is designed to do—to heal itself.

One of the most powerful tools I have used during the process of forgiveness and healing is the four questions and the turnaround which form the foundation of 'The Work' by Byron Katie. In her book, *Loving What Is,* Katie uses the questions to inquire into the thoughts where we remain stuck and causes us to suffer.

Here are how I have applied the questions to my past life so that you get an idea of how they may be useful for you.

My thought: *It is my husband's fault I have depression.*

1. *Is it true?*

My response: Of course, the thought is true. He did things which contributed to my depression.

2. *Do I absolutely know that this is true?*

(This is where things go a little deeper.)

My response: Well, no, I can't say with absolute certainty that my thought is right.

3. *How do I react within myself and towards my husband when I think this thought?*

My response: I shut down, I become angry and depressed. I hurt and I want to numb myself with social media and alcohol. I want to disappear into my bed and stay there. I shut out my family and the people who I love. I act with anger and resentment towards my husband.

4. *Who would I be without this thought?*

My response: If I do not have this thought as the lens from which I viewed the world, *who would I be?* I am loving and open towards my husband. I would seek love and connection with him, see his bids of attention as ways to show me love. I'd be open to receiving love and focus on healing instead of holding onto anger, resentment, hurt, and shame.

Then comes the turnaround. This involves flipping my original thought in as many ways as I could and inquiring into each alternative statement for the nugget of truth it may contain.

Some turnarounds might be:

- *It is not my husband's fault I have depression* — When I look for the ways that this statement may be true, I can see that no person is responsible for another's experience of depression.

- *It is my fault I have depression* — This is also true. I see how I am responsible for my choices, my lack of boundaries, and my poor self-care which led to my experience of depression.

- *It is no-one's fault I have depression* — This also holds some truth. There are many factors, (some of them outside of my control), which contribute to whether we develop depression or not.

Rebuilding trust is what comes after forgiveness. It is the action part of the healing process. As with any relationship, learning to trust yourself after you have let yourself down is a gradual process of healing and forgiveness.

About eight years ago, I took a two-year break from teaching so I could open a cupcake shop. This was during the height of worldwide "cupcake mania". Shows such as *Cupcake Wars* and *Two Broke Girls* were extremely popular TV shows and people could not get enough of these beautifully decorated sweet treats. It was safe to say I was a tad obsessed. I scoured cookbooks and cyberstalked online cupcake celebs. I watched endless amounts of YouTube videos and I practiced my piping and cake decorating skills. (It is really amazing what you can learn from YouTube.) I convinced my long-suffering husband to tag along with me to cupcake shops in Auckland so we could conduct "market research". We debated business ideas, cupcake flavours, and decorations. I started an underground cupcake bakery online, one thing led to another, and before we knew it, the business became successful enough that I was able to convince my husband that the idea had enough merits for me to give up my stable day job and open a shop of my own.

The start of something new is always my favourite part, and I was so excited to see my dreams take their shape in a concrete form. A good decision can lead to a bad outcome and a bad decision may surprise you as it does not always guarantee a bad outcome. The jury is still out as to which category my cupcake shop fit into. But there are no absolutes or guarantees once we bring our aspirations to life and allow them to fly free into the world.

The shop sales picked up and although any new business is slightly tough for the first few years, we were able to upkeep eighteen months of steady success. I developed a strong social media following and a good reputation within the community. The café was child-friendly, and it was just the place for those frazzled mums who could meet in a cute, trendy shop for a cuppa and relax as they indulged in a treat while their children were entertained. However, this success did not last. I am sure there are many factors that played a role in this—hospitality businesses are always fickle and risky. But if I am truthful here, I made a lot of bad decisions. Within only a couple of months of opening my shop, my business partner decided to leave and endued with the wound of my Huntress. I mistakenly told myself I could do it by myself. I was *too proud* to ask for any assistance. Asking for help meant that I would have to admit I was not my "perfect" avatar. Living in the rosy shadow of the Maiden, I pretended everything was fine on the outside but in reality, it was a struggle to pay my rent. I was so riddled with shame that even my husband and family were not aware of how bad things were until it was too late. The shop was sold two and a half years after it opened, and I never set a foot back into it again.

I can say that this was one of the lowest points in my life. I was left with severe clinical depression, adrenal fatigue, and burnout. My marriage was hanging on by a thread due to my deceit. My children were traumatized because our family had changed so much. I had so much debt stacked up that we were in danger of losing our home. To say that I had created a mess was a *huge* understatement.

From this experience, I had created the following shame stories:

- I suck at being business owner.

- I was a worthless, no good human being who didn't deserve love.

- I was a bad wife, worthy of the verbal abuse her husband was hurling at her.

- I was a bad mother, and everyone would be better off if I died.

- I could never trust myself to own a business again.

- I am the type of person who was better off working for someone else until I retired and died.

For some time, I defaulted to my Danger Chicken mode. I was looping around in circles of self-destruction, and I even contemplated taking my life—it seemed so damned hard. However, a short time later, my cousin hung herself in the family home and I was able to witness how devastating this was for her children, her husband, her parents. I knew I could not do the same thing to my family, so I chose to stay. I decided to get up, get dressed, and show up every day, and I eventually got better. I started work as a centre manager at a small, early childhood education centre. I slowly paid back my debts. I became interested in personal development, and I was able to start picking up the pieces in order for me to get my life back on track.

Ultimately, we should all be able to stand in the knowledge of our own worthiness. However, when your sense of self is at an all-time low, when you have made so many poor decisions which have hurt yourself and the people you love, then you often need the people around you to believe in you first. People who see the value in you and will hold this space for you until you're able to see this for yourself again. With the help and support of friends, family, colleagues, and managers who saw the potential in me, I regained confidence in myself.

Slowly, I began to forgive and trust myself through the act of making and *keeping* promises to myself. The exploration of this particular cave was not my favourite adventure. I sustained many learning injuries along the way. However, there was gold too. The stumbles, the sprains, and the fractures hurt but the injuries heal. If you take the time to look amongst the rumble of your broken dreams, you will find treasure in your cave, and long after the injuries have healed, the golden nuggets of wisdom will remain.

I believe in all our relationships we set up "trust accounts". We consistently top up these accounts with acts that inspire trust. As illustrated in my story above, we can easily allow our own trust accounts to become overdrawn. Fortunately, we can remedy this by taking time to intentionally deposit funds into your trust account.

She AWAKES: Your Trust Account

Take some time to take stock up the funds in your trust account with yourself.

- **What is your balance with yourself?**

- **What constitutes a withdrawal for you?**

- **Looking back at your past, which withdrawals have been the most significant from your trust account with yourself?**

- **What constitutes as a deposit for you?**

- **How can you make it a priority to make more deposits into your trust account?**

- **Complete the following sentence: I am willing to trust myself even though……**

Affirmation: *I forgive myself for the wasted years I spent believing I wasn't enough.*

Stages of Grief

A part of the healing process is recognising that something died. Women hold onto dreams and versions of themselves that were either stillborn, aborted, or conceived but miscarried. We may arrive at a time where we wake up and realise, we have completely lost a version of ourselves that we will never get back. For as long as we hold onto a future self that will not be realised or a past self that we will never be again, we will get stuck and find that we cannot unfold into who we truly are. This is a place we can get stuck in for decades. There is a grieving process which much take place where only time can heal. I believe that one of the primary reasons we become so stuck in our lives is because we do not allow ourselves enough time and space to grieve these unborn or disowned versions of ourselves. Many of us cannot even admit to ourselves that they ever were, or even if they existed somewhere in our imaginations.

Part of the healing process is grieving, according to Elisabeth Kubler-Ross and David Kessler. There are five stages of grief: *denial, anger, bargaining, depression,* and *acceptance.* David Kessler later published a sixth and final stage, finding meaning, as discussed in his book, *Finding Meaning.* This is not a linear process, and we can move from one stage to another multiple times throughout the process. As Kessler said, *"the stages of grief are descriptive, not prescriptive."* (This is my experience of the stages of grief, even though I present them below in a linear fashion, this is for the ease of you, the reader.) There is much backwards and forwarding, dipping in and out, and twirly-birding between stages—sometimes at a pace that would have you gasping for breath and seeing stars.

Grief occurs when we are least expecting it. Grief is never-ever ending, it morphs, and shape shifts along the way. It is not intended to be a place to stay in. Grief is a mirror that we hold up to ourselves, much like a magnifying glass to help us focus on a path that we want to walk on. Our grief presents what is dear to us. It is the price we pay for the beauty of loving completely.

Denial

According to Elisabeth and David, *denial* is the first stage. When women are asleep, they are in the state of denial. It is a sense of disbelief when you think to yourself, *'I am fine, my life is fine—really!'* It is clinging onto being a Danger Chicken for dear life, refusing to see ourselves as who we truly are, in pain and suffering.

In the stage of denial, we have not yet become conscious of the promises we made to ourselves but did not keep, and the true extent of this has damaged our relationship with ourselves. We are in denial to the fact that we have been violated in some way—physically, but also spiritually—and we have chosen to stay with our rapists. We are oblivious to our "shark music" and how this soundtrack is impacting our lives.

It is like ignoring the fly shit on the wall and we just hope that it goes away. It is our stoic insistence that we are "okay" or "I don't need help" in our steadfast belief that we need to be strong as our world crumbles around us.

Anger

Anger happens as we wake up to our new reality and we look for someone to blame our situation on.

Do we blame other people in our lives?

Do we blame society?

Do we blame our family members?

Do we blame ourselves?

How could we have been so gullible—so stupid? How could we have wasted so many of our precious years with someone who didn't love us in return, a child who has rejected us, or in a life that no longer serves us?

We are enraged by life or by God for allowing this to happen. And it is often the disappointment in our lives that stokes the flames of anger and shame. Often, we do not allow ourselves to feel anger as we fear we will lose the approval from others as a consequence of our outrage. So, it simmers destructively in the pits of our stomachs turning into a cauldron of poisonous, lukewarm mush which we are forced to eat like week-old gruel.

My personal experience of anger is tightly interwoven with fear. My childhood lessons of anger was that it was an "okay" emotion for adults to have and not for kids. Anger in my family meant *danger*. The fear and unpredictability of my father's outbursts of anger caused me to become hyper-aware—permanently in a state of preparedness for anger to show itself when you least expected it. Anger in my family meant walking on eggshells and a constant scan of the room for any hints of disapproval on my father's face. Anger caused me to become sensitive to the emotional frequency of the room in case I had to retreat quickly. My experience caused me to feel frightened of my own anger, so I tried extremely hard to never let myself feel or acknowledge this emotion. When I look at my parenting, I have spent much of my adult life appeasing others, so they won't get angry, and shielded my children from the anger of their own father.

Let me normalise this for you:

- You may have been taught to fear your own anger, to only strive for positivity and the happiness in everything.

- You may have been raised on the virtue of "blessed be the peacemaker".

- You may have learnt from well-meant adults who were intent on protecting you from your emotions and that anger is a dark part of yourself you should fear.

- You may have been told that this is a part of yourself that is unwanted and unworthy of love.

These were lies.

When we suppress what we perceive as "negative" emotions and only allow ourselves to experience the "positive" ones, we leave no space to acknowledge or honour our feelings. This minimises our experiences. *It minimises us.* When we are stuck, and we allow the anger to control us, this is where we behave in ways which are abusive to ourselves and others. Dear wild heart, you *are* allowed. It is your birth right to experience the full, emotional kaleidoscope of *you*. It is natural and healthy to permit yourself to feel anger.

In the section of this book in the "Empowered Self", I will give you tools to process your anger, and other emotions, in a way which empowers you. Just know for now, recognise that it is okay to experience this emotion.

Bargaining

Bargaining is the stage where we delay our sadness by creating "what if?" and "if only" scenarios. We can unintentionally get trapped in this stage for years when we look back at our former dreams or the life that we wish we had, all while imagining how things *could have* or *should have* gone.

In bargaining, we "Facebook-stalk" old boyfriends and school friends to compare our lives with theirs. Imagining and wishing for a life that is different to the one we lead now. When we are in the bargaining stage, we reach for the "quick fixes", the things we can buy, or consume, babies to mother, and relationships which will momentarily make us feel better about our lives.

All of these things are a superficial fix. There is no external cure for an internal hurt.

Depression

During the depression stage, our sadness kicks into full force. As with anger, sadness is another emotion that we have traditionally been taught to fear. Thinking back to my formative years, sadness was either dealt with by finding the "silver lining", distraction, or ultimately, with anger. Dwelling on sadness was seen as a waste of time and self-indulgent. There were times when sadness was deemed acceptable, such as when someone passed away. However, there was a time limit on how long you could be sad for before you had to get over it and move on. Childhood tantrums were often met with the back of a wooden spoon or a slipper where I was *'given something to cry about'*.

I recall having an argument with my mother in my teenage, angsty years as I moped around my room about some boy or teenage miscarriage of justice. My mother, at her wits ends, yelled at me, *'You have so much to be grateful for, why can't you just be happy!'* Where I yelled back at her, *'What's wrong with being sad, why do I always have to be happy?'* As a rebellion from the happiness dream, I would find the most depressing song imaginable with words, which are now so laughably depressing, I would listen to it on repeat, and I would cry and cry and cry, all in the effort to feel sadness. This act of intentionally feeling sad was my way of "cutting" myself. Micro cuts to allow the mounting poison that I was not allowed to feel to leave my system, a way to feel real, raw, and human outside of the happiness avatar.

It was not entirely my parent's fault. My father had lost his mother to an aneurism when he was seven years old, and he suffered a horrendously abusive childhood. Anger was the only acceptable emotion he was allowed to feel, he was forbidden to display any sadness. My mother lost her father at the tender age of fourteen, and the youngest by many years of six children, experienced a rather sheltered and lonely childhood. Looking back at the circumstances they came from and knowing what I have learnt about how childhood trauma shapes us; I express nothing but gratitude to my parents for the stable, and mostly, happy childhood they provided for my sisters and me. I know they did the best they could with the limited emotional coping strategies they had in their toolkits.

As an adult now, I can step into my mother's shoes in the moment of our argument so many years ago and think about how this must have felt for her given her experience. Here was a child that she had sacrificed for to provide the things that she didn't in her own childhood. A child who had both parents, a comfortable existence, and yet she still was not happy. I can only say that it must have felt like a slap in the face to my well-meaning mother. I have never met a parent who did not want the best for their children. However, we are only able to give from the resources we have at our disposal.

One of the reasons that sadness becomes so challenging for many of us is that we were never taught to just sit with the emotion of sadness. Sadness is so potently painful that we hurry past it in order to push it down away from us and towards something or someone else. We attempt to numb it down instead of allowing ourselves to just *feel* it. It has taken me a while to catch onto this, but I have since learnt that we need to give permission ourselves and others to feel every single one of our emotions because this is vital to the human experience. The emotion of sadness reminds us of something we loved a part of us, or something that was important to us which has now been lost. Allowing ourselves to sit with sadness is our way of honouring the significance of our loss. Tears are healing in nature, causing our bodies to release the nurturing chemicals of oxytocin and endorphins. Permitting ourselves to experience the full weight of our sadness will aid our body to shift the trauma.

Perhaps we are frightened that the intensity of our sadness will overwhelm us or tear us apart so ferociously that we will never recover from it. However, as Oscar Wilde so eloquently put it, *"The most terrible thing about it is not that it breaks one's heart—hearts are made to be broken—but that it turns one's heart to stone."* Andrew Harvey reminds us that our hearts break repeatedly so they can burst open again and again meaning our hearts can hold ever more wonders. I believe we must experience sadness and heartbreak in order to love stronger and for our hearts to grow bigger. In denying ourselves to feel sadness, we become less human. We deny ourselves a beautiful rebirth from the ashes of our grief, a life with more love not less. Depression is what occurs if we do not allow ourselves to experience and sit with feeling sadness and anger.

To me, depression feels like a constant, never-ending headache, a tiredness that no amount of sleep can remedy. A constant fog over your mind that will not lift. It is knowing I have a hundred and one things to do and not feeling like I can accomplish any of them. It is seeing the world in monochrome, as if all colour and joy have been sucked out of the technicolour universe. It is feeling as if there is no end in sight, living in hopeless for the impending future. Everything is just too hard; you feel like the ball in the pinball machine who is being bounced from one difficult conversation to another; one crisis to another. You are just so, so tired and just so, so heavy.

Some days, the best that you can hope for is to just hang in there, get through today with the hope that tomorrow will be better.

Acceptance

Acceptance is often the hardest stage of the grieving process. It is natural to resist acceptance with every fibre of our beings. There is often a sense of shame in moving to the stage of acceptance. The fear is that acceptance means that we must agree with what happened, or say that what happened is okay, especially when we so desperately wish that things were different. We may find ourselves viewing our lives, our children, our careers, our bodies, our broken dreams, the death of our fairy tales lying like rotting fruit at our feet and *wanting* them to be different. Oh, how we want them to be different! However, not accepting is fighting with reality–fighting with ourselves. Fighting against reality is exhausting. Trying for a different outcome from reality is exhausting. Byron Katie says, *"When I fight with reality, I lose 100% of the time."* When we fight reality, we become a Danger Chicken–compelled to continue blindly, to behave in the same way expecting a different outcome.

As a child, I was naturally thin. My family was not well-off, but my parents always made sure we had the common staples like bread, milk, fruit, vegetables, and meat. Growing up on a budget meant that everything was cooked or baked from scratch. We hardly ever enjoyed the luxury for takeaways or junk food. Although I was never particularly athletically inclined, I spent most of my days outdoors playing in the garden with my sister, swimming with my neighbours, roller skating down in the garage, bicycling with friends, or playing in the nearby park. Many people think about South Africa where people are locked behind six-foot-high fences and burglar bars on the windows. However, the South Africa of my childhood was a vastly different place to how people may imagine it to be now. In many ways, it was idyllic, free, and safe for children to walk to school and play outside until the streetlights turned on and that was your cue to return home for dinner. When I turned eleven, like many girls, my body began going through the change to reach puberty. The first sign to show that I was shifting from "girlhood" to "womanhood" was that I gained a layer of hormonal plumpness which lasted for about six months until it disappeared just as suddenly as it appeared. *Six months*—such a short time in my young life. However, it was long enough to do irreparable damage to my body image.

I learnt from a young age that *thin* always meant *beautiful*. This was part of the description of the female avatar. The eighties and nineties were the age of the *Supermodel* and the *Heroin Chic*. Images portraying glamourous, tall, flawless, and impossibly skinny girls and young women jumped out at you from everywhere. They were on the television shows we watched, in the books and magazines we read. My mother believed this too and would pull my sisters and I aside if she felt we were getting slightly chubby, and she would suggest diet modifications to help us to get "back on track". The ladies at church would talk about this diet and how to get rid of the dreaded extra five kilograms. I stopped eating breakfast, I took lunch to school, but I gave it to the boys—they always seemed hungry—and I made excuses as to why I would not eat dinner. I would check-in on my weight several times a day to make sure I had not gained any more weight than the day before. I took up smoking because I read somewhere that models lived on cigarettes and black coffee to curb their appetite—*and who didn't want to look like a model, if it worked for them then it must be the right thing to do.* I knew I had reached my goal when mother would praise me with, *'You are looking so beautiful and slim. Look how nice you look in that dress. Your wrists are so tiny.'* Or when my dad would jokingly call me, *'Spine and Eyes.'* Or when the boy I fancied called me, *'Hot!'*

I think I would have continued to starve myself in this manner if it had not been for my aunt dying of cancer. My dad's younger sister was short and stocky—pleasantly plump. She had a quick wit about her, a wicked sense of humour, and soft brown eyes. I barely remember her face, what she wore, or how she did her hair with anything other than fuzzy details, but I remember how kind, warm, and generous she was. She *was beautiful.* My aunt was the one person I would run to when things were tough at home, I would talk things through with her because she always had a way of putting things into perspective for me, making it okay to go back home. My aunt and my mum were really close too, she used to visit on Saturday afternoons for tea and we would chat as we sewed clothing or permed each other's hair. *How I loved to hear her infectious laugh.*

One Saturday afternoon, I overheard my aunt describing to my mum the excruciating abdominal pains she had been suffering, and she explained that she was seeing a specialist about it because she was worried. A few weeks later, she was diagnosed with bowel cancer and was booked in for surgery and a course of radiation and chemotherapy. My courageous aunt put up a valiant fight but was eventually bed-ridden as the cancer came back stronger which made it harder for her to eat or drink anything. My mum doted on her and spent every day of my aunt's last few months next to her, nursing her and caring for her until she eventually passed away from thirst and starvation due to the size of her tumour. My aunt was only in her forties when she passed from this life into the next. Watching someone whom you love so dearly literally starve to death has a profound effect on how you view health, vitality, and even beauty. I learnt first-hand during this experience just how incredibly short life is and how utterly unimportant and temporary outward beauty is. Near the end of her life, my aunt had hardly any hair, her skin hung from her bones, but yet she still had her warmth and grace which radiated from inside her. I learnt that inside beauty, the kind my aunt had even though she was not the "ideal" body shape, was a far more accurate definition of *worth.* I decided there and then that I wanted to live my life, and I no longer wanted to starve myself. I accepted myself for what I looked like, and I made peace with my body. Once I was freed of this obsession to fit a certain body shape, it gave me the freedom to pour my energy into other important areas of my life.

When we practice self-acceptance, we relinquish the power that our circumstances have over us. Freed from the bonds of our hurt, we create peace inside of us which shines out of us like a bright light attracting blessings into our lives. Others around us are drawn to this light as our acceptance opens the door to accept those around us for who they are.

Finding Meaning

Awareness of a problem is always the first step to solving a problem. Byron Katie says, *"When we stop opposing reality, action becomes simple, fluid and fearless."* The grieving process is a cave; a cave that holds our treasure.

What is the gold under layers of clay waiting for us to unearth?

What is the meaning that our grief is pointing us to?

The word crisis has its roots in the Greek word, *krisis*—a turning point in a disease, a point to get better or worse. I read somewhere in one of Glennon Doyle's books that crisis can also mean "to sift". Acceptance is the turning point, but it is also the moment we receive the gift of "sifting out" the unimportant things in our lives. The opportunity to strip away all the unnecessary fillers in our lives, and to focus our attention with precision from inside out.

Acceptance is nothing more than an access point to where we transform. It is only when we stop raging from the war within that the meaning can reveal itself. After the grief has passed, and our acceptance has taken hold, within shaking off the glamour and the breaking open of our hearts, we are able to form a deeper and more authentic connection—a purpose, a meaning within us.

She AWAKES: Moving from Grief to Healing

Think back to the *you* you were before you became a mother, a wife, or a partner.

- **What did you dream that *her* life would become?**

- **Are you still holding onto a past *you* that you would like to be again?**

- **How are these lives different to the one that you have now**

- **Have you given yourself the opportunity to grieve the dying of these versions of you?**

I invite you to use this chapter to work through any unresolved grief that you may have in these areas of your life, allowing yourself the opportunity to observe and sit with any previously unprocessed emotions such as anger or sadness.

One way of doing this is journaling. Referring to the questions above, journal your thoughts and feelings, being sure to hold nothing back.

- As emotions come up for you give yourself permission to feel your emotions. (You may have a temptation to suppress them but stay steady with yourself. Allow yourself to simply sit with them until they naturally start to lift.)

- Do not try to fix or solve anything at this stage, just allow yourself to observe and feel.

- Once you have journaled your experience, rip up or burn the pages.

Repeat this process over the course of a few days and/or weeks.

As you journal, you will notice yourself going deeper. You will find new thoughts and emotions may surface, ready to finally be released. This is normal and part of grieving and healing. Done over time, you will eventually reach a place where you can recall your grief without having it cause you the same emotional reaction as you had previously, and all that is left is the lessons you learnt along the way.

Affirmation: *I honour all versions of myself with my attention, my grief and my emotions.*

who says that you can't?

we are constantly limiting ourselves
trying to appease the mythical they
have you ever stopped to think that your they
might be YOU?

Allowed

AT WHAT STAGE OF OUR LIVES DID WE START LIMITING OURSELVES?

Silencing our voices?

Shrinking down to fit?

When and where did we learn the lessons of "not allowed"?

My father tells a story of a baby elephant who was sold to a man who harvested trees in the forest.

When the elephant was a calf, the man placed a cuff and a chain around its foot. The man secured the chain to the ground with a big steel pin. As he was a little elephant, he the wanted to do what little elephants do. He wanted to follow his mother, play with the other baby elephants, splash in the nearby waterhole, or go for adventures in the lush, green jungle nearby. But because he was young and weak and the chain was strong, as much as the baby elephant tried to escape from his cuff, he couldn't set himself free. Fun, play, and adventure called to the baby elephant, but as much as he pulled, the chain and pin would not budge. The baby elephant learned that escape was futile, and he resigned himself to the fact that he would never be a free, wild elephant. He became an obedient, compliant worker elephant lugging wood by day and sleeping each night chained to the ground by the cuff, chain, and pin. As the calf grew, the cuff expanded but the size of the chain and pin stayed the same. He eventually grew stronger than his bounds. However, it never occurred to the now grown-up elephant that he could be free if he wanted to, all he had to do was lift his leg.

We are that baby elephant. We were once young, wild, and free, full of adventure, fun, and mischief. When we were young, we were chained to the dream with invisible bounds of expectation, which were our parents' limitations. Boundaries set in place intended for our safe keeping from the "danger of the jungle". What few of us have realised is that we have long outgrown our limits. Even though we are still wearing our cuff, chain, and pin that holds us in place, all we need to do is lift our leg.

I recently explored one of my limits. I, like so many, have been taught to fear the dark of night. Somewhere along the way, I learnt that indoors and light means safety and dark and outdoors means danger. I also recognise I am, to some extent, still bound by the bedtime curfew of my childhood, and the belief that says I should be in bed and not outside at midnight on a weeknight. Perhaps because it was warm, or I was just restless, I decided to get up out of the pillowy cocoon that was my bed and pad down the hall to the kitchen for a glass of water. In the darkness of my kitchen, I glanced out of my uncovered window and saw the stars calling me to join them for a night-time adventure. My first reaction was to shut down the invitation to be wild, so I denied the call. However, on this night, the call was stronger than the chains of my childhood boundaries and so I stepped outside, placing my bare feet on the cold, hard concrete. A gentle breeze caressed my naked skin as the warmth of the day gave way to the cool of the evening. As I made my way over to the grass, the wetness of the night dew made me jump with it's refreshing cold. I, however, resisted stepping back onto the concrete, and instead allowed myself to fully feel the sensations in my naked, goose-bumpy body.

It was dark. But this night, there was no moon—a new moon.

And then I saw it!

With the absence of the moon, I was able to see and absorb the full splendour of the stars in the heavens above me. Swirling majestically so bright and densely together that they appeared to form thick, celestial clouds. What I was witnessing reminded me of a hologram as the stars twinkled in a multi-dimensional way. I stood in awe; my head tilted up to the sky, my viewing pleasure accompanied by a symphony of cheerful crickets. A warm wave of gratitude rippled over me. I knew in this moment that the same magic which resided in the beautiful, amazing stars that captivated me resided in me too. The truancy of the moon made this spectacle possible. There was no doubt in my mind that miracles were possible. This is a simple story, a seemingly insignificant moment in the grand scheme of a lifetime. I could have easily stayed within the programming of my baby elephant and mindlessly followed my beliefs about the night. However, I was aware, awake, and willing to challenge these childhood boundaries. I recognised that I had the power to lift my foot up.

I am now starting a new story for myself about darkness, night, and bedtime curfews. This same feeling of "not allowing" restricts us in so many areas of our life. It keeps us petrified in fear and it controls our behaviour, our thoughts, and our actions. Not being allowed controls the work or the careers we choose to pursue, or how much money we allow ourselves to make. It tells us untruths about the success we feel we deserve and are capable of. It limits the adventures and experiences we have. It is the choke hold around our sexuality—our ability to fully submerge into our sexual desires—to receive and give pleasure. It cuts us off from our emotions, as these too, are not allowed. And in our hurt and fear, we abandon ourselves.

Self-care is another way we restrict ourselves. We tell ourselves about different kinds of falsehoods such as taking the time to care for ourselves is "selfish" or it will make us a "bad mother". We must give all our time and energy to prove our love to others. Generally speaking, taking time to look after yourself is not in the job description of the "good mother" or the "good girl" avatar, but once we start to **AWAKEN** up from the dream, the acceptable notion of self-care can be a sneaky hook back into the dream. A way to reinforce the avatar of what it means to be a woman. Ads in magazines, on television, and social media posts scream out loudly to us, "Buy this cream, go to this spa, get this outfit–then you will be better, then you will be *happy*."

Self-care is not about other people, and it is not about pleasing others. As Diana Vreeland writes, *"Prettiness is not the rent you pay for occupying a space marked 'female'"*. Self-care is about caring for *yourself*. Connect to yourself courageously and unapologetically stay with yourself. Give yourself the time and space you need to percolate your thoughts, feelings, and process your emotions to re-energize your body, mind, and spirit without restriction or shame. The simple truth is that we care the most whole-heartedly for others when we need to take care of ourselves first. True self-care makes us feel more like ourselves, and once we have tapped into it, we embrace the renewable well-spring of love and energy that we give to ourselves and others. "Not allowed" can also permeate into our ability to permit ourselves to be visible and loud–especially as part of the "seen and not heard" generation of girls who are now women. This can be the destructive force behind self-protecting behaviours, especially as the layers of clay begin to break away revealing the vulnerable *golden self*. We receive so many messages about what it means to be female and "lady-like" that it throttles our ability to speak up to own our truth and be loud.

Often our children are our greatest teachers, and I learnt a beautiful lesson from my daughter about the power of being "allowed to be loud". I had just been to visit one of my children in the hospital, the feelings of fear and anxiety were consuming. When we arrived home, I remained in the car awhile to compose my thoughts and process my feelings, while my other children went ahead towards the house. I was roused from my pondering by a loud scream, and I immediately imagined the worst. We have livestock on our property, including three-week-old piglets, so my first thought was that her screams were in relation to finding mangled piglets. I could already see their bloody, decapitated bodies in my mind…

'Oh no, what else could go wrong?' I muttered as I sighed with resignation to myself, as I warily trudged out of the car towards her. To my utter astonishment when I reached

my daughter, she was just standing there by herself letting out loud heart-wrenching screams.

'What's wrong?' I asked in exasperated shock and dismay.

Elated, she turned and smiled at me, *'Wow it does work!'*

'Come Mama, scream with me; it will make you feel better'.

I felt silly, and I wanted to make an excuse to go inside. However, she pleadingly looked to me, expectant for my approval. I didn't want to reject her, so I gave into her request to join.

'One, two, three', we counted together and then we let it all out in a loud, unrestricted scream, *'AHHHHHHHHHHH!!!!!!'*

We repeated this process several times that afternoon. Her sister found us and screamed with us too. A rush of euphoria tingled through my body. Release and relief washed over me.

In her book *Cassandra Speaks*, author Elizabeth Lesser, recounts the legend of the classical Greek princess Cassandra.

Cassandra was the daughter of Priam, the last king of Troy and his wife Hecuba. Cassandra was extremely beautiful and caught the eye of the God Apollo, who promised her the gift of prophecy if she submitted to his desires. Cassandra accepted the gift but when the time came to satisfy Apollo's desires she refused. Enraged, Apollo spat in Cassandra's mouth and cursed her with prophecies that would never be believed. Cassandra accurately predicted the fall of Troy, but no one believed her. She was later dragged from the Goddess Athena's altar, raped and killed.

Lesser philosophises that this is one of the many origin stories about the impotence of a woman's voice, which I tend to believe.

As girls, we are taught to mute ourselves, to be quiet, and polite. Emersed in our patriarchal culture we learn through repeated experience that we will not be believed. We are told to silence our howls, our roars, and our callings to the full moon. We swallow our big, impolite, socially unacceptable emotions, our "too-much-to-handle-ness". We bottle it down until it builds up like a cancer leading to our emotional death.

Losing myself in that moment and allowing my wild woman roar was both liberating and intoxicating.

My daughter is right, screaming does *feel good.*

She AWAKES: Allowing Yourself to Be Loud

We can restrict ourselves in many ways, so today, I invite you to accept the challenge to be loud.

- Find a space where you feel comfortable, it may be indoors or outdoors.

- Count to three, and then simply scream at the top of your lungs.

- Repeat this until you feel you have let it all out.

You may feel silly at first. You may not be used to hearing your voice, but please push through the resistance.

Once you have finished screaming, stand with our eyes closed and feel into your body. You can reflect on these questions below and write down your answers in your journal.

- **How do you feel after screaming out loud?**

- **How can you allow yourself to be loud in other areas of life?**

- **Can you allow yourself to sing?**

- **Can you allow yourself to write a poem or a short story and share it with a friend?**

- **Can you allow yourself to speak up at work?**

- **Can you be loud in the bedroom and explain to your lover what you would like?**

- **Can you allow yourself to tell others what you desire to make you happy?**

- **Can you allow yourself to set some boundaries around your time and energy and articulate this to others?**

- **Can you allow yourself to say "no"?**

Affirmation: *I am allowed to be loud, to speak up, and take up space.*

Allowing Yourself to Fail

As we waken, we move out of our comfort zones and we begin to peel away layers of clay, we start to expose our brilliant, golden self. Letting go of the façade of perfection can stir up emotional discomfort in us. It has often fascinated me that we have learnt to fear our mental and emotional discomfort in this way. When it comes to our physical selves, it has been my observation that we welcome and embrace physical pain but yet, we have to reject emotional or mental pain.

We attend the gym and say things like, *'no pain, no gain'* as we do burpees, squats, and lift weights. We use the stiffness of the next day as confirmation we worked hard enough and are building muscles. One of the ultimate physical indulgences for many women and men is a massage. One woman relayed her experience to me, *'I love a firm massage'*, she exclaimed enthusiastically, *'It hurts so good!'* Why are we not taught to embrace our emotional discomfort in the same way? Why are we not taught the lessons of "hurts so good" when encountering our emotional pain? Why do we avoid encounters with doing hard things which will build our emotional muscles and make us stronger and more resilient human beings?

Do you think that the process of becoming a butterfly is easy and pain-free for the caterpillar? I can only imagine the discomfort the caterpillar must feel—growing, splitting itself open again, and then shedding layers of itself. Spending time still and alone in the darkness of its chrysalis before morphing into the splendour of the butterfly.

In our ordinary, avatar world, failure or the perception of failure can rip away our golden stars and feel like a death. When we remove ourselves from the dream and stand in our sovereignty of our Queen, we are going to make mistakes. When we are learning new things and growing as a person, failure is inevitable.

So, how do we do it?

How do we allow ourselves to fall, get up, yet still show up day after day?

In the following exercise, I am going to offer you a way to work through your fear.

She AWAKES: Everyone Starts at Zero

I am not usually an advocate in comparing ourselves to celebrities or other social media influencers, however, I do believe this exercise can be a force for good.

Think of a famous person who you admire. (In my life it has been Oprah, or Brené Brown).

- **Look back at their career or where they were in their lives ten or twenty years ago?**

- **You can take a look at their social media and scroll back to their very first post or read interviews they did a few years ago.**

- **How much have they grown in the last decade?**

- **What circumstances, obstacles, mistakes, and failures have they overcome to become the person they are today?**

- **Can you imagine what their life would be like if they had given up the first-time things got tough?**

Go back to the dream which you wrote for yourself in the exercise back on page 60.

- **What would it mean to you if you had the life you created for yourself in that dream?**

- **What would be more painful for you, staying safe as you are now or taking risks and growing into the person in your dream?**

- **What is one area in your life where you experience fear, but you know if you act in opposition to this fear it will result in mental and emotional muscle building?**

- **What is one action you can take today to move in opposition to this fear?**

Affirmation: *Mistakes and failures are proof that I am growing and learning.*

The Art of Receiving

Another way that women limit themselves and where the "not allowed" shows up for us in the shadow of the Maiden or the selfless wounded Mother, is allowing ourselves to receive. We can severely limit our ability to receive, whether it is in allowing someone to do something for us, opening ourselves up to money, career opportunities, the abundance we deserve, receiving pleasure in the bedroom, or being able to accept a compliment. If this is a problem for you, from an archetype perspective, the best way to balance this wounded or shadowed energy is to learn at the feet of the Lover. The healthy embodiment of the Lover knows that receiving is her birth right, and she actively seeks this out for herself. Now if you have been living in the darkness of the selfless Mother this idea might be as foreign and uncomfortable to you as walking around naked on the main street of your town.

The best way I have found to accomplish this is to start with the art of receiving compliments. *Isn't it strange how we find it so difficult to accept a compliment or a feeling of genuine appreciation when someone shows us?* Over the years, I have become better at receiving compliments by imagining they are beautifully wrapped gifts, given from a generous, loving heart. *Would I give a physical gift back to someone or act in an ungracious and unkind way?* No, I would not. So, a compliment shouldn't be any different.

I have found that for me it takes both respect for others and myself as well as the courage of a vulnerable, whole heart to receive a compliment.

She AWAKES: Receiving Praise from Others

The next time someone praises you or gives you a compliment, even if it feels awkward at first, just push through the resistance and try to have fun with allowing in the praise and adding to it.

- **Compliment:** *'I really like that presentation you gave today at work'.*
  Response: *'Thank you, I really appreciate you saying that because I worked hard on that talk'.*

- **Compliment:** *'I really like your dress'.*
  Response: *'Thank you for noticing, I really like it too, it makes me feel joyful when I wear it.*

Be sure to maintain eye contact with them and smile.

Affirmation: *I can be humble and receive compliments with worthiness, grace, and gratitude.*

Dear Wild Heart,

If no one told you that you were allowed, then I want to be the first to sow a new seed in the garden of your soul. You are allowed.

You are allowed to be who you were born to be—with your messiness, your imperfections—the beautiful flaws that make up you.

You are allowed your golden centre, your sensitive heart, your old wild, wise soul.

You are allowed to love your body, to take care of your body, to give and receive pleasure with your body, to create with your body, to enjoy your body in all its many stages and forms.

You are allowed to feel your emotions, your tears, your secrets, your dreams, your desires.

You are allowed your too muchness, your hard thorns, and your soft curves.

You are allowed the full promise of your potential, the softness of your whispers, the loudness of your roar.

You are allowed to be happy, to make space for love and joy as it is your birth right to feel this way.

You are allowed to be successful, to have money and beautiful things.

You are allowed to protect yourself, your body, your energy, your heart.
To create boundaries and to defend them.
To say no when no is required.

You are allowed to not know, to grow, to fall, to make mistakes, to change and to reinvent yourself over and over and over again.

You are allowed to take up space.
You are allowed to be YOU.
You are allowed to sing, to dance, to spend nights outdoors when you should be indoors.

You just have to raise your foot.

To hear this poem read out loud to you go to:
https://tanyavalentin.co/You-Are-Allowed

the dark and sinister alter egos
the unhealed wounds
the parts of our mothers and fathers
we swore that we would never become

but here they are
seeping out from the shadows
bringing our childhood nightmares
into flesh and bone

Awareness

Self-awareness is the first step to healing, as we cannot hope to heal ourselves of something that we are not even aware is there. This means becoming aware of your thoughts, your beliefs, the ways in which you speak to yourself and about yourself, as well as your default behaviour patterns as illustrated in my example of how I become so accustomed to verbal abuse in my relationships that I, in turn, started verbally abusing myself.

It is important thing to approach awareness with the spirit of objective curiosity and not self-judgement, and this too is something to become aware of. The trick is to become aware of when we have slipped into self-judgement and not punish ourselves about it. We can give ourselves permission to do the best that we can *today,* and then focus on doing better when we know better or can do better. If we fail to do this, we can slip into a destructive cycle of causing ourselves to feel shame, which will eventually breed more shame.

Bruce Lee once said, *"Don't speak negatively about yourself, even as a joke. Your body doesn't know the difference. Words are energy and cast spells, that's why it's called spelling."*

The word, *Abracadabra,* generally used in magic spells, gets its origins from the Aramaic phrase, *Avra Kehdabra*—I create as I speak. Ergo, if you want to transform your life, then you need to transform the way you speak, especially about yourself. This means you need to pay close attention to your thoughts, the words you say to yourself, and about yourself creates your reality. The seeds we sow with our words are the seeds of the fruit we will eat. It is simple biology, if we want apples, we need to plant apple seeds. We cannot plant cactus seeds and hope to grow apples. Our brain pays close attention to the spells we cast, and it uses them to create our reality—the fruit of the seeds we sow.

As Don Miguel Ruiz mentions in his book, *The Four Agreements,* this requires from us to make the agreement with ourselves to be impeccable with our word.

What spells have you cast over yourself minute after minute, hour after hour, day after day, week after week, year after year without realizing it? You don't need a fairy godmother to reverse the spells you've cast on yourself, you already have the magic inside of you. You already know the way to break the spell once you reconnect with yourself. You have the ability to sit quietly and use the power of your awareness. You do not need to pay a magical guru in order for you to find it.

One of my coping mechanisms which has been with me since childhood has been writing. It has been the key to my growing self-awareness. It is through the cathartic practice of journaling where I began to make the unconscious *conscious* in me. Meditation has also become a way for me to become aware of my thoughts so I can let them go as I strengthen the witness part of my psyche.

In the following exercise, I will share a way for you to start to cast better spells over your life.

She AWAKES: Casting Powerful New Spells

You already contain the magic in yourself to break the curse of the unintentional spells you have cast in your life. For this exercise, I would like you to use the reflections you recorded when you eavesdropped on our thoughts in the exercise Tending Your Soulish Garden back on page 76. (*If you have not done this exercise, please stop reading this chapter and return to this page and complete the exercise.*)

Please use a clean page in your journal and divide the page into two columns.

Write down any negative thoughts or limiting beliefs you recorded in the above-mentioned exercise in the left-hand column. Look out for sentences that start about yourself with, *'I am just…'*, *'I am only…'* or, *'I am not as good as…'*. These are the spells you have been unconsciously casting.

- **What stories have these spells created in your life?**

- **Thank these stories for being in your life and let them go.**

Now use the right-hand column to reframe these thoughts or stories into positive affirmations. These are your new spells. (*Hint: you have already been doing this if you have been practicing the affirmations from the exercises in this book*).

Ways to make your spells super powerful:

- Start your new spells with *"I am"*.

- Take your time with this. Infuse emotion into your spells, for maximum potency.

- Even if you don't yet believe your new spells, continue to cast them. Remember, you are creating your new reality.

- Just like I said to write out the affirmations from this book, write down your new spells on beautiful pieces of paper, in your best handwriting, and place them all over your home, your mirror, your car, and your office for you to find like love letters to your soul.

Affirmation: *I am creating magic with my words.*

as I sat on a bench looking out at the ocean
I asked God why he had allowed me to experience such pain

did he not love me?
had he forgotten I was his child?

dear soul
he answered

I haven't left you
be rest assured dear one

I only gave you as much as you could handle
so that you when you helped others with their pain
so you would understand what they are going through

you were given exactly the right
life apprenticeship
to crack you open
and reveal the unfolding of the treasure
that is you and your beautiful soul

Your Life Apprenticeship – Acknowledging Past Versions of You

AS MUCH AS WE WOULD WISH IT SO, *life is not easy.*

For the majority of women, the transition between child to adolescent, adolescent to woman, and woman to crone is not a trauma-free experience. We make many mistakes and some mistakes we must make more than once before we can fully comprehend the lesson from our learning injuries so we can move into the full promise of our whole integrated selves. We accumulate multiple layers of emotional and psychic scar tissue through our experiences in life.

This is our life apprenticeship.

As poet Courtney Peppernell advises us, *"You can't skip chapters, that's not how life works. You have to read every line, meet every character. You won't enjoy all of it. Hell, some of the chapters will make you cry for weeks. You will read things you don't want to read; you will have moments when you don't want the pages to end. But you have to keep going. Stories keep the world revolving. Live yours, don't miss out."*

When we are in our Danger Chicken state, we spend most of our time thinking things are happening to us and we curse life for all its injustices. As we prepare to awaken our Wild Woman, we begin to see just how our life apprenticeship has equipped us with the exact skills, tools, and gifts we need to be the person we were meant to be. We recognise that our lessons and stories are a blessed treasure for us to share with the world. 'Oh', we exclaim, as the realisation hits, 'life was happening for me all along.'

One of my sources of energy is a regular yoga practice. Yoga is one of the ways I am able to embrace the wisdom of my body and still my mind. If you are a yoga practitioner, you will be aware of the asana pose, the *Warrior* or *Virabhadrasana* in Sanskrit. These poses are steeped in beautiful storytelling and myth. Whenever I practice them, I am reminded of how we can embody strength and acknowledge ourselves in all our stages of life–future, past, and present.

Warrior One starts in *Mountain* (Tadasana) Mountain pose. I am strong with my feet grounded to the earth; hips are square in line with the mat; I am the mountain. As I step back, I raise my arms to the heaven, and I am reminded that although I am grounded to the earth, I am connected to the heavens and all that is. As I transition into *Warrior Two*, I bring my hands to the prayer position on my heart centre, and I remember my true nature is love. I move my arms to float, one in front of me and one behind me representing the divine timeline. The past behind me, my physical body in the centre, and my future in front of me—brimming with untapped potential. At this stage of the pose, I can't help but resist to visualise my amazing future I am yet to experience. As I arch my back, and bring my bent arm, palm towards me over my head in *Reverse Warrior*, I imagine looking at myself in a magical mirror. This is my opportunity to thank and acknowledge the past versions of me.

We can see miracles everywhere if we choose to look. Let me show you three of life's such miracles:

1. We can never inhabit the same body twice. In fact, the body I inhabited today, is different from the one I inhabited yesterday. On a cellular level, the body from my twenties is gone, my forty-five-year-old body is a totally different body.

2. You cannot waste time in advance. As poet, Arnold Bennett, points out:

"The chief beauty of time is that you cannot waste it in advance.
The next year, the next day, the next hour are
lying ready for you,
as perfect, as unspoiled,
as if you had never wasted or misapplied
a single moment in your life.
You can turn over a new leaf every hour
If you choose."

3. The third miracle is a happy collaboration of the first two. Since we do not inhibit the same body twice and we are not able to waste time in advance, we are in a constant state of reinvention and rebirth. If our body has already let go of the past, then why do we still hold onto the baggage from our past?

We are literally one minute, one day, and one decision for a different life. However, before I explore the exciting future ahead of me, I want to pause to pay a tribute to the past versions of myself. Her triumphs, the missteps, and the truths she already knows. She birthed the current me into existence, and I would not be here without those bodies.

It is a powerfully releasing exercise to acknowledge and forgive your past selves. This was my experience of this inspired by the work of artist Jen Sievers:

*dear six-year-old me—***You are a poet**

yes I know
you say as you staple scraps of paper together to make a book
and you scribble the words that you know how to write in clumsy pencil block letters
you know in your soul that words are in your blood and writing is what you are meant to be
doing
You are a poet

*dear ten-year-old me—*You are a poet

you love to write stories and poems but you are starting to question this part of yourself
your teacher calls you out for daydreaming and scribbling words
in the margins of your exercise book
you inwardly shrink every time the clever girl at the desk at the front of the classroom gets called
up to share her amazing stories with the class
you look at your work and you know that you will never be as good as her
don't let these thoughts of self-doubt seep into the fabric of who you are
You are a poet

*dear fifteen-year-old me—***You are a poet**

you love all things dark and melancholy but hide this from your parents and their preoccupation
for happiness and light
you rebuke yourself for not being able to write pretty prose with words that rhyme
like some of the other girls in your class
instead you have a penchant for the classic poets who killed themselves in
gas ovens or died from heartbreak poverty and venereal diseases
mesmerized by their beautiful words strung together on the page before you
fascinated how mere words can evoke such a powerful emotional response in you
you spend hours listening to alternative rock
paying close attention to the stormy lyrics
while you pour your soul onto the page
You are a poet

*dear eighteen-year-old me—***You are a poet**

many a heartbreak or teenage drama has been overcome by the healing magic of poetry
you wear your heart on your sleeve as you write for hours like a woman possessed
but you know deep in your heart that being a poet is not a real job
it is not going to pay the bills
your mother informs you that your parents just don't have the money to send you to university
you take on a part time job and study english literature via correspondence
but you eventually give up
you decide to put aside your dream of writing and take a sensible job at a bank
but remember dear one

You are a poet

*dear twenty-three-year-old me—***You are a poet**

you have met the love of your life and you have married him
life around you becomes violent and unsure and you decide to move to a new country
you leave your poetry
you leave it behind in a cardboard box
in your parent's attic to gather dust
even though you are leaving this behind
remember

You are a poet

*dear twenty-five-year-old me—***You are a poet**

you have tried your hand at many different jobs but nothing seems to fit
you use this to convince yourself that you are failing at life
you berate yourself because you can't stick with anything for long
but we both know that this is because You are not
a waitress
a shop assistant
a jewellery designer
a banker
a pharmacist
a baker
a teacher

You are a poet

dear thirty-year-old me—**You are a poet**

you are very busy
you have two children under three
you are suffering with post-natal depression
some days are particularly difficult as you battle to even just get out of bed although you deny it
and would never burden anyone else with this knowledge
the survival of everyday life has left your once beautiful marriage in tatters
poetry is the furthest thing from your mind even though we both know that you could use it as
an outlet (just as you did in your earlier years) for all that you are feeling and going through,
you are tired
your gift lies dormant pulsing under the surface
but never fear
your heart is absorbing all the experiences and emotions which you are too afraid to confront and
storing them in your heart bank
ready to unfold when the time is right
You are a poet!

dear thirty-four-year-old me—**You are a poet**

your sister finds the box of your poetry
that you left in the attic when you immigrated
and returns it to you
you look over all the poetry that you wrote throughout
your teenage years
some of it makes you weep
some of it makes you cringe
but it is all beautifully You
keeping these poems is too painful
a constant reminder of the potential that you never lived up to
a painful reminder that you are a failure
that you are not good enough
so you tip it all into the paper recycle bin as if it no longer means anything to you
but never fear you are just letting go of the past
and making way for what is to come
You are a poet!

*dear forty-year-old me—***You are a poet**

your depression is at the worst that it has ever been
you are sad all the time
but you don't know why
you have a successful career
the family
the house
everything that is enviable of a life
but it brings you little joy
you go on a personal development course through work
and you meet a remarkable woman who causes you to stop
to challenge your very existence
peel back the layers of who you are
she helps you to listen to the whisper on your soul
the call to be a writer
a poet
you weep as this realization hits its mark
even though you aren't quite there yet
there is no doubt
You are a poet

*dear forty-four-year-old me—***You are a poet**

you have made some changes in your life and about to make more
you have rediscovered writing
even though it isn't poetry
you have begun to write blogs
safe little glimpses of your inner self that you allow the world to see
one day when you are out walking
your creative genius decides to make herself known
as much as you had tried to mute her, she is a persistent creature…
at first she starts by whispering in your ear
you try to ignore her
silence her as you had before with the deafening noise of life
but she persists
and then you start to hear them
the trickle of ideas - words that have been dormant for so long
which becomes a stream

which then becomes a torrent of

> *life*

>> *emotions*

>>> *experiences*

>>>> *pain*

>>> *your creative genius was literally spamming you*

>> *free after decades of isolation and disuse*

> *you turn and sprint home*

> *repeating the strings of words in your head as not to forget them*

> *not caring that you may have appeared to be possessed*

so desperate is the need for pen and paper

to scribble down all that you could remember before the magic leaves you

in this moment you can feel her reassuring warmth as it radiates through you

the realization dawns that

You are a poet

you have always been a poet

you have just come home.

She AWAKES: Acknowledging Past Versions of You

It is now your turn to journey back in time and acknowledge the past versions that were once you. I offer you this exercise to deepen your thinking. Think back along the timeline of your life and in your journal, write down the spiritual journey, or hero's journey, you have taken to become the you that you are now. Create a timeline and mark in the following types of events with the symbols provided:

- **A Star:** A tool or skill set you have gained.

- **An Arrow:** A turning point.

- **A Heart:** Something learned from a family/loved one.

- **A Triangle:** Breakdown/breakthrough moment—a paradigm shift.

How has life been happening for you all along?

How might this life apprenticeship have prepared you for the next part of your life journey? Now use what you have learnt about yourself to write yourself a letter, a poem, draw or paint a picture, or create a dance that honours who you are, who you were, and who you are becoming. *Take your time with this, this type of introspection can bring up memories, thoughts, and emotions so hold yourself gently and give yourself space and time.*

Affirmation: *I embrace and celebrate the past versions of me.*

being different is a good thing

it means that you have held onto enough of yourself

Alone

WHEN WE BECOME A MOTHER OR OVER IDENTIFY WITH THE MOTHER ARCHETYPE, one of the many things we sacrifice on the pyre of motherhood is our solitude. I have always identified strongly with the independence of the Huntress and so my loss of solitude came to me at a high cost to my mental health as I battled against my "good mother" avatar.

it is the nature of mothers
to lament over the loss of solitude

to longingly reminisce about the time when we could go to the toilet alone

to seek it out

to crave our own precious space

    and feel the shame of needing it

A born introvert, I require solitude like others would require oxygen. There are two types of exhaustion, one commands rest, but the other commands stillness, aloneness, and peace, but I crave the latter. One of the side effects of belonging to the dream is that you eventually disappear.

As a child, one of my favourite television shows was *Star Trek*. I don't know if you are a fellow *"Trekkie"*, but when I think about belonging to the dream, I think about the *Borg*. The Borg are a group of cybernetic organisms linked in a hive mind called *"The Collective"*. The job of the Borg was to collect and assimilate other life forms. There was no room for individuality or original thought if you were part of *"The Collective"*.

The dream is our version of the *"The Collective "*. One of the reasons which makes the dream so attractive and addictive is that it does not require any effort or any energy, so you can just go with the flow. In contrast, unhooking yourself from the dream relies on a lot of effort, inner strength, courage, determination, and perseverance, which is why one of the challenges for the Wild and Wise Woman is a perceived lack of belonging due to the loneliness of deep introspection. Choosing not to be part of the dream can be a scary, cold, and lonely place. For many people, including myself, the dream is so comfortable that it is easier to blindly blend in. *"The Collective"* is not a new concept. Shakespeare wrote about it in *Julius Caesar* when Mark

Anthony delivers his iconic speech, and the crowd turns into a mob which insights civil war. We saw this happen when the crowd decided to crucify Jesus Christ. Even Jesus's most loyal disciple, Peter, denied knowing Jesus three times as it was easier and safer to be a part of the crowd instead. The dream is why we do not wear our insides on the outsides, it is why we hide our witch marks, and hide under layers of clay. It is why we are so afraid to show up as our authentic selves, and why we make the decision to disconnect ourselves from our Wild Woman. It is why we hold everyone else's opinions as gospel while we ignore the truth that is already inside of us.

In my parents' generation, being part of *"The Collective"* was the most important thing. Women were selfless and men stayed at jobs which robbed their joy, their lives, and their very soul because the happiness and fulfilment of the individual was trivial compared to the expectation of the hive. For most of my life, I have been *living the dream*, so afraid of what others would think of me as if the worst thing that could happen to me was not to be liked. We no longer burn witches at the stake; however, the words, actions, or disapproval of others can burn hotter than flames. Aldous Huxley said, *"If one's different, one's bound to be lonely."*

Our fear of rejection is why we try to blend and hide in plain sight. It is why we fear being different, authentic, or original. We have been taught that there is safety in numbers. We mistakenly believe that our happiness and belonging hinges on the opinions of others, so that is why we subscribe to the dream in the first place. Being alone outside of the dream can seem like a fate worse than death. I used to hate being alone, but now I crave it. Needing time alone is one of the signs of the **awaken**ing woman. My Wild and Wise Woman call me to be solitary and sing out seductively like a siren's song calling sailors out at sea. I have come to recognise that alone does not necessarily equal being lonely. Lonely is a matter of perspective, a purely subjective experience. We can be surrounded by people and feel desperately lonely, or we can be alone and feel a warm glow of contentment, love, and connection. The roots of the word "alone" originate from the middle English word "all one", which reminds us that you are one with your Wild Self and all existence. You already have everything inside of you. It comes with the assurance that there is nothing greater outside of us than what already is within us.

Alone is where I can still hear the noise of the world competing for my attention, but I can hear her, my creative genius, my Wild and Wise Woman reconnecting me with my needs. The inner callings of my heart. Alone is where I learn to trust my inner knowing and create happiness within myself, recharging my energy and taking my power back from other people.

She AWAKES: Intentional Solitude

Does solitude call out to you?

Hopefully, by taking this adventure with me, you have been setting aside intentional time to embrace your silence and rediscover yourself through the power of introspection. As busy women and mothers, we are often time poor. But if solitude calls to you, you must permit yourself to answer.

Some ideas of intentional solitude may be:

- Wake up half an hour before your family and use this time to read, reflect, meditate, or journal, and allow yourself to set your intentions for the day.

- Going for a walk alone is very beneficial for you in many ways. Exercising, breathing in the fresh air, and being alone with your thoughts can be a magical combination.

- Intentionally unplug from your phone and social media. It is a sad fact that we can go a whole day without a single moment of stillness. We can fill our life with unnecessary noise and forgo a single moment of reflection, deep intentional thought, or connection to our inner selves. There was a time where we had space for thinking, times where we would go for walks or a drive in our car, and we would have time to reflect on our day or our lives. We could assimilate the lessons of the day and integrate them into our hearts. There used to be a time when we were bored, but just as the forests and green spaces are disappearing from our communities, so are the times we spend in the forest of our minds.

- Garden or clean your house. You will be amazed at the level of reflection available to you during mundane household tasks.

- Take a shower or a bath. Shower thoughts are a real thing. My shower or bath is a place I can hear my Wild and Wise woman the loudest.

- Masturdate. Take yourself out on a date to a movie, restaurant, or for a picnic.

- Spend time alone connecting mother earth.

- Take yourself away for the weekend or a holiday—*by yourself*.

Affirmation: *When I love and accept myself, I am never lonely.*

I snuck off at lunchtime
for some afternoon delight
tucked away
curled up in my muse

every time I think that we are done
she pulls me close once more in inspirations tender embrace
and fills me with thoughts and delicious imaginings

I am pregnant with possibility

Awakening Woman

WE HAVE REACHED THE MIDPOINT OF THE MOUNTAIN. The midpoint of the mountain represents our awaking selves. The challenging of our stories, our thoughts, and beliefs, our bonds are loosening, and we are beginning to have dominion over ourselves and our lives.

As you invite in to embrace your Wild Woman and other feminine energies into your life, as you become more connected with yourself, you may notice some of these signs of the **awaken**ing woman.

You may notice you are experiencing an increased sensitivity and tingling sensations in your body, but also increased emotional sensitivity.

You may feel a pull to spend more time outdoors.

You may desire more purpose and meaning in your life.

You may need more time alone to pray, reflect, or meditate.

You may notice your sleep is filled with vivid dreams, even nightmares of predators which often is the case when a woman is transitioning to a high consciousness.

You may experience a shift in perception and priorities as you let your old habits and beliefs go.

You may find yourself caring less about other peoples' opinions about you.

You may have started seeing synchronicities and feel a deeper connection with your intuition, emotions, and psychic gifts.

Some of these changes can be overwhelming and even scary, but you are unearthing and waking up parts of yourself which have been dormant for a long while.

Take heart, you are exactly where you need to be. This is happening *for you*.

Trust yourself and trust the process of your new becoming.

She AWAKES: Signs of Your Awakening

Reflect on your journey as you arrive at this part of the book. Take a moment to locate yourself.

- **Do any of these signs ring true for you?**

- **What emotions are you experiencing?**

- **Have your dreams changed?**

- **Have you had a shift in beliefs, perceptions, or priorities?**

- **How do you feel in your body?**

If this feels too overwhelming, pause and take some time today to journal, be gentle with yourself, and practice some self-care.

If you feel excited, turn the page.

Affirmation: *I am awakening.*

PART FOUR

Knowing Self

if something inside you is dying
let it die

but then let it go
don't let its decaying corpse lie around
rotting you from the inside out
slowly hollowing out your soul

instead make space
for the part of you wanting to be born

and where shall I meet you, my love?

in the between
the space of now and tomorrow

I shall meet you in my dreams

there I shall meet you

there in the never

Knowing Self

WHEN I FIRST FOUND OUT I WAS PREGNANT WITH JESSIE, I began reading everything I could about pregnancies. I joined a website that sent me daily emails like:

"Day 12: Today your baby is the size of a..."

And I read books like *What to Expect When You're Expecting.*

During my subsequent pregnancy, reading and searching the internet which helped ease my anxiety, became my obsession. Every twinge, every niggle, every pain I felt would be researched and examined for its "normalness". Deep down I thought that if I could find an explanation to what was happening inside of me, I could somehow control the outcome of my pregnancy because my knowledge would keep us both safe. However, I now know that this only added to my stress and anxiety levels. After I gave birth, my obsession with reading and researching kicked into overdrive. Early motherhood was a time of great trepidation for me, and it was an extremely lonely time. My husband worked ten-hour days to support us. My mother and my husband's mother, who have strong Mother archetypes alive in them, were still discovering how to shift from mother to grandmother and they were not getting along well.

As the unnamed Maiden was still a strong archetype for me, I was desperate to please and didn't want to seem to favour one over the other. My sisters and friends did not have any children and bereft of a reference point, or a guide, I had to place my trust in sources outside of me. I needed constant reassurance, but none was on hand.

My first baby had died. *'Could I keep this one alive?'*

'Was I doing a good enough job?'

'Was I a good mother?'

'Was I good enough?'

As my Mother started to activate, I came to recognise that books and the internet could only ever give me knowledge. Wisdom was something I already had inside of me. The knowing, self-taught, hard won from living from the collective intuition of my past lives and the lives from the women who went before me. I realised that no matter how much research I did, no matter how many groups I belonged to, no matter how many people I asked… No one was going to be able to make my choices for me. I could ask for advice, and I could weigh up the options, however, sooner or later, I was going to have to trust myself and my own knowing or I would have to live with the consequences of living in the purgatory of indecision. Over time. I came to the conclusion that I *knew* myself and I *knew* my baby, so the rest was just noise. Time and time again I had to go back to what I felt was right in my body, my heart, and my soul.

When studying the archetypes, I encountered some confusion when comparing traditional Goddess interpretations of the archetypes as mentioned in Jean Shinoda Bolen's book, *Goddesses in Everywoman*, and contemporary expressions of these energies. For example, the traditional expression of the Wise Woman is the Sage or the Goddess Athena—Goddess of wisdom, crafts, and strategies. Athena is a head-centred seeker of truth, she is a father's daughter who is driven to be "one of the boys", and sides with patriarchal culture norms. There has been debate as to whether this is a true feminine archetype or just an expression of a woman's animus, (her natural male energy). This is in stark contrast to the modern archetype of the Wise Woman who is a heart-centred keeper of women's intuition. At first, this caused much confusion and I struggled with how to apply this archetype in my life and how to write about her. After much consideration, I decided on the interpretation of the Wise Woman in this book since it is the one which makes the most sense to me. My understanding is that the Wise Woman archetype is an archetype in her own right, however, the other feminine energies all hold their own unique gift of knowing to share with us.

The Queen of the Underworld has an innate wisdom which guides a woman though the trauma of meeting her shadow and allows her to use this to be a guide for others. The Mother is imbued with the gifts of maternal instinct, connected to, and passed down to her from all mothers before her. The Lover knows her body, she knows what she likes and allows herself to seek a pleasurable life with sustaining experiences that make her feel good. The Wise Woman represents a woman's intuition, reason, thirst for knowledge, objectivity, and strategy. The Queen knows how to build and maintain partnerships and alliances, she knows her worth, how to invest in herself, uphold boundaries and delegate to her team to grow and protect her energy. The Huntress knows what is important to her and how to focus her attention and energy on her mission. She knows she can rely on herself, and she already possesses what she needs to be the Queen in her own story. The Wild Woman is a woman's connection to her psychic gifts, she is the keeper of a woman's dreams, and the inextinguishable fire at the centre of her inner hearth.

When these energies work together in unison for the woman they inhabit, they are an unstoppable force, a secure and stable foundation of knowing that is the birth right of all women. All of us, *even if you think you don't,* possess this sacred and magical part of ourselves. Some call it our muse, our creative genius, our knowing, our intuition, our gut, or our GPS. Our inner Goddesses commune with us, they nourish our souls and enrich our lives with life sustaining and ambrosian meals of love and inspiration. We are all equally blessed. The only way we differ is in our ability to listen and to take heed. In this section of the book, I refer to this accumulation of collective wisdoms as the fusion archetype of the *Knowing Self*. I will provide you with keys tools to guide you in accessing aspects of your inner Knowing Self, to support you in rebuilding the bridge to trusting yourself and your intuition.

The first of these keys lies in the deceptively simple lesson of "Yes" and "No" knowing.

She AWAKES: "Yes" and "No" Knowing

I would like to take you back to a time, right back to a time when you were a child, where you were connected with your body and your intuition. Can you remember a time when you didn't need to think, deliberate, or ask for everyone's advice and opinions before making a decision? When you just *knew*?

Close your eyes and bring to mind a person from your childhood who you disliked, and in your imagination, look at their face.

- **What does it feel like to be in their presence?**

- **Pay attention to the expression that naturally comes to your face. And then pay even more attention to what is happening in your body.**

- **Can you name the emotions you felt?**

- **What sensations did you feel?**

- **Where did you feel it in your body?**

This is the feeling of **"*No*"**.

Now, close your eyes and bring to mind a person from your childhood who you love, and in your imagination, look at their face.

- **What does it feel like to be in their presence?**

- **Pay attention to the expression that naturally comes to your face. And then pay even more attention to what is happening in your body.**

- **Can you name the emotions you felt?**

- **What sensations did you feel?**

- **Where did you feel it in your body?**

This is the feeling of *"Yes"*.

In the coming weeks, spend time tuning into your body's "Yes" and "No" messages.

Affirmation: *I am learning to trust my inner knowing.*

Disconnection from Our Knowing Self

As illustrated in the exercise you just completed, this feeling of "Yes" and "No" from your childhood is still very much alive in you. You can tap into this knowing and extend the wisdom of what instinctively feels right and good to you, and what doesn't, in all areas of your life. I would like to point out that this "knowing" has nothing to do with fear. Something can ultimately *feel right* and good for you, but fill you with fear, we may just be so disconnected from our true deep knowing that we have forgotten how to trust ourselves.

What caused you to stop trusting the knowing of your body?

What caused the disconnect of your heart and your soul?

We all have and keep secrets, and we all tell lies. Denial is a form of deception. In this type of prevarication, the first victim of the lie is more often than not the perpetrator of the untruth as they are often lying to themselves too. Fabrication is the deliberate invention of a false story, then there is the lie by omission, where we know something about someone or something that can cause hurt to a person we care about or ourselves, so we choose to keep it secret. The intention of a lie is almost always not to inflict pain on another, but rather to protect ourselves or others...

Oh, the secrets we keep.

It was a beautiful moonlit evening on a beach on the northern coast, now known as KwaZulu Natal in South Africa, and it was in my eleventh year around the sun.

It was a Friday in March, and the hot and humid day had continued into a hot and humid night. The moon was full which meant a 'spring' tide—a time when the tide was either exceptionally high or exceptionally low and crayfish could be hunted in the exposed rock pools. My dad and his fishing buddies decided to spend the night camping out at the beach, surfcasting and hunting in the exposed rock pools for octopus and crays. I have always adored the beach, so my sister and I begged my dad to take us along on this coastal adventure. The men built a bonfire on the sand, and we ate frikadelle and tomato sauce sarmies which my mum had lovingly prepared for dinner. After dinner, my sister and I ran off to play hide and seek in the nearby sand dunes with our cousins and other childhood friends. We loved going on these rare adventures with my dad, because unlike my protective mother, my father allowed us more freedom when she was not around. I am not sure how I became separated from the other children, but I remember being alone on the beach and stumbling into him, My uncle. The husband of my favourite aunt and the father to my much-loved cousins.

'You haven't said hello to me yet', he scolded. 'Come here and give me a cuddle.'

He smelt like stale beer, and he was slurring his words. I really did not want to cuddle this man, but he was my uncle and a grown up, and I was taught to respect and obey adults. So, even though every fibre of my being screamed out to me not to embrace this man and my immediate urge was to turn and run the other way, I was a "good girl" who played by the rules. My fear of getting into trouble for being rude to my uncle won over my urge. I ignored my inner knowing, I walked over to him and gave a hesitant hug.

'Oh, that's lekker', he slurred, 'give me a kiss.'

I obediently did as he asked, and I gave him a peck on the cheek as I had done many times before. But this time felt different. This time made it the hairs on the back of my neck stand up in fear and revulsion. I tried to pull away, but he held me in his grip and slipped his hands under my bathing suit, caressing my newly forming breasts with one hand, his other hand tracing the edge of my bathing suit near my groin, before slipping a finger into my suit and stroking the outer lips of my labia, and then moving it to slide on the inside of my vulva. Petrified, frozen in disbelief, and confusion were the emotions I felt in this moment. Somehow, I snapped back into my body and managed to wriggle free from his grasp.

'I think I can hear my dad calling'.

This was my feeble excuse I gave before I began running a stumbling race on jelly legs, as fast as I could towards the light, towards other people. Once I was back amongst my peers, I was shaken but with my avatar firmly in place, I pretended the incident didn't happen. Later, as I lay in my sleeping bag under the tepid night sky looking up at the moon and the stars, next to the dying fire. I shook and shivered despite the warmth of the evening or the proximity of the fire. I was too terrified to close my eyes and sleep. Watching, waiting, dreading to hear if he was coming near me.

By the time dawn broke, I had decided several things about myself.

It was *my* fault.

There was something *wrong with me* that made him act this way.

I was broken, dirty, and evil and that was why he did that to me.

Sex and my body were dirty and disgusting, and I unknowingly moved into the shadow of the wounded Lover. I could not trust myself or my ability to make good decisions. If I told anyone what took place on the beach, they wouldn't believe me, or I would hurt and humiliate my parents, cousins and my aunt, who I adored. This experience did not fit in with the avatar of "the example" and in my mind I saw their sadness and disappointment. I felt the sting of their rejection.

This was a secret that I *had* to keep.

In the light of day my uncle pretended that it never happened.

'Perhaps it didn't happen?'

'Perhaps I made it up?'

'Maybe it was a bad dream?'

Although this experience should have taught me how I could trust myself, it had the opposite effect. My childish lapse in judgement caused me to lose faith in myself and others. It severed my connection with my Wise Woman and from that day I lived in a fractured state of constant fear. I did not trust myself to be alone with him or any other grown-up man again. After a while, I convinced myself I was the liar, that the incident was just a dream, a product of the overactive imagination of an eleven-year-old child. This is a secret or a lie by omission I kept with me into my adulthood. It was not until after my aunt died of cancer, and I was married, that I plucked up the courage to confess what had happened to my mother.

The secrets we keep do not lie dormant, nor do they benignly wait until we release them. They are not contained to the part of us where we keep them hidden. There is a price we pay for being a secret keeper, a curse that our secrets use to change the shape of us. They grow and metastasize like a tumour, wrapping themselves around our hearts, invading the crevices of our minds, and weaving themselves into the fabric of who we are. I can still sense the tentacles of my secret in my marriage, my sexual identity, my relationships with others, and my ability to trust. The secrets we keep become our night terrors, our sleep paralysis monsters, our shame demons, the secret self we keep hidden from even those who are the closest to us. Yet, it is another layer of cold, earthen unworthiness to hide behind. Secrets and shame feed our private fear that no one could love *all* of us, because if they knew all that we are, they would reject us because they find us unworthy and utterly unlovable.

She AWAKES: Your Moment of Disconnection

You may not have had such a dramatic severing of your connection with your intuition. Or perhaps your story is deeper and more soul-destroying than mine that you cannot remember when and how you lost connection with your Knowing Self.

I encourage you to reflect on your moment of disconnection and write, draw, paint, or create movement about this.

If you are unsure when this happened to you, I invite you to simply write on a piece of paper:

"The moment of disconnection from my knowing self was..."

And leave this statement open to percolate and allow it to come to you in its own time.

Affirmation: *I am whole when I trust my intuition.*

the room is aglow with the warmth of candlelight
the goddess stands in front of me
naked and beautiful
smooth amber skin
silky dark hair falling
over full ripe breasts

her palm is extended as she beckons me to come nearer
entranced I comply

  she bends her head
    her lips
      caressing my breasts
  her tongue moving in lazy eights around my nipples
  she smiles at me
in a knowing seductive way
    snaking her hand down my belly
until she reaches between my thighs
  her fingers find and touch the source of my womanhood

I wake
gasps escape
my heart racing
my body slick with sweat

  wet and throbbing
begging for release

I touch myself

    my body writhing in an intense climax
  as tears roll silently down my cheeks

mothers are not meant to think this way

Keeping Council
With The Lover

IT IS THE WAY OF THE DREAM to give a woman false information about herself, her sensuality, and her sexuality that she becomes frightened of this awesome force which is alive inside of her. It is the way of the dream to place high value on the seemingly "safe" and docile archetypes of the Maiden and the Mother to warn us away from dangerous, uncontrollable archetypes such as the Lover or the Wild Woman. We have been taught that you we can only choose between two options damsel/old hag, mother/whore. The stories that we grew up with lead us to believe in cookie cut two-dimensional view of women and men. If our culture were an ice cream shop, we may be led to believe that the only flavours available to us are chocolate or vanilla. However, in reality we have a whole rainbow of colours and flavours to sample. The thing about archetype work is that it gives us options.

During our womanly initiation towards the Lover, many women either disconnect from this archetype, suppress her, shut her down, or move into the wounded Lover to engage in overtly sexual behaviour which does very little to honour and nurture the woman she is. At various times of my life, I must confess that I have fallen into both of these shadow Lovers. As discussed in the first part of this book, our Lover archetype is not just a woman's sexual self, she is also a woman's ability to experience joy and pleasure in life as well as being connected to her creative self. When we disconnect from our Lover, joy, pleasure, and creativity dwindles away and eventually dies. We cannot be fully **AWAKEN** and disconnected sexually.

(This next part may be confronting but stick with me.) The majority of women whom I speak to who feel stuck or tell me they feel as if they are living their lives with little joy, excitement, and purpose. They are joyless and uninspired in their sex lives too. Many women feel as if having sex with their husband or partner is a chore or that sex is not a priority, and they can do without it.

Here is my story:

Sex, or rather the lack of sex, has been a bone of contention for the longest time in my marriage. My younger pre-baby, self-enjoyed sex, she basked in the glorious power she could wield with her body, her lips, and the promise of her vagina. But like many women, for some reason my libido dipped when I became a mother. Don't get me wrong, I still enjoyed getting my inner goddess on once I was in the flow of things. However, I found I was just so tired all the time and I very seldomly initiated sex with my husband or with myself. I searched for clues—*was I not attracted to my husband anymore?*

Yet, the truth, and if I was being totally honest with myself, was that I didn't desire sex with anyone. At first, I thought it was my hormones, so I went to my doctor and asked her to run some tests. I was hopeful there was going to be a magic pill I could take which would just make me want *it* again. When I got the test results back it said, "reproductive hormones in normal range", and reading this made my heart sink. *'Damn, it's me!'* I knew from my research I was not alone in this. Female sexuality is more complex than just "popping a pill". But if it was not a hormone problem, *then what could it be?*

Here is what I have figured out so far: My observation has been that our feminine sexuality, which is tied to our ability to 'bring into being' can be focussed in so many different ways. We can use it to birth children, 'idea children' or in the pursuit of sexual expression. Often the birth of a new 'child' diverts our nurturing life force from our other creations. Once activated the Mother archetype can be an all-consuming force in a woman's life. In the last twenty years, my body has been taken over, it has been stretched out, filled out, and demystified. My body has made and been home to four humans. My vagina was the portal of their entrance into this world. My breasts were the implements from which I kept them alive. During the past two decades, I have been pregnant, sleep deprived, depressed, and lactating. My body no longer felt like it belonged to me, to the point where I didn't even recognize myself sometimes. Even though sex made me a mother, in my mind, my Mother and my Lover did not inhabit the same body. I must confess that when my husband suckled on my breasts at times, I recoiled as all I could think about was breastfeeding babies and this filled me with disgust.

There is a psychological fallout from the moving consciousness of being desired to being needed. A woman, when she is already depended upon so completely by her children, does not require a lover who requires something from her too. It is essential to her life force for her to find rejuvenation in her attachments. She does not need another demanding child to take care of. I realise that I came to see sex as another act of "giving" and since I had become so transparently selfless, I had nothing left to give. Our Lover wants to be desired—not needed– "needed" is in the realm of the Mother.

Our relationships are holistic organisms just as we are. One part of our relationships affects the other. When my husband and I were feuding with each other during our darker years, our children were not the only collateral damage of our war, we were damaged too, individually, but also in our collective self too.

Did I come to distrust and despise myself and him to such an extent that I believed I was no longer worthy of pleasure?

Was this distrust a reason why our relationship was no longer a source of my pleasure?

Did I allow my shame demons to convince me that if I enjoyed making love with their father, it meant I was somehow betraying my children?

Was the anger and the damage that occurred during this time in our lives was okay if I let him back inside of me?

Would my choosing to take pleasure in sex make me a bad mother?

Was it possible that our sexuality was another way that the fairy tales we grew up reading or Hollywood has programmed us to believe in unrealistic expectations of what life and sex should be like?

Part of the *"And they lived happily ever after"* blights on our collective psyche.

Very few of us know what goes on in some else's bedroom. Movies and pornos are not real life. However, many of us hold onto the belief that everybody else's sex life is way more interesting, passionate, and fulfilling than their own, but most of the time, this is not the case. We spend so much time comparing ourselves to our imaginations. *Is trying to fulfil our expectations of how our sexual selves should perform is another way for us to prove to ourselves that we are not good enough?*

These are all good questions when I look at them written down on paper, and I do believe that some of these questions are going on for me, and I think for other women too. However, when I think about it, the suppression of my Lover happened long before I became a mother. And even before I was a victim, of sexual assault by the hand of my uncle, (which I know wounded my Lover). When I look back, I can recall I have always had a skewed view on sexuality. There is nothing I can point a finger to as a defining moment, however, I learnt from an early age that sex was something no one talked about. Sex was disapproved of. Sex was embarrassing. Sex was secret. Sex was dirty. I learned that we are either a mother—saintly, proper, and lady-like. This was greatly contrasted against the alternative of the "loose" woman—someone to be reviled and feared by other women and are taken advantage of by men.

In my experience, childhood exploration was severely frowned upon and punishable. This was further compounded by my first sexual encounter–the sexual assault of my uncle when I was a child. *But what did these childhood experiences teach me?* It taught me to fear my sexuality, my desire, and my womanhood. It led me to believe that my body was a source of sin, disgust, anguish, and pain. The central emotions that shaped how I experienced the Lover Archetype were fear and shame. However, as author, Clarissa Pinkola Este's, says in her book *Women Who Run with The Wolves,* "*The problem of secret stories surrounded by shame is that they cut a woman off from her instinctive nature, which is in the main, joyous and free. When there is a black secret in the psyche, a woman can go nowhere near it, and in and in fact comes in contact with anything that will remind her of it or cause her already chronic pain to crest to an even more level.*"

Through my teachers, fear, and shame, I learnt that I couldn't trust the knowing of my body and so it was a lot safer to simply shut down this part of me.

She AWAKES: Your Initiation into The Lover

Take time to slow down and give yourself full attention to sit with the following questions and record your thoughts in your journal.

- **How were you initiated into the Lover Archetype?**

- **What were the predominant messages you heard from your parents, other adults, and your community about sexuality when you were a child?**

- **What were the greater messages you heard about desire, pleasure, and joy? (Sexually and non-sexually)**

- **How did your earliest experiences with your sensual and sexual selves shape how you experienced the Lover archetype?**

Affirmation: *I am grateful for my body and the pleasure it provides me.*

Embracing The Lover and Reconnecting With our Whole Selves

Many books will teach you to engage and live from your heart space. There are countless books which encourage logic and head-centred thinking. Our bookstores and libraries are full of books that inform you on how you can take care of your body. Religious texts and spiritual gurus emphasise the importance of your soul and spiritual health. However, this is a book about **awaken**ing and reconnecting with your *Whole Self*. It is so tempting to look at the feminine archetypes and think Maiden, Mother, Huntress, Queen–check–and think we've got it down. But our Wild and Wise Woman is a harder sell because we shy away from the discomfort of emotional growth, (although, I hope I have convinced you of the importance and transformational power of doing this work).

So many women view their Lover with a sense of apathy, shame, and disdain. To be whole women, we need to embrace every one of these aspects of ourselves, including the reconnection with and healing our Lover. The Goddess who most represents the Lover is Aphrodite. Aphrodite was an alchemical Goddess, capable of transforming a woman's life. In history, it was thought that through alchemy, base metals such as lead, or copper could be transformed to precious metals such as silver or gold. It was also speculated that through alchemy, one was able to cure diseases and extend life. The Lover does not only transform a woman's life, she is also the force that attracts the beauty and abundance into a woman's life.

As Regina Thomashauser says in her book, *Pussy: A Reclamation*, *"So many of us were taught to keep a lid on anything and everything outrageous. To just turn it off. We turn off our life force, turn off our feelings, turn off our sensuality, and as a consequence, we turn off our power."*

Just so I can clear any misunderstanding, this has nothing to do with having lots of sex or being overtly sexual, (unless you want to), neither is this about your relationship with anyone else but yourself. What I do know is that we are wonderfully, holistic beings and when we sever a part of ourselves from ourselves, or we are fearful of a part of womanhood, we can never authentically step into our power and become the Queens of our lives. My goal is for you to reclaim your body for *yourself,* to take back this power to ignite the life in you again. To "turn on" and know yourself in the most intimate sense. I am giving you permission to de-objectify your body, and to lovingly restore it to the sacred, creative sanctuary that it is for you. Intimacy is so much more than just sex; intimacy is feeling safe with someone enough to share the most vulnerable parts of us. To be naked in front of each other, stripped of all our layers of clay. We cannot hope to do this in front of another if we cannot accept and love ourselves in this way first.

when the initial passion of the bodily act of sex
has faded it is no longer a matter of lust
but rather matter of trust.

I know this can be scary, especially when there is so much messaging about a woman's sexuality being "taboo", something that is unmentionable and wrong. For so long, we have been led to believe that we are victims in our Lover stories, receptacles for men's lust. Just think about the words used to describe our sacred feminine parts and how they are hurled around as an insult. Our long, HERstory, is that women are objects to be traded. Our sexuality is something to be owned, conquered, and exploited. So many women can't even name their genitals or talk about their sexual selves without feeling shame. The idea of pleasuring ourselves, looking at our vulvas in the mirror or getting to know our way around our own pussy disgusts so many of us. Can we whole-heartily love and accept ourselves when we hold such fear and contempt around this part of us?

Regena Thomashauser, lists the following five stages of our sexual awakening and the reclamation with our pussy in her book, *Pussy: A Reclamation*.

- **Stage One:** Complete and utter revulsion.

- **Stage Two:** "Scientific researcher".

- **Stage Three:** Natural curiosity, an affectionate researcher, a woman who recognises that there may be a whole world which remains unknown to her if she doesn't investigate this further for herself.

- **Stage Four:** A woman who owns and takes pleasure in her pussy, and therefore owns her life.

- **Stage Five:** Rapture. She feels at awe at being connected to the seat of all life.

Where do you range on this list of stages?

If you are at stage one, and wish you were further along, don't be discouraged, so many women are at this stage too. This is merely a place to grow, not a place where you think you have failed. But if you are happy being there, that is okay too. However, let me give you my best argument for getting better acquainted with your pussy, you have nothing to lose and then at the end of this chapter I would have either convinced you to reclaim your Lover or we can agree to disagree on this subject.

Let's take a look at the miraculous pleasure wonderland that is the female body. First, the vagina is the place from which all life starts, the passage of all creation. But the vagina is also a source of delight for her owner as it is home to rich nerve endings which are mostly located in the first third of the vaginal entrance including the g-spot, (located two to three inches from your vaginal opening on the front wall of your vagina). However, the "crown jewels" of a woman's pleasure centre is the clitoris with eight thousand nerve endings. This is double the amount of nerve endings in a penis. The clitoris has no other use other than to give her owner an orgasm. Strangely enough, although early scientists theorised to the contrary, an orgasm is not necessary as part of the procreation process. As far as scientists know, the female orgasm has no other use other than to create a powerful rapture for the body she inhabits. Whereas men have been given a penis, a multi-tool, for many uses such as sex, urination, and procreation, your clitoris is purely part of your body to provide you with joyful gratification. An orgasm has so many alchemical benefits for a woman's health and overall well-being. When a woman experiences an orgasm, her body is flooded with oxytocin, endorphins, serotonin, and dopamine and the cortisol levels in her body decreases. This can have the following health benefits:

- Better sleep.

- Improved circulation.

- Reduce pain.

- Spike in DHEA which promotes tissue repair, a stronger immune system and healthy brain function.

- Improves your body's lymphatic system.

- Keeps you looking and feeling younger for longer.

- Reduced stress.

- More energy.

However, our amazing female bodies have more gifts for us on the pleasure front. We have many erogenous zones, (pleasure zones), all over our bodies. (I once watched a Ted Talk where a woman could be brought to orgasm just by touching her left ear.) It might surprise you that women have thirty-four nerve fibres per square centimetre of facial skin, while men average just seventeen. Women are literally wired to feel in our DNA, and we are designed to feel pleasure. When John Meyer sang, *"Your Body is a Wonderland"*, he was spot on.

So, why do we not tap into this powerful, restorative life source that is our body?

Why are there so few women who are comfortable enough in their skin to get comfortable with their pussies?

Why are young girls still taught that it is dirty to touch themselves instead of being taught about the health benefits and the power of staying connected to their sexuality and their bodies?

If you reclaimed your body and truly believed that pleasure, joy, and creativity were your birth right, how would your life be different?

How would you treat yourself?

What choices would you make for yourself?

How would you feel?

I used to put off buying new clothes until I "lost my weight". If I bought clothes, I would buy them in a size sixteen, instead of the size eighteen that I really am just in case someone would see the label and think I was fat. I would step off of the scale or look in the mirror at my extra chins, my saggy boobs, my stretch marks, and my rolls and sigh with disgust—wishing I were different. Just wishing I were younger, skinnier, firmer, and sexier. I repeatedly told myself what a lazy, unmotivated, undesirable, undeserving slob I was. I used to do these things, and I was miserable. But one day, I saw an ad on Facebook for a plus size clothing brand. I fell in love with the stunning dress the model wore. It was feminine, floaty, colourful; just stunning. The model, roughly a size eighteen, looked exquisite, confident, and radiant. You could see she was completely comfortable in her own skin. And so, I decided, even though the dress was more than I would usually spend on myself, to place an order and I waited in anticipation for my new dress to arrive.

A couple of weeks later, a parcel arrived in my letterbox. I excitedly ripped open the package and gleefully put the dress on. *It was perfect!* For the first time since I could remember, I looked in the mirror and I felt gorgeous. That small moment was a huge turning point for me, it dawned on me that I could look beautiful no matter the size I was. From that day, I vowed to, (and religiously stuck to), only buying clothes which made me feel good. Outfits that made me feel the same as I did in that one dress. Slowly, but surely, I began purchasing more clothes that made me feel beautiful. I stopped dyeing my hair brown and let myself go lighter, and for the first time in my life I became blond. And it stayed that way until I made the colour grey my friend. Instead of using the mirror, the scale, or my too tight clothing as a way to confirm my "not good enough" status or wishing that I was different, I looked in the mirror and choose to see myself as beautiful woman I was.

It was easier said than done on some days, where I could only find one small thing about myself to like. Giving myself compliments and choosing to see the beauty in me felt so unnatural—I wasn't raised to think that way. As girls, we receive the message very early on in our lives that we have to act or think in a certain way. We are admonished for being vain and are taught to be ashamed of compliments. We learn that the most desirable feminine attribute is selflessness… However, I persisted through my discomfort and I began practising radical acceptance, and from that I found was that the more I accepted myself, the more joyful, confident, and comfortable I felt in my own skin. Once I was no longer at war with myself, I found that had so much more energy to create the types of things I wanted in my life, and I could make space to discover new things about myself.

I stand firm in this because I believe many women are still trapped in the puritan, patriarchal thinking of our mothers and their mothers before them. What we learn about our Lover is very much an unhealed mother wound. We are taught that sex and sensuality is purely an act of giving, pleasing others, in our culture's expectation that women should all be Maidens or Mothers, and sex is something we only do with others and for others but never for ourselves. Just think about the stories we have been told as girls, the story of *Sun, Moon and Talia* at the beginning of this book. The innocent Maiden waiting for the prince to rescue her. The passive victim of uninvited sexual acts.

In the fairy tales we grew up with, the sexually awakened women are painted as evil. The evil queen in Snow White and Maleficent. Women who are in touch with their magic are painted as witches corrupted by dark debauchery. Thankfully, many of the stories we tell our daughters, and will tell to our granddaughters, are evolving. However, the message that a woman who belongs to herself is "wild" and "uncontrollable" is still very much alive and something we are fearful of. When a woman can fully embrace the healthy expression of her Lover, she recognises that she is valuable as she is. She comes to know that her joy and pleasure is precious, and she is worthy of not only receiving these things in her life, but also able to create her own magic in the world.

She AWAKES: Receiving and Creating Your Own Pleasure

There are many exercises you can explore that will enable you to get in touch with your Lover and to explore pleasure, sensuality and sexuality. I offer you a gateway back to your Lover, back to the amazing YOU.

Masturdate yourself. I encourage you to plan an intimate date for yourself with yourself as you would with an exciting lover.

- Take a sensuous candle lit bath with luxurious oils and bath salts that make you feel pampered.

- Groom your body, do your hair, and apply make-up as you would for a date.

- Prepare for yourself or order a dinner with foods and drink that you enjoy.

- Light candles and set the table as if you were having dinner with a Queen.

- Take your time to be present with your meal—take your time and savour the flavours in every bite.

- Once you have enjoyed your meal, put on your favourite music, close your eyes, and allow the music to move you.

- Stand in front of the mirror and then slip out of your clothes.

- Look yourself in the eyes, smile, and say, *'Hello Beautiful'*.

- Then look at the rest of your body and find parts that you like.

- Give yourself compliments and accept your compliments.

- Then lie down on your bed and begin to touch yourself, starting from the crown of your head moving all the way down your body.

- Feel into your body, take your time and exploring each pleasurable sensation.

*A word of caution: As a survivor of sexual trauma, I know how important consent is, even if it is consent we give to ourselves. Please tune into the "Yes" and "No" knowing of your body. Seek your body's permission and only touch the parts of your body that feel safe and pleasurable to **you**. You can always repeat this experience allowing yourself to explore as you feel your confidence and consent grow.*

Reflect on this experience in your journal.

- What did you discover about yourself during this experience?

- For the next twenty-one days write yourself a love note about one thing that you adore about yourself. (Mine is over the page.)

Affirmation: *I am the worthy creator and recipient of my own joy and pleasure.*

Day one: I love how resilient you are darling you are soft on the outside but you have a tungsten-like core running through you.

Day two: I love how motivated and persistent you are you have worked really hard on yourself to make your dreams a reality I am proud of you.

Day three: I love how you are more compassionate with yourself. I love how you are teaching yourself to be self-curious instead of self-critical.

Day four: I love that you are kind to others you always try to find the best in people you are a generous friend.

Day five: I love that you trust easily. I love how fiercely loyal you are to those whom you love.

Day six: I love that when the going got really tough with your marriage and many would have given up you managed to find the smallest glimmer of hope a part of your relationship worth saving.

Day seven: I love that you found the courage to reflect on your life and make changes that were needed for your own happiness. I know how difficult this has been how at times you wept and nearly gave up but you kept going I am so very proud of you.

Day eight: I love how you found your voice each day you are learning to trust yourself a little be more.

Day nine: I love that you have let writing and poetry back into your life and that you are once again embracing the wisdom of your creative genius with a wild open brave heart.

Day ten: I love the mother that you have become you might not be the perfect mother but you are the perfect mother for your children.

Day eleven: I love how you are able to look in the mirror and instead of shrinking away in disgust you are able to find beauty.

Day twelve: I love what a good listener you are your family and children know that you are a safe place where they can just *be* without fear of judgement.

Day thirteen: I love how you are able to appreciate the smallest beauty in life a walk on the beach a flower given to you by child a night spent outside under the stars.

Day fourteen: I love how you are able to smile and laugh once more do you remember when you wondered why your happiness was important? when you used to think that it was a selfish waste of time? wow, look at just how far you have come.

Day fifteen:	I love that you are using your experiences and your pain to help others how by embracing your vulnerability you can connect with the common humanity of others.
Day sixteen:	I love how you have embraced your own need to solitude that you are able to indulge yourself with stillness and peace without guilt.
Day seventeen:	I love that you have started to embrace your lover energy that you have been able to claim carnal pleasure as a right I love how more attuned you are with your body you are no longer your enemy.
Day eighteen:	I love that have been able to forgive yourself and others that this no longer a heavy load that you carry with you day in a day out.
Day nineteen:	I love that you are open-minded and flexible you, my dear, have an insatiable love for learning love how you have embraced gratitude and how this has transformed your life.
Day twenty:	I love how sensitive you are a few years ago you would have viewed this as a weakness you now know the truth that this is actually your greatest strength.
Day twenty-one:	I love how beautiful your spirit is you are beautiful inside and out don't let anyone convince you otherwise.

Twenty-one days of noticing the things that I love about me on my forty-fifth birthday.

Knowing Yourself

WHEN MY DAUGHTER, MADI, WAS YOUNGER, she and I used to play this game where she would test how well I knew her. She would set up questions for me about her favourite things that I was required to answer. She would quiz me on phrases and sentences that she would often say, "Madisims" I would need to complete.

Hopefully, during the reading of this book, the completion of the accompanying reflective exercises, and the shedding of layers, you are making space to know yourself one intimate layer at a time. It has left you to rediscover *Her*, the knowing and divine self that you were before the big sleep and the *her* you would like to become. Hopefully you are coming to realise that this person matters and is allowed to take up space in your life.

I have prepared some questions for your own version of the "Do You Know Me" game:

- How many decisions do I make out of habit, or to please others?

- What sparks life in my heart in a way that radiates warmth throughout my body and lights up my eyes?

- What do I really need in my life?

- What are the desires of my soul?

- What am I afraid to give myself because I know that once I have experienced it, I know I can never go back?

- Why or how have I ended up where I am now?

- Why do I struggle to give up old destructive behaviours and adopt new more life-enhancing ones?

- Why is my **awaken**ing so important to me?

I have since discovered that my answers have a lot to do with my core values. If you look around your home, you will see vital clues about what may be important values for you.

For example, if you look at the walls in my home, you will see a lot of art and many family photos, a dedicated meditation space with a yoga mat, an area for my crystals, and my gratitude journal, heaps of indoor plants, scented candles, and books on self-improvement. From these things in my home, you would be able to conclude that I value beauty, family, spirituality, and personal development.

Once you know what you value, you can use this information to make choices and decisions which are aligned with what feels right for you. This creates an ease and a sense of flow in your life. And if you would like to dig deeper into yourself and your core driving value, I offer you the tool of the *seven layers of why*.

To begin your reflection, first, set a timer for ten minutes. Then start with something that you would like to examine further.

(My question for introspection is: *Why am I so passionate about writing this book and supporting other women to* **AWAKEN***?*)

Each time you answer your question, you reframe your answer into a why question.

1. *To empower women who feel stuck.* WHY is it important to empower women?

2. *Because I was once stuck.* WHY is it important not to feel stuck?

3. *Because when you are stuck, you are a victim.* WHY do you not want to be a victim?

4. *Because victims have no power, no choices, and no voice.* WHY is it important to have power, choices and a voice?

5. *It is important to have the power to change things and to be able to have control in my life.* WHY is control important?

6. *Because I don't want to be helpless, I want to be free to choose.* WHY is choice important?

7. *Because when I was growing up, I was never allowed the freedom to choose.* WHY is freedom important to me?

You repeat this seven times, answering instinctively with the first answer that comes to your mind.

This is how I realised that Freedom is my number one motivator, which doesn't particularly surprise me since the two key archetypes I identify with, at this present moment, are the Huntress and the Wild Woman, both of which value freedom. It also makes perfect sense as to why I am unable to stick to a strict exercise or diet regime, why I prefer to be self-employed, and why I have always felt the compelling pull to stand out and rebel against convention.

Freedom is my number one, most important value I hold but when I was growing up, I had none.

8.   My mother chose what I wore.

* I wasn't allowed to cut my hair until I was a teenager.

* I felt God was always watching me, and I felt trapped in my religion.

* I had to be the person everyone expected me to be.

* I wasn't allowed to choose a career I was passionate about.

* My father had to sign me over to my husband like a piece of property.

* Women's work is a career in caregiving or administration.

* Women belong at home, barefoot and pregnant….

And this is why projects like writing this book and guiding women who feel stuck ignites a fire inside of me, and roars to set itself free. When I carry out this work, I am in the natural flow of my highest value–*freedom*. The flow we encounter when we live in alignment with our highest value feels effortless, warm, and wonderful. When we are in a state of flow, magic moves through us like liquid lighting. We can enjoy our magic and use our golden selves for the highest good.

She AWAKES: Knowing Yourself

Knowing yourself on a deeper level can give you powerful insights into your motivations, choices, and decisions. It may also explain why things might feel "off" for you if you have been living out of alignment of these values.

For this first part of this exercise, I welcome you to take stock of your home.

* **What does your home or personal space say about you and your core values?**

* **Do your choices and behaviours align with your core values?**

* **How can you live more in congruence with your values?**

Some women whom I complete this exercise with cannot find anything in their home or personal space that resembles them; they often find that their home is too full or cluttered with other peoples' stuff. If this is true for you, then be gentle and kind towards yourself, it simply means you have a bit of digging to do. What an exciting adventure awaits you as you rediscover the woman that is *you*.

Referring to my example, try *the seven layers of why* to get to know yourself on a more intimate level. If you are feeling unsure of the question you would like to explore, I suggest you begin with, *why did I choose to read this book?*

- After completing this exercise, what did you experience and what did it reveal to you about yourself and your number one motivator?

- What did this exercise reveal to you about the dominant archetypes in your life?

Affirmation: *I love every single layer of me.*

Meeting and Consulting Your Guide

We hear the voice of our Knowing Self in various ways. We may hear her in our prayers, or in meditation. We may hear her in the shower, or when we clean the house. We may hear her in our mothering moments, or in moments of anguish when we ask for an answer to a problem and a solution suddenly appears— as previously discussed in our "Yes" or "No" moments.

When we are coming to know our Knowing Self, many of us may ask ourselves, *'What is the difference between my Knowing Self and my Inner Critic?'* Or *'How do I know if I am hearing the voice of my intuition or my fear?'* Intuition is borne out of an accumulation of our experiences and a deep tuning into our needs. We experience this as confidence in our gifts, strengths, or our beliefs in something bigger than us that is able to meet our needs. Although fear and intuition are both experienced in our gut, when we make a decision from our intuition, the emotions surrounding this decision are calm or confident. When we make a decision from fear, we experience doubt, and possibly relief. If and when we allow fear to cloud our knowing or judgement, we are projecting our past psychological wounds, our emotions, and our anxiety towards the future onto our decision-making. Intuition feels freeing and expansive and springs forth from the golden Knowing Self. Whereas fear can feel restrictive and causes us to retract, and when we make a fear-based decision, this becomes the offspring of our avatar. But when we are connected to our Knowing Self, we are in the present moment. We are neutral and unemotional.

When I was writing this book, my fear would yell out to me, *'Don't do this. Give up. You will never succeed'*. My intuition would calmly and quietly whisper to me, *'You've got this. I trust you.'*

Always be aware of the state of your physical well-being when discerning between fear and intuition in the moment of your decision. If you are tired, hungry, or in a state of fight or flight, your Wise Woman may tell you that this moment is not the right time to be making big life decisions. You may need to eat, rest, or allow yourself to return to the call before committing to a next step. Honour that voice and honour yourself. Press the pause button, return to yourself and your decision once you can hear your intuition clearly without the background static. We can so easily lose ourselves in the source of our momentary chaos, often leaving us to feel utterly trapped and alone in the experience of our overwhelming emotions. These strong emotions generated in our hearts or in the pit of our stomachs can completely overrule any sense of reason that our brains are so desperately trying to scramble for.

Robert H. Schuller was famously offered this sound advice, *"Never cut down a tree in the wintertime. Never make a negative decision in a low time. Never make your most important decisions when you are in your worst moods. Wait. Be patient. The storm will pass. Spring will come."*

Why is this sound advice? Our brains get sucked into the worst possible scenario when we are feeling angry, sad, depressed, anxious, or in shame. When nothing seems to be working, it seems broken and unfixable. So, when things are shit, we tend to paint everything with the shit-brush. In these bleak wintery moments, I admit I question everything.

'Am I in the right marriage?'

'Am I in the right career?'

'Am I in the right life?'

'Should I run away and leave it all behind me?'

In my winter of discontent, I doubt myself as a wife, mother, daughter, sister, and friend. I tell myself how useless I am, how I will never work again, and that everybody secretly hates me. Our minds can reach the most barren and desolate of places amid our frigid winter.

I'm going to share a story of where my mind took me recently.

My daughter calls me at two o'clock in the morning from the hospital. She is scared and alone because the hospital is short-staffed, and there are not enough nurses or health care assistants to care for all of the patients. I feel disorientated, fearful, and panicked. The Mother in me feels shame because I chose to sleep in my comfortable bed at home instead of choosing the martyr's way of sleeping in a recliner next to her bedside.

The Mother in me is hyper alert, and instantly awake. My husband, on the other hand, is hard to rouse and never wakes up easily. He is always foggy for at least an hour after he has been woken—*especially at two o'clock in the morning.* When he doesn't immediately fight me for the right to rush to the hospital and rescue our baby in the early hours of the morning, I get angry with him, and I storm out of the house while telling myself what a terrible father he is, and he doesn't care. In a rage, I even dictate this tirade into my voice notes while I tear off along the country roads towards the hospital.

'Because, we both received the call for OUR daughter, and your first instinct was to abdicate any responsibility. How could you hear this and allow yourself to roll over and go back to sleep?'

'Because, when I told you I was going, and you weren't worried enough to fight me to sit with her even though you knew I needed to work in the morning. Instead... instead, you gave me reasons why you should stay in bed....'

'That is why I know this marriage is over for me. We've tried very hard to keep this marriage together with hard work, prayers, Blu Tack, and bits of yarn. I know and you might look at my reasons and you might judge them as a poor reason to end a marriage.

But I just know.

I know and I see.

I can't pretend to unsee and unknow.

I don't think I can swallow this venom back down and pretend that it isn't slowly killing me.'

(Yes, I know, I can be ever so slightly dramatic! LOL.)

The truth of this is that this was just a story. My shit canvas, painted with my shit-brush. My mind is going to a bleak and terrible place in one of our family's dreary, winter moments. Knowing when I am caught up in the source of my fear and have produced a shit canvas is an important area of growth as I strengthen my connection with my Wise Woman. An hour after recording my dramatic voice notes, my husband woke up and realised how he had acted, and he apologised. And luckily, I came to my senses too before I chopped down this particular tree.

I offer you the following exercise as a way to strengthen your connection with this calm, confident, knowing Wise Woman. This exercise was introduced to me when I did a *Transforming Trauma* course presented by Dr James Gordon, director of the *Centre for Mind Body Medicine*. It allows us to access this archetype through visualisation and to speak with her—in her many forms—and ask questions if we wish too.

If you would prefer to listen to this exercise as an audio recording, please go to https://tanyavalentin.co/Meeting-Your-Guide *where I will guide you through it.*

She AWAKES: Meeting Your Guide

- **Sit in a comfortable position in a place where you won't be disturbed.**

- **Close your eyes.**

- **Focus on your breath and allow your breathing to slow and deepen.**

Imagine you are walking down a country road. This may be a place you have been before, or a place in your imagination. Continue to walk down the country road until you reach a safe place where you feel calm and comfortable outside in nature. This place could be a beach, a clearing in a forest, a campsite by the fire, a cave, or a desert or any place that feels right for you. As you are sitting there, you are visited by a guide. This guide could be a male or female, an animal, an insect, another version of yourself or a being of light. Introduce yourself to each other and ask your guide your question.

Calmly sit in this experience with your guide and have a conversation with them to ask all the questions you would like answers for—allowing them to answer everything in turn. Once you are finished speaking to your guide, thank them for appearing and allow them to leave. Now it is time to leave your special place, pack up, put out your fire, and walk back along the country road to where you started your journey.

Open your eyes and step back into the ordinary world.

- **What did you see in your visualisation?**

- **What form did your guide take?**

- **What were your questions and how did your guide answer?**

- **How did this experience make you feel?**

Take a moment to record your experience in your journal, because as with a dream, the details will eventually become hazy once you return fully to the ordinary world.

Affirmation: *When I am feeling stuck or confused, I can tune into the knowing power of my intuition.*

My Experience with My Guide

Below is my experience during the first time I performed this visualisation exercise:

I walked down a gravel road lined with wire fencing and trees alive with the orange autumn leaves. It was dusk and the sky was a golden hue as the sun said its farewells and slid below the horizon. At the end of the road was a calm lake, so I built a fire and sat waiting at the water's edge for my guide to arrive. As the first stars appeared in the heavens, I was visited by a she wolf with vivid, yellow eyes. Our eyes locked as she slowly approached me. I was fearful at first as I had been taught to fear wolves, but she lay down next to me and rolled over like a playful Labrador to show me the grey-white fur on her belly. She told me that her name was Sharay, and I could ask her anything.

I asked her my first question, 'Who are you?'

She replied, 'I am your wisdom, I am your wild'.

I then asked her, 'Am I on the right path?'

'You already know the answer to this. I would not be appearing to you if you were not.'

'Why am I so afraid?'

And she answered, 'Because this is new to you, you have been closed off to me for so long. I will not hurt you if you respect me. I will only harm you if you mistreat me.'

'But what if I fail?'

Sharay blinked her big, golden eyes and urged me to look at the stars up above as she quietly and confidently said, 'Trust the one who created all of this beauty. When you work with Him and I, we will not let you fall.' She rose to her feet and curled her big, furry body around me. I felt so warm, loved, and safe in that moment. She licked my face as she would a pup and she whispered in my ear, 'Access this guide any time, I am your birth right. God's nature is love, joy, kindness, and forgiveness.' She unwrapped herself from me and she disappeared.

I came back to myself into the ordinary world. I was sitting in my sunny meditation space on the couch in my family room. With her words still resounding in my ears and my body tingling from my experience, I recorded everything in my journal. After this experience I recognised the following synchronicities:

- The wolf symbolises guardianship, ritual, loyalty, and spirit. The wolf has an ability to form quick and deep emotional attachments and is blessed with keen knowing. As guides, they teach us to do the same. The wolf's message is to trust our hearts so we can take control of our own lives and destiny.

- The second synchronicity was in the name of my wolf guide. According to the Hebrew origins of *Sharay*, the name means *releaser*.

I have since travelled several times to this spirit world and met with my guide. Sharay has not visited me again, although I have been visited by a bear and a being made entirely of light. This first experience with my guide will live forever in my heart and memory.

sometimes we all need to speak to a friend
we all need a kind soul to listen
and feed us love
until we are able to do this for ourselves

Kindred

FIVE YEARS HAVE PASSED since I made the decision to start unearthing bits of myself which I had left behind. Precious parts of me were sacrificed on the altar of motherhood, wifehood, and religion—expected sacrifices of womanhood. Five years since I uttered *'Fuck it, not another day more!'* I started counting summers and made a conscious decision to make my life more meaningful instead of *perfect*. To make the sum of me count for something—to live a life of joy and purpose.

My **awaken**ing has been a paradox of bittersweet emotions, fear, elation, sadness, anger, and joy. A journey of receiving, letting go and acceptance. As I unearthed these treasures within me, I arranged them on my cave floor, side by side in an uneven mosaic and I realised I was building was a mirror… a mirror to reflect, confront, and allow myself to truly see *me* for the first time in years. When I first began this process of rediscovery, my mirror initially presented other women to me. I wasn't used to focussing on myself. I would see other women whom I admired greatly, and I longed to be like them. I would repeatedly hold their image next to mine and compare myself. I would use my mirror as we do when we are in a clothing store changing room and look for all the ways we fall short.

Comparison is yet another vehicle for our shame demons to overwhelm us with fear. It is a sneaky trap to hook us back into the dream, spurring us to measure ourselves against our idealised version of someone else—their avatar—to reinforce that we are not good enough. Our Authentic Self is not as good as their projection. Many a brilliant idea, a dream, a kindness, a loving intention, or relationship has died at the feet of comparison. Through my experience when I compare myself to another, not only shame shows up, but it brings along its friend, envy, for the ride. Envy highlights in my mind what others have and what I desire. Treated with curiosity, envy is a vital emotion for pointing things which are important to us. We are seldom envious about things that do not matter to us, however, when wielded in the hands of our shame demons of "not good enough" and even "who do you think you are?" The destructive force of envy becomes a yardstick for comparison to others and the continuous measurement of how we fall short in our own lives. We do this without realising that the thing we are envious about in others is something that already exists inside of us.

In this particular gamble, the dice are loaded but they are not in our favour. *The house will always win.* I have observed that as parents we constantly play the comparison game. We compare, measure, and shame ourselves by counting how many "gold stars" we have been awarded. We only used to compare ourselves when we visited someone or met with them socially, but the advent of the social media age has been so insidious to our fragile sense of self. We now have a readily available feed of comparison, shame, and envy on tap twenty-four-seven to scroll through each other's highlights reels at four o'clock in the morning when we can't sleep—an unattainable illusion of perfection. We can easily fall into the trap of comparison in other areas of our life too, and we can even fall into this trap by comparing our **awaken**ing journey with others.

I was raised to be a "nice" person, so I do not turn my anger which is a by-product of my shame and envy onto others. I internalize these emotions until I can find no redeeming qualities within myself. I compare myself to others and beat myself up as I resent the hell out of others because they have something that I so desperately desire for myself. When we don't love and accept ourselves or we are unable to recognise our own gifts, we cannot celebrate the amazing human beings around us with a whole heart. We are unable to genuinely express what an amazing job they are doing as all we see in them is a reflection of our own flaws and shortcomings. This builds an impenetrable wall around us and created a separation between ourselves and others. This is the root of the loneliness so many women feel. So many women have been taught to compete and be frightened of the "too muchness" that they encounter in other women.

I have had a turbulent relationship with my mother-in-law over the years. One that I, because out of respect for her, I will not recount in this book. Instead, I will express my gratitude for her. I am grateful that my husband had a strong-minded feminist for a mother. I know it was not easy to be a feminist in the male dominated, conservative society of early apartheid South Africa. She is an intelligent woman with the courage to speak her mind and stand up for what she believes in, and motivated to create actions in order to better her life and the lives of those around her. It is because of his mother that my husband has always supported my dreams even though some of them were slightly left field and sometimes downright crazy. This relationship with his mother influenced him to see our relationship as a *partnership* instead of a dictatorship, prevalent in many South African marriages. It is because of her courage and foresight that our family, including my parents and sisters, were able to build a better life in New Zealand.

A woman who stands up for herself and claims her sovereignty is often shunned for her opinions or labelled a "too much" woman and can cause people to forget that she is kind, loving, and generous too. Sometimes, we only see her "too muchness". Even though a "too much" woman is often challenging to be around, she allows other women the permission to have courage to stand firm in their "too muchness" too. I am grateful for what I learnt by knowing her as my shadow teacher and for the son that she raised. I am grateful that my daughters have her as a role model in their lives and can share some of her "too muchness" as part of their genetic makeup too. When we love and accept ourselves with a whole heart, we can stand vulnerable, yet secure in our worthiness and our **W**ild **A**uthentic **K**nowing **E**mpowered selves, we arrive in a place where we find our true belonging. The type of belonging that does not rely on the approval of others, where there is no judgement, no need to compete or compare with anyone else. Where taking up space feels natural, and it doesn't take space from another. Then, we are able to stand firm with a strong back to support us and accept others with a wild, open heart.

When we arrive at this place, we allow other women to do the same. We naturally call those who are our kindred to us. We were born to recognise truth, and as young children, we unapologetically speak the truth. We point out the truth as it unfolds around us in bold, blatant innocence. Childhood truth is unfiltered and undiluted. We remark on the fat person sitting on the bus. We tell strangers that our mother is on the toilet "doing poos". So unfiltered we are as children that we embarrass the adults in our lives with shameless telling of the truth. Red-faced, they shush us, punish us, silence us, and teach us to water down the truth—even sometimes to bury the truth. We learn that our truth is shameful, something to fear, and our truth speaking is banished to the shadows of our hearts.

But our souls will always remember. We feel it deep down in our bones that we were meant to speak out the truth.

When we witness truth in someone else, we feel it in our bodies. It pulls at our gut, our heart, the seat of our very soul.

To the uninitiated it can feel like discomfort, coloured with anger, envy, and fear.

Icy hot nausea.

Disgust.

Shame.

But truth can also feel like a shiver. Like the frisson which takes over our bodies when we are stirred by music, poetry, a piece of writing, a work of art. It can feel like an exhalation after holding your breath for a long time.

To me it feels like relief.

When I see courage, and the undiluted truth in another this is reflected in me. Like a caged bird who hears the song of the free, wild, birds I want to sing too. A voice inside applauds, *'There it is —Truth!'* My joyful soul wants to shout out, *'The truth in me sees the truth in you'*. Our shame says, *'I will be rejected, I will not fit in'*. Our ever-knowing Wise Woman reassures us that through our coming in and subsequent coming out, we make it okay for others around us to be reconciled with themselves too.

This is a privilege denied women for far too long. "Witch-mark" psyche frowns on women meeting with other women for anything other than socially agreeable events. Women sitting in circle with each other as was observed in ancient cultures is still now considered by some to be "weird" or "otherworldly".

Through our community with other women who are on the same adventure into their selves as we are, together we can shift the heavy layers of clay which we cannot lift on our own. In doing this, we find a home in our own hearth and the hearth of one another.

She AWAKES: Freeing Yourself from the Comparison Trap

Comparison and fear of judgement is one of the greatest obstacles that stop women from befriending other women. To heal from our wounds of comparison, we first have to cast our loving gaze of awareness in this area of our lives. Reflect on areas in your life where you feel envy and naturally compare yourself to others.

- **What desires and areas of significance is your envy and comparison highlighting for you?**

- **Thank your envy and comparison for the lesson they have given you.**

- **Look for evidence in your own life of how the object of your envy is already abundant in your life. For example, if you are envious of someone's creativity, look for ways in your life in which you have been or already are creative.**

- **How can you reframe the object of your envy to acknowledge it is already part of you? For example, *"I am already creative."***

- **What is one action you can take to build the evidence to back up this reframing statement and move closer to your desires?**

- How can you be genuinely happy for and compliment another woman for the things she has in her life that you would love to have in yours?

- How can you use your truth to attract like-hearted sisters to you?

Affirmation: *The truth in me sees and acknowledges the truth in you.*

Part five

Empowered Self

it is okay to admire the talent in another
to marvel at the beauty of their gifts

sometimes the gifts of others can make us feel small
and insignificant when we compare

but don't let fear and comparison
rob you
of your passion

your individuality

Empowered Self

We have now reached the part of our journey together where we find ourselves moving into the territory of the *Empowered Self*.

Many years ago, I received the same invitation that you did at the beginning of this book, when I woke up and realised I was no longer the timid Maiden who was tolerantly waiting to be rescued so her new life could begin. I was no longer stuck in the role of the obedient wife and selfless mother, being content to serve and live her life vicariously through others. My Wild Woman welcomed me with open arms into the womb of my cave. She grasped me by the hand, and one by one, introduced me to my shadow creatures. I roamed, I raged, I roared, I explored, and when I thought I was done, that I couldn't possibly go any further, my Wild Woman drew me into her lap. She comforted me in the circle of her fierce embrace and affectionally whispered tenderness's to me. She firmly sent me back out to play until the creatures became my friends. She revealed to me the place where the soft glow of my inner hearth resided, and there, we were joined by my Wise Woman, Together, they showed me how to ignite the fire with the parts of myself which no longer served the woman I was becoming, and they held me while I grieved. My guides within the special world helped me feed the flames until my hearth blazed brightly. Fuelled by the bonfire of my vanities, I allowed the fire to grow so big, so fierce, so hot, that I was entirely consumed. My clay, my avatar, and my trophy cases who were devoted to gold stars had to be sacrificed in the flames so that the *golden me* could emerge.

Your Huntress, who stirred inside of you when you accepted the call to adventure waits for you outside your cave. She is the energy you need in your accession of the mountain so the warrior can be crowned the *Queen*. This is where you learn to stand confidently and regally, firm in your worth. In your cave, you were met with guides who supported you in sacrificing parts of your avatar and you were able to discover treasures within yourself. This has spearheaded the reconnection with your **W**ild, **A**uthentic, **K**nowing self. You are now ascending the pinnacle of your mountain symbolising your transition back into the ordinary world, taking forward with you all the wisdom you have gained as you continue down your path. Once you arrive back in the ordinary world, you will stand in your sovereignty, no longer an apprentice, and begin the stage of practice and mastery. This may not be the last mountain that you will need to climb, it's inevitable that there will be others. You are a Queen of two parts. The Queen of the Underworld, gifted with the treasure of your lessons and stories, and the Queen of the ordinary realm. This will not be your last adventure into yourself, there will be many more, however, the difference between this quest and the ones yet to come is that you now know the way. Once you know how to access your cave in the special world, it is always available to you. Now you have activated your divine feminine energies, they will forever be available to you to support and guide you whenever you require. You may find that you no longer feel the same as you did before you started your quest as a transformation may have already started to take place. You may notice many of the signs of your **awaken**ing in you as discussed in the chapter, *Awakening Woman.*

I am so grateful that you have allowed me to accompany you this far. Our journey is nearing a close, however, before we part ways, I would like to equip you with tools and arm you with a sword which you can take with you on the next stage of your quest.

and I saw it in the stars

I saw it in the leaves
as they transformed from green to gold

I heard in the breeze
as it whispered my name

behold

a new Queen is born

Embracing Your Queen Status

Imagine a Queen, who knows what she wants and sets about getting it.

A Queen standing sure and true in the confidence of her worth and divine sovereignty.

A Queen who is whole and does not need the approval of others to lead or define her.

A Queen who does not discount herself, diminish who she is, or hide behind her clay

but vulnerably and courageously allows herself to shine in all of her golden splendour.

A Queen who does not need others to pick her as she knows she can choose herself.

A Queen who is not waiting for a hero to save her, because she knows she is the hero she has been waiting for.

Imagine a Queen, who knows she is valuable, so she invests in herself.

A Queen values her own energy, and she sets and maintains firm boundaries in order to preserve these for herself.

A Queen who invites beauty and abundance into her life because she recognises this is what she deserves.

A Queen who surrounds herself with a team of advisors, mentors, and ladies in waiting.

A Queen who trusts herself and her decisions.

A Queen who trusts her team, not only outside of herself, but also within.

A Queen who confidently calls on her team when she needs them because she recognises this is how to show up as the best version of herself in all instances because she knows this is the birth right of the fully integrated Queen.

Imagine a Queen, who lives in her heart and knows that her gold is for sharing with the world and is not afraid to do so.

A Queen who knows that when she heals and uplifts herself, she makes it possible for other Queens to rise with her.

A Queen who is a protector and champion of other Queens.

A Queen who knows that there is enough room, gold, and treasure in the world for all to share and that she doesn't need to hustle, compete, or put others down in order to be a Queen.

A Queen who uses her life lessons and shadows as tools from which to grow with wisdom and humility and for the greater good.

A Queen who learns from her mistakes and practices using her Queenly skills, because she knows this makes her a better Queen.

Imagine a Queen, who wears her crown with dignity, confidence, and pride.

A Queen who knows she is a Queen and that all Queens rise.

Imagine this Queen is you!

Rise Queen, [your name], rise!

To hear this poem read out loud to you go to:
https://tanyavalentin.co/Imagine-a-Queen

The Imposter in the Shadow of the Queen

If the words in my poem provoked you with inspiration and passion to put on your crown, drape your regal cape around your shoulders, and get going–great! However, you may be feeling a tiny bit of self-doubt and fear or even feel the presence of my old friends, *'I'm not good enough'* or *'Who am I?'* You are not alone. It may not surprise you, and it may perhaps sadden you to hear that most Queens feel like a big, fat fake from time to time. In fact, as you venture forth, back into the ordinary land as a newly crowned Queen, you may feel this *a lot,* especially if you have been a wounded Maiden or Mother for the majority of your life. You may have encountered powerful women in your life and felt intimidated by them, raised on evil Queen stories, or have been frightened by the threat of "Karen". Of all the archetypes, a woman's sovereignty can be the most frightening. We are not taught to value ourselves, our ideas, our creativity, or our softer compassionate feminine style of leadership. Women are not taught to stand up for themselves or to speak out. Our golden "first fruits" are not nurtured or allowed to shine. Instead, we learn lessons of shame and hiding behind a clay wall. This is why there is so few examples in the world of feminine leadership and why our world strains under the burden of male-dominant power.

Embracing our Queen demands that we sacrifice old, outdated versions of ourselves, which can be petrifying. Embracing your Queen is a choice, it is a sacred claiming of your realm and choosing the real estate of your story. It is trading in your running shoes for slippers, a bow and arrow for a crown, and invisibility for sovereignty. Allowing yourself to be brave and uncertain, giving yourself divine permission to be seen, heard, celebrated, and criticised. Even if you are fortunate enough to be graced with the presence of a strong Queen in your life, this too can fuel your imposter Queen. You may look at other beautiful Queens in your life doing their Queenly work with calm, confident efficiency and think you could never be like them....

... And you won't.

Because the truth is, no one will rule your realm like *you*. Your crown will not be identical to the crown of other Queens. There has never been another Queen like you before and there never will be. You are uniquely qualified by the mountains you have climbed, caves you have explored, and the treasures you have discovered. But take heed dear one, you can confidently acknowledge your strengths, talents, and gifts *and* be humble. You get to choose how you want to rule your realms.

As a Queen, you already deserve your desires. You are already worthy in so many ways. Owning your Queenly status attracts other kindred Queens to you, *'But how?'* You may wail as your hands, wring your crown, and your mascara may run down your cheeks. But the answer is that self-confidence comes from the same as with building trust with yourself. *It happens in the doing.* Among many of the things we have mistakenly been taught, is that *we must first be confident before we do.* However, we must first *do* and then we build our confidence. So, stop comparing, and start taking action. We do not need to know all of the steps right away, just the next one. Just showing up and taking the next imperfect step is enough to create results to allow your confidence and trust to grow in leaps and bounds.

If you still feel stuck, I invite you to go back to the chapter on Awareness and repeat the Casting Powerful New Spells exercise on page 190.

To further support you with this I have created a royal lesson as part of your Queenly finishing school.

She AWAKES: Embracing Your Queen Status

In this four-part exercise, I will support you in identifying your Queenly traits and your royal mission to help you to craft your new *Royal Mission Statement*. We will finish this off with anchoring and lessons in deportment.

For the first part, I invite you to think about three Queens whom you admire.

- Write their names on a page in your journal and think of five traits about these Queens which you admire.

- Then check what three traits each Queen may have in common.

- Write these down. Now you may not believe me, but the very reason these traits stand out for you is because these qualities are already alive in *you*.

For the second part of the exercise, I would like you to reflect on the following:

- What are you most passionate about?

- What is your zone of genius? (The things which come easily to you, but others struggle with.)

- What are you most alive when doing?

- What dream about your life keeps you up at night and refuses to let you go?

- What would you like to help others with?

- What was the value that you identified in your seven layers of *why* exercise?

Using the information from this brainstorming session, think about what your mission or purpose may be. How are you going to use your passion and zone of genius to serve others and make your dreams come true to satisfy your highest value?

The third part of the lesson is crafting your *Royal Mission Statement*. It should look something like this:

I, [Your Name] am a [Quality One], [Quality Two], [Quality Three] Queen. Here to [mission or purpose] so I can manifest [dream] into the world and can live with [value].

Here is mine for inspiration, adapted from the statement which I left with after my unearthing:

"I, Tanya, am a beautiful, passionate, creative Queen. Here to co-create magic with others in the world so I can manifest creative abundance can live my life with freedom."

Once you have crafted your statement, you are ready for the final lesson.

For the next month, practice your statement in the mirror until you believe it. In order to complete this, I suggest the following:

- **Write your statement on a piece of paper and stick it on your mirror.**

- **Every morning and every evening, I invite you to look yourself kindly in the eyes, smile, and then to practice saying your statement with as much emotion and energy as you can muster.**

I also invite you to think about how else you may evoke your Queenly energy.

- **How does a Queen walk?**

- **How does she carry herself?**

- **What does she wear?**

- **How does she take care of herself?**

- **What types of decisions does she make?**

- **How can you best embody the qualities in your statement?**

- **What is the first step can you take to fulfil your mission or purpose?**

Affirmation: *I am ready to be the Queen of my own life.*

I am here

I am the Queen
weaving magic
with my thoughts and my words

Equilibrium

IN MY YEARS OF PERFORMING THIS WORK ON MYSELF as well as working with other women, I have noticed it isn't the things outside of us that disempower, but rather what is inside of us that ends up being what trips us up. After all, it is not the water that surrounds the boat who sinks, but rather the water in it.

Earlier in the book, I mentioned the *Witness* archetype or energy. However, we also have the Judge and the Victim alive in us too. Both are made up of a combination of our disempowered shadow selves. The Witness is an expression of our Knowing Self. When we are in the Judge, we are both critical and self-critical. The Judge, when working with the Witness, is a useful archetype for helping us develop our critical thinking and discernment. Yet, when we are purely in the Judge, our thinking is full of "should's" as we judge both others and our own actions according to our values and beliefs. Our Judge is also present in our inner critic, ready to mount an attack on us from the inside. When our Judge is particularly working, it activates our Victim. The Victim tells us how helpless and powerless we are about changing ourselves and our circumstances. The Judge and the Victim have an unhealthy, co-dependent relationship which leads to the disempowerment of self. The Witness is empowered energy, it is objective, impartial, and curious. When the Witness is activated, you are able to control and use the energy of your archetypes to nurture yourself to create more space, more opportunities, and a life free from the valley of despair.

The exercises in this book were created to support you to strengthen your Witness. When we fully embody the Witness, we are freed from the suffering of our Judge and Victim. It is like wearing Wonder Woman's armbands, and the bullets just bounce off us.

She AWAKES: Your Victim, Judge, and Witness

Reflect on your life and your experiences, and in your journal, write about a time when you were in the *Judge,* the *Victim,* and the *Witness.*

Affirmation: *I am ready to step into my full, empowered self.*

By now, you would have recognised which archetypes are most dominant for you. You would have come to realise that even though you align strongly with these dominant archetypes, it is your birth right to have access to the full range of powerful energies each archetype holds.

In this chapter I will walk you through each archetype and help you, with the support of your Witness, to access ways to restore equilibrium to your life by utilising your feminine forces. This is particularly helpful if you find yourself acting out of the wound or the shadow of a dominant archetype.

When Your Maiden is Out of Balance

If your Maiden is out of balance, you may have reached a crossroads in your life and lost all sense of who you are. You allow others to make the decisions and you are waiting for someone to rescue you or to make your life better.

You can rebalance the nameless Maiden's influence in your life by calling on the energies of the other archetypes in the following ways:

- **Evoke the independent energy of the Huntress, set yourself goals to focus on, and practice self-discipline.**

- **Embrace the knowing energy of your Wise Woman and learn to trust your intuition about what is right for you.**

- **Call in the courage and introspection of your Wild Woman and reflect on ways that life is happening for you instead of to you. Embrace change and step outside your comfort zones.**

- **Embody your Queen, create healthy boundaries, and practice making clear, confident choices for yourself.**

- **Embrace the loving Mother and practice taking responsibility for nurturing and parenting yourself.**

- **Evoke the Lover, and practice self-love and acceptance.**

When Your Mother is Out of Balance

If your Mother is out of balance, you may notice that you are exhausted, you have no time for yourself, and you can't remember the last time you did anything you enjoyed. You feel guilty anytime you do something that is not a productive use of your time or isn't for the kids. Your children are getting older and don't need you as much which has left you feeling sad and confused because you don't know who you are without being somebody's mother. You spend a lot of time comparing yourself to other Mothers or trying to control your children. This is also true if your "child" is a business or employees if you are in a leadership position.

You can rebalance the Mother's influence in your life by calling on the energies of the other archetypes in the following ways:

- **Evoke your Wild Woman, spend time prioritising your healing and growth and learning to be yourself.**

- **Call in the energy of your Lover and practice self-care, self-love, and self-pleasure—rekindle the flame of your sensuality and creativity.**

- **Embrace your Wise Woman and learn to rely on your inner knowing of what is right for you and your "family", instead of comparing and judging yourself with others.**

- **Evoke your Queen to invest in yourself and your personal growth. Make time for yourself, delegate household tasks that you don't enjoy to others, or bring in outside help.**

- **Call in your Huntress and pursue finding your purpose outside of your role as a mother. Prioritise what makes you happy and discover who you are as a woman.**

- **Embrace your Maiden invite spontaneity into your life and be open to new ideas.**

When Your Huntress is Out of Balance

If your Huntress is out of balance, you may notice that you live for and are super focussed on your mission in life. However, you have begun to feel burnt out because your need for control stops you from trusting others. Your commitment to your work keeps others from getting close to you, you feel alone and disconnected from friends and family, and are unable to ask for help or accept support when it is offered.

You can rebalance the Huntress's influence in your life by calling on the energies of the other archetypes in the following ways:

- **Call in the energy of your Wild Woman to explore your wounded Huntress so you can drop your armour and allow yourself to heal and grow.**

- **Embrace the energy of your Mother and nurture your relationships, especially with other women. Practice self-love and give yourself permission to take a break as the Huntress can spend a lot of time in survival mode which becomes exhausting.**

- **Evoke your Lover, practice letting down your guard, opening your heart to others, and experiencing pleasure, joy in your more sensual side.**

- **Embrace your Wise Woman and learn to discern your fear from your intuition.**

- **Call in your Queen, practice delegating jobs and trusting the people in your team to do their jobs.**

- **Evoke your Maiden and allow yourself to be open to receive.**

When Your Lover is Out of Balance

When your Lover is out of balance, this can manifest itself in your life in two ways:

Firstly, there is the repressed Lover. If the repressed Lover is the dominant energy in your life, then you may notice a disconnection from your physical body and find you spend most of your time in your head, reliving the past and worrying about the future. You may not have a desire to have sex, see sex as a waste of precious energy, or as a chore.

Secondly, there is the fragile Lover. If the fragile Lover is a dominant energy in your life, you will constantly feel the need to be adored so you can feed your sense of worth. You use sex as a way to get people to love you and you find it difficult to be single or by yourself.

You can rebalance the Lover's influence in your life by calling on the energies of the other archetypes in the following ways:

- **Evoke the energy of the Queen so you can feel confident in asking others for more of what you like and creating healthy boundaries in your sex life about the things you don't like.**

- **Call in the energy of the Wild Woman, explore your own sensuality, and spend time naked. Spend time noticing past patterns of the wounded Lover energy and spend time healing so you can create space for new, healthy intimacy in your life.**

- Evoke the energy of the Huntress and give yourself permission to spend time on your own, showing yourself some physical love and pleasure—you are allowed to receive. Let yourself explore the things which bring you pleasure and joy.

- Embrace your Wise Woman and have mindful solo sex. Take some time to tune into your body and what you enjoy.

- Evoke the curiosity of the Maiden and allow yourself to be open, experiment, and try new things.

- Embrace the energy of the Mother, practice accountability and responsibility in your sex life.

When Your Wild Woman is Out of Balance

If your Wild Woman is out of balance, you may notice that your life is chaotic, and you are at the whim of your desires. You have created a life without boundaries which has left you feeling shaky, insecure, and isolated in the realm of your own special world.

You can rebalance the Wild Woman's influence in your life by calling on the energies of the other archetypes in the following ways:

- Call in the wisdom of your Wise Woman to ground you with her objectivity and reason.

- Evoke the energy of the Huntress to support you in focussing some of your chaotic wildness.

- Embrace the Mother and allow her to nurture the relationships in your life.

- Call in the leadership of the Queen to harness the insights gained in the special world of the Wild Woman to create success and abundance in your life.

- Evoke the creative carefree energy of the Maiden to remember to play, to be light-hearted, and to have fun.

- Embrace the Lover and allow yourself to use your insights into yourself to push past your barriers in your relationships and sexuality.

When Your Wise Woman is Out of Balance

If your Wise Woman is out of balance, you may notice that you feel superior to others because you have this wealth of knowledge they don't. You take life a little too seriously and you only want to have long, deep meaningful conversations because you see no value in fun, frivolous interactions with others. You feel isolated and out of place as if nobody understands you.

You can rebalance the Wise Woman's influence in your life by calling on the energies of the other archetypes in the following ways:

- **Call in the energy of your Queen, stand in your worth and take on more leadership in your life.**

- **Embrace your Maiden and look at your life and the things around you with renewed awe, gratitude, and wonder.**

- **Evoke the Lover and allow yourself to have pleasurable new experiences. Allow yourself to be open to connections with other women so you do not isolate yourself.**

- **Embrace the energy of the Mother to serve others with your wisdom and nurture the relationships in your life.**

- **Call in the energy of the Huntress so you can use your knowledge to advocate for others.**

- **Evoke the energy of your Wild Woman and allow yourself time for reflection for the integration of your stories and lessons.**

When Your Queen is Out of Balance

If your Queen is out of balance, you may notice yourself slipping under the influence of the evil Queen and you may recognise that you look down on other women and feel bitter and envious towards their achievements in life. You feel superior to other women, or you feel threatened by other women and fear they are plotting to destroy your relationships or hard work. You spend your time thinking of revenge or spend time gossiping about other women.

You can rebalance the Queen's influence in your life by calling on the energies of the other archetypes in the following ways:

- Embrace your Mother to prioritise healing and nurturing relationships.

- Evoke your Maiden, allow yourself to trust others, and be playful.

- Call on your Lover and embrace your vulnerability by allowing yourself to enjoy the pleasure of relationships with other powerful Queens.

- Embrace your Wild Woman and connect with nature the spirit realm.

- Call on your Wise Woman and allow your knowing to guide you. Share your knowledge and wisdom as a way to enrich your community to uplift other Queens.

- Evoke your Huntress and allow yourself time to go on an adventure.

She AWAKES: Harnessing the Power of Your Archetypes

A powerful Queen knows the value of surrounding herself with a dedicated team, and that's why she contains a powerful team of archetypes inside of her who are available to do her bidding anytime she chooses.

In this exercise, I will show you how to harness the power of your Witness to identify an out of balance energy in your life to help call your other archetypes so you can create equilibrium in your life.

- Give yourself the presence of your full attention.

- Sit comfortably with your hands on stomach and heart.

- Gently close your eyes if it feels comfortable for you to do so. Or you can focus softly on the flame of a candle or the space in front of you.

- Connect to our breath and focus on breathing slowly in through your nose and out through your mouth.

- Slowly deepen your breath, and feel your stomach gently rise and fall.

- Feel into your physical self.

- Scan your body from head to toe for the vibrations of your emotional being.

- Asking yourself one simple question, *'What am I feeling?'* Then allow your inner self to respond in turn.

- I invite you to name the emotions you can feel moving around in your body and allow yourself to lovingly sit with them. Allow yourself to feel discomfort and healing of tears if these show up for you.

- Ask yourself, *'Whose energy is this?'* And once again, allow your inner self to respond. *(For example, the energy of worry, self-doubt, and need to control is the energy of the wounded Mother.)*

- Then finally ask yourself, *'What other energies could I access in order to empower me today?'*

In my example above, I could evoke the energy of the Lover to remind me to stay in the present moment and find joy in the little things. I could call in the knowing of my Wise Woman to trust myself and intuition as a mother. I could call in the introspection of my Wild Woman to reflect on the wounds which still need healing. I could call on the nurturing of the integrated Mother to mother myself. I could call on my Queen to recognise I don't have to do this alone, and I am able to ask for help.

Affirmation: *Each day, I step into the promise of my sovereignty.*

to pause

to hear

to recognise the murmuring of my soul
and to slow down

to stop

to allow the gentle time and place
to look inward deeply and to feel

to allow tear to well up on resolute eyelid
and to spill down

the tender pull of heart

to weep unfettered and unhinged
to open up to the healing of the moment

Emotions

ONE OF THE PRIMARY WAYS WE BECOME DISEMPOWERED is through the experience of our emotions. As newly crowned Queens, we need the power and strength to obtain mastery over ourselves. Queens rule, they do not allow the energies outside of them to rule them!

Many of us have learnt through our life apprenticeship that certain emotions are bad, undesirable, and something to fear— that emotions are dangerous. Somewhere along our life's journey, we came to believe that our sensitivity and the "too-muchness" of our feelings–expression–of our vulnerable whole selves was a weakness. And so, we made the deliberate decision to shut down this part, leading us to abandoned ourselves. This became our meta emotions philosophy–our feelings about our feelings.

In the chapter, on *Allowing Yourself Time to Grieve*, I expressed to you how I was domesticated to feel about anger and sadness. You may have experienced similar messages about your emotions., so I invite you to explore your meta emotions philosophy in the exercise below.

She AWAKES: Your Meta Emotions Philosophy

Think back to your childhood.

- **What was your family of origin's way of dealing with sadness, anger, anxiety, fear, and happiness?**

- **What did you learn about these emotions?**

- **How has this formed the way you deal with these emotions now in yourself and with others?**

I invite you to journal each of these emotions separately. There may be some overlap but that is okay since this is a powerful way for you to explore how your meta emotions philosophy on certain emotions impacts the other. If writing doesn't feel right for you, then you can draw about your experiences.

I urge you to take your time with this, practice self-care with your energy as this is deep work and it can be confronting.

Affirmation: *I am allowing myself to be open to the healing power of my emotions.*

Emotions Coaching

Excuse my crudeness but in a way, emotions are like farts. We all fart. Women are taught that it is impolite to fart and so we keep them in. In a way, our farts—although loud and smelly—when allowed to move out of us, they keep our bodies healthy and functioning as it was intended too. It is the same way the energy of our "e—motions" are also meant to be experienced, and then *move through us*. Neither farts nor emotions are meant to be stored inside the body. However, when we suppress our farts, they begin to build up in our intestinal system wreaking all kinds of havoc and causing us to experience a world of hurt. The exact thing happens to us when we suppress our load, smelly emotions.

In Brené Brown 's book, *Dare To Lead*, she describes the ways we may have been taught to store or offload our hurt and disempowering emotions:

- **Last Straw:** Packing our emotions down so far that it is impossible for them to resurface until a seemingly innocent comment sends us into a rage or a crying fit.

- **Bouncing Hurt**: Using anger, blame, and/or avoidance when getting close to our emotions.

- **Numbing:** Using food, television, social media, drugs, alcohol, or sex to numb us so we do not have to feel our emotions.

- **Stockpiling:** Firmly packing down our emotions until our bodies start to shut down.

- **High-Centred**: Getting ourselves stuck in our emotions where we can't move forward, and we can't move back.

- **Fake Nice**: Being overly accommodating on the outside but resentful, hurt, angry, and frustrated on the inside and then exploding for no apparent reason.

I would like to add an additional offload strategy to this list from the work of as mentioned in Miriam Greenspan's book, *Healing Through the Dark Emotions*:

- **Emotional Bypass:** Using our faith in our relationships in religion or another person to bypass our emotions.

The good news is that as awful as the experience of these emotions can be, they do not have to be a disempowering force. Even if we have used these emotional offloading techniques many times before, we are capable of changing this disconnecting behaviour to one which connects us to ourselves and the people who we love. When we view our emotions through the lens of the Witness, they can be extremely helpful and empowering, even the so-called "bad ones".

All humans have needs, however, through the dream of our domestication, we come to believe that it is wrong to have needs. Even as babies, we learn the lesson that we shouldn't be "needy". Men receive the message that they don't have needs—other than sexual ones—and it is weak to admit their needs. Women are led to believe that they have to sacrifice their needs for the sake of others, that wanting to have their needs met is deemed selfish. Our emotions are simply our body's way of giving us information about our needs.

When we permit our Judge or our Victim to have access to our emotions, it can cause a disconnection depending on how you were taught to deal with them. But when we engage the curiosity of our Witness, we can be open to the following information about our needs. *(Your needs may be different depending on your values; however, this example illustrates what may be going on for you.)*

- **Fear:** *I need to prepare for something outside of my comfort zone. My need safety and security are not being met.*

- **Anger:** *Something that is important to me, a value or a boundary has been violated. My need for justice is not being met.*

- **Hurt or Disappointment:** *I had an expectation of someone or a situation which was not fulfilled. My need for predictability and order is not being met.*

- **Sadness:** *Something that was important to me has been lost. My need for love and support is not being met.*

- **Guilt or Shame:** *I am out of alignment with my values. My need for integrity with my values is not being met.*

- **Envy:** *Someone else has what I want for myself. My need significance is not being met.*

- **Frustration:** *What I am doing isn't working. My need for clarity is not being met.*

How do we engage our Witness?

How can we let go of our old ways of disconnecting and abandoning the important information of our emotions?

A copy of a needs and emotions list can be downloaded at
https://www.tanyavalentin.co/Needs-List

There is a way, it is called "Emotions Coaching". This is a technique I learnt during a parenting course that my husband and I took to better support our teenage daughters with their anxiety. According to John Gottman, there are five stages to emotionally coaching your children:

- Tune into your child's emotions, especially the lower frequency emotions.

- See this as an opportunity to connect and turn towards your child.

- Listen with empathy and validate your child's feelings.

- Help your child label their emotions.

- Support your child to problem solve it into a solution, (if appropriate).

She AWAKES: Emotions Coaching and You

Think of a situation when you felt a strong emotion. How could you use the five steps of emotions coaching below to process your emotions?

- **Tune into *yourself*, especially during the lower frequency emotions.**

- **See this as an opportunity to connect and turn towards yourself.**

- **Listen to the emotions that are alive inside of you with empathy and self-compassion and validate your experience of these emotions.**

- **Name and label your emotions. Pay attention to where you feel them in your body.**

- **Problem solve your emotions through accessing the information that your emotion has for you about your needs or practice the emotional release technique.**

Work through the five steps and record your reflections in your journal.

Since learning these five steps, I found that the application of these steps is endless, and I have used them to be a better partner, sister, friend, mentor, and leader. I found through the process of practicing these steps, the best way to learn to be and emotions coach for others is to first learn to emotions coach yourself.

Here is an example of how I applied these emotions coaching principles to myself during a recent experience with the emotion of frustration.

Frustration is part of the anger family. Frustration is a less intense emotion than anger, however, if we do not resolve the source of our frustration, it can quickly escalate into anger or even a full-blown rage.

Today, I am feeling extremely frustrated. One of my children is feeling frustrated, her mental health team is feeling frustrated. It is a hot, and humid sticky afternoon. We are all eating a giant helping of prickly, fibrous, hard-to-digest frustration. My daughter is frustrated that the medication, therapy, and other interventions for her depression are seemingly not working. I am frustrated with her, but I am also frustrated for me as I am trying so fucking hard and everything, I am doing apparently has no effect. I know, rationally, that my daughter has no control over how she feels, however—and I would never say this to her—there is a part of me who angrily thinks she isn't trying hard enough.

Frustration can be a challenging emotion to navigate. The solution to frustration is to find another solution to try. Yet, when we are in frustration, we can easily trigger much bigger more intense emotions. When we are in this state of mind, our irrational thinking brain is no longer engaged, so trying to form a new solution can seem nearly impossible. The other frustrating thing about frustration is that we may not be happy with our alternative solution, so this can further exasperate things just like adding matches to an already lit fire.

How to navigate this emotion?

Firstly, I recognise that I am in a disempowered, emotional state. *My frustration is a bid for connection with myself.* Secondly, *I see this as an opportunity to turn towards myself and connect.* Recognising I have the ability to pause here and engage in some self-care like intentional stomach breathing to support me to feel grounded and calm.

Making space for the pause is an important step in the process. According to Dr Harriet Learner, our brains are so programmed to defend, that most of us don't even realise we have the option to pause—to disengage from an argument, to find a moment to settle ourselves emotionally—before we continue with our discussion or move onto problem solving. This is the vital step to keeping ourselves grounded, and not abandoning who we are or who we would like to be, so we show up as the best possible version of ourselves.

I then explore what I was feeling with *empathy, curiosity, and self-compassion. Naming my emotion of frustration.* Validating my emotions by telling myself that I am allowed to feel this way. It is normal and everyone feels this way from time to time as it is human to experience frustration. *I then gave myself the permission to simply sit with the emotion* of frustration until I had processed it and it had passed.

The first few steps of this process are designed to support you to connect with what you are feeling and engage your Witness so you can pay attention to the message that frustration has for you and problem solve, if appropriate. Which is, *"what you are doing isn't working, try something else."* As with the stages of grief, this process of emotions coaching is not linear. You might do the third step before the fourth, and you might bounce back and forth. The object here often isn't even to solve the problem.

The final step of fixing or problem solving is optional as there may not be a clear solution by the time you reach this point. The object of emotions coaching is to simply allow yourself the time and space to be with your emotions and to process them in a way which doesn't cause hurt and shame to ourselves and others. This is a practice of being able to "be with" ourselves and our emotions without having our emotions control us. The ultimate goal is to gain a greater understanding of ourselves and an emotional connection to all parts of our often-fractured selves.

Emotions are part of being human, the only humans who don't experience them are dead people. Strong emotions, failures, and mistakes are part of our contract with life; they cannot be avoided. As terrifying as these loud, smelly, and strong emotions can be, they cannot harm us if we allow them to do what they were naturally designed to do which is to move through us, imparting important information about our needs. According to Marc Brackett, director of The Yale Centre for Emotional Development, *"Our emotional intelligence largely impacts whether we approach or avoid the decisions we make, our intellect, mental health, creativity and performance. How we deal with life has the biggest impact on us in the long term."*

Affirmation: *When I allow myself to sit with my emotions I grow in the discomfort.*

Learning to Identify Our Emotions in Our Bodies

One of the most important steps in reconnecting with our emotions and using their power as information is learning to recognise where our emotions manifest in our bodies. Even though we may think our emotions live in our head, our bodies give us vital clues that we are having an emotional response *before* our brains may register that we are. Once we are able to tune into our body's cues, we are able to be better emotions coaches to ourselves.

She AWAKES: Tuning into Your Body's Emotional Clues

For this exercise you will need blank paper or your journal, crayons, felt-tip pens, or colouring pencils. On the pages in front of you, I invite you to draw yourself experiencing the following emotions:

- **Sadness**
- **Anger**
- **Worry**
- **Fear**
- **Loneliness**
- **Joy**

In each drawing, draw yourself and then draw the emotion as a symbol or a circle in the places on or in your body where you feel them.

- **What did you notice about yourself and your emotions?**

Affirmation: *Noticing emotions in my body allows me to grow into an empowered Queen.*

Emotional Release Technique

As painful as it can be sometimes, we all have the strength to sit with the full potency of our emotions. We have been gifted the blessed power of releasing them once their lesson has been received. Each and every one of us has the ability to sit quietly and use the power inside of us.

It starts with the connecting to our breath. Focus on our breath, slowing and deepening our breath. Hands on stomach and heart. Feel into our physical selves. Feel our spiritual selves come alive. Feel into the vibrations of our emotional being, and ask ourselves one simple question, 'What am I feeling?' Then allow your inner selves to respond in turn.

I know that at this very moment, if I searched myself, I would find sadness, worry, and fear lurking in the inner garden of my heart. My limiting beliefs are a gift. My fears, my sadness, my worry, my anger, and my envy, they too, are a gift. They come up for me to show myself areas of my life which need my tender, loving care, and attention for the purpose of healing. I see these as an opportunity to inquire into my worry and fear. If these emotions could speak, *what would they say to me?* If they were voices, they would speak of my fear for my eldest going off to university and living by herself without the support of her family. They would speak about the fear for my children and my desperate longing for them to be okay, of my Mother's heart which is yearning for my children to be happy, healthy, and to succeed in life. My emotions would speak of the sorrow and sadness that I feel for my daughter leaving, of the shame I feel for not being the mother that I hoped I would be.

I take a moment here to sit and hug myself.

I allow my emotions to rise to the surface.

I give myself permission to feel everything, to cry and, that to me, feels like a blessed release.

I then address my emotions, the part of me which longs to protect and keep me safe. I say to my sadness, my worry, my fear, and my shame,

"Thank you for being my sadness, my worry, my fear, and my shame."

"Thank you for doing your job and for showing me what is important to me."

"Thank you for loving me and protecting me. I no longer need you; I release you."

I imagine my emotions evaporating from me like spirits following the light, and then I expand my reality and visualise what else might be possible. I visualise my eldest in her Maiden archetype, moving to university, blossoming into who she was meant to be as a woman. Embracing her Huntress, her Mother, her Queen, her Lover, her Wise Woman, and her Wild Woman as an integrated creative being. I visualise my other two children starting their respective new schools—making new friendships, being challenged, and thriving. I visualise forgiving myself and being the most loving, beautiful version of myself I can be.

I know this can happen because I have magic inside of me.

Each day I can create my day, my life, and my future.

There is magic in my thoughts, there is magic in my words.

She AWAKES: Your Emotional Release

Now, dear one, it is your turn to sit with the fullness of your emotions and practice their loving release through the magic of your attention.

- **Gift yourself the presence of your full attention.**

- **Sit comfortably with your hands on stomach and heart.**

- **Gently close your eyes, if it feels comfortable for you to do so or focus softly on the flame of a candle or a space in front of you.**

- Connect to our breath. Focus on breathing slowly in through your nose and out through your mouth.

- Slowly deepen your breath and making your stomach gently rise and fall.

- Feel into your physical self.

- Scan your body from head to toe for the vibrations of your emotional being.

- Asking ourselves one simple question, *'What am I feeling?'* Then allow your inner self to respond in turn.

- Invite yourself to name the emotions you can feel moving around in your body and allow yourself to lovingly sit with them. Allow yourself to feel discomfort and healing of tears if these show up for you.

- Ask yourself, *'If these emotions could speak, what would they say?'* And allow your inner self to respond.

- Take a moment here to embrace yourself and just be. Allow your emotions to come and bubble up towards the surface.

- Give yourself permission to feel everything.

- Thank each of your emotions for choosing you and for the message they had to bring, and then lovingly tell them that you now release them.

- Imagine your emotions evaporating into the air until they have disappeared.

- Now, allow the power of your imagination to create an expansion of your reality. A loving and beautiful version of your story and your life. This reality is just as true as the one you imagined in the first place.

Affirmation: *There is magic inside of me.*

I lie in bed
my fingers trace the lines
the pink ribbons scars
the silvery stretch marks on
well-worn skin
this forms the roadmap of my existence

this has oft been the source of
self-loathing and pain

I have been relentless in the admonishment
of my body
criticizing it
for not being thin enough
pretty enough
perfect enough
as if that was ever attainable

I move inward
and wrap myself in a warm embrace
I forgive you
I accept you
you are loved by me
I say as I show my body love

Embodiment

ANOTHER WAY WE CAN BECOME DISEMPOWERED is by spending too much time in our conscious minds and thereby ignoring the wisdom of the body. We disconnect from our body in so many ways, from ignoring our basic needs such as using the bathroom when needed or eating when we feel hungry, to disconnecting from the signs in our body that relates to our intuition or ignoring the signs in our bodies about how we are feeling.

In many spiritual practices, we can focus solely on the heart and the soul. In mindset training, we tend to focus on the power of the mind, however, the body has wisdom of its own. In the wisdom of embodiment theory, the mind does not only influence the body, but the body influences the mind. The body has many lessons to teach. Becoming an empowered, integrated woman requires us to have full access to all our body, mind, heart, and soul.

In this book I have touched on many practices which support all parts of us and will support you to access and heal yourself holistically.

- **Connecting with your breath.**

- **Meditation.**

- **Mindfulness—training yourself to observe your body and your mind.**

- **Movement practices like martial arts, tai chi, yoga, walking, or running.**

- **Noticing moments of flow.**

- **Tapping into what feels intuitively right for you by paying attention to the "yes" and "no" sensations in your body.**

- **Emotions coaching and emotions release.**

In this chapter, I want to support you with deepening your practice in tuning into your body in a powerful way through the process of active meditation. Many of us associate meditation with sitting or lying still and focussing on either a mantra or a guide. There is a way we can meditate by being active and immersing ourselves into the sensations in our body.

She AWAKES: Active Meditation

For this exercise, we will explore the healing power of dance so you will need access to some music, choosing two songs. One song with a good drum or bass beat and a second song which is a flowing piece of music that encourages free movement.

You can use a playlist on your computer, mobile device, or an app like Spotify.

- **Push play on the first song and close your eyes.**

- **For the duration of this song, I invite you to shake your body to the beat of the music.**

- **Starting from your feet, moving upwards to your head, and then shaking your entire body.**

- **Once the first song ends, I invite you to stand for a few minutes with your eyes closed and just feel into your body.** *What are the sensations you experience? Where do you feel them?*

- **Then push play on the second piece of music and with your eyes closed again, allow the music to move you.**

Once the music is finished, take a moment to reflect and to record your reflections in your journal.

Affirmation: *I am alive in my body.*

in this world where the only sure thing is change

I want to spend the remainder my life changing with you

Educate and Equip

DURING OUR JOURNEY TOGETHER, you may have unearthed parts of yourself that have lain dormant in your cave for years, or even decades. Amongst the rumble, it is my hope you have found many wondrous treasures of *you*, and that one of those treasures has been your curiosity.

As I mentioned in my introduction, it is unrealistic that by reading one book, or twenty, will be enough to stave off your growing inquiry into yourself. This book is just one part of your journey. (I have included a list of books you can use to explore yourself further at the end of this book.)

You may be leaving this journey with more questions than answers and that is perfectly normal and allowed. This life is an endless quest of exploring, unearthing, unfolding, and awakening. If you are feeling unsure about what you would like to do next and this frightens or overwhelms you, don't worry, this is natural. Fortunately, as you have discovered in this book, you do not have to climb the whole mountain in one bound. You only have to inquire into yourself as to what your next step may be. This may begin with the question, *"What am I curious about?"*

Self-exploration is like receiving a never-ending pass-the-parcel present. Each layer reveals a new little surprise. Some surprises are delightful little embellishments, some of them are sweet, sugary treats. Some surprises are mirrors to reflect back on yourself. Some are not what you expect, some hold a disappointment, or even a disaster. But nothing is permanent, dear one. There is always another layer waiting to unwrap until you are left with the prize in the middle. The rediscovery of the *golden you*.

She AWAKES: Educating and Equipping Yourself

What are you curious about? If you were able to allow yourself the full measure of your curiosity, *what would you want to know?*

In this exercise I invite you to explore your curiosity, to give yourself over to your inquisitiveness.

- Ask yourself, *'What am I interested in exploring further?'*

- Make a list of ways that you may educate yourself in the area of your curiosity.

- Take inspired action—do one thing that will move you closer to the area of your interest.

Affirmation: *I am allowing myself to explore my curiosity.*

Resistance to Investing in Ourselves

When we are claiming our Queen status, we can experience a deep ingrained resistance to the idea of investing in ourselves. This is especially true if you have spent decades in the shadow of the self-sacrificing Mother. I have witnessed in myself, and others, that mothers will purchase the best shoes and clothing for their children while being content to recycle a ten-year-old wardrobe. Mothers will seek out classes and extramural activities for their children, sit by as their partners join social sports teams, or make their gym time a priority while telling themselves there is no money for their own interests. They spend their free time driving children all over town to this or that activity and the tell themselves there is not time for themselves.

We live in a world where mothers are shamed for taking time for themselves, where selflessness and long-suffering are rewarded with "gold stars". When we are caught up in this shadow of the Mother, it can feel challenging to change gears and to start investing in yourself. This thinking can be hard to shift, so you may need to spend some time communing with your Wild Woman and digging in the shadows of your cave as to why this is true for you and integrating your stories and creating new ones. The way we interpret our life stories depends on the lens we use. The important thing to remember is that lenses are merely tools. Sometimes they are useful for helping us see or focus on something important in the here and now, but ultimately, they are a filter for our emotions, and in particular, our shame and fear can taint these filters.

For example, I could tell myself the story that investing in myself is selfish and motherhood is all about sacrificing. *Or...* I could recognise that the legacy I am leaving with this story is one of self-sacrifice and suffering for my children. I won't want them to live this way, and so, I could tell myself a new story that when I invest in myself, I am providing a new example of what it means to me a woman and mother to my daughters. They will no longer have to carry the heavy load of beliefs that we have outgrown.

Now it's your turn...

She AWAKES: Healing the Self-Sacrificing Mother Wound

In your journal, use the following prompts to uncover and heal this wound.

- **What did you learn about what it means to be a mother from your mother?**

- **What did you learn about what is expected from mothers from your culture?**

- **What are the stories you told yourself about motherhood because of this?**

- **What are the unconscious rewards you are getting from living in your old stories about motherhood?**

- **What new stories could you create instead?**

Affirmation: *I can invest in myself and be a good mother too.*

Money Blocks

Another way we sometimes struggle to ascend into the full potential of our Queen is through our blocks around money. During our many years in the dream, we may have heard and lived the following messages:

- People from our family aren't successful and wealthy.

- It is my destiny to…

- People from our family are plodders, we work hard for our money.

- You must stay in the same job or career until you retire—even if you hate it.

- Being poor is virtuous, but wanting money is evil and shallow.

- Money will ruin you.

- Being creative and having fun is not a *real* job.

These were certainly prevalent in my upbringing. You may have encountered similar and/or others depending on your upbringing or culture.

As Queens in business, some of these stories left over from our dream of domestication can sneakily be running in the background of your subconscious causing self-sabotaging blocks around money. According to the work of Denise

Duffield-Thomas, these are common money blocks we may get caught up with from time to time:

- Giving others our services for free or undercharging because we feel we are not experienced, qualified, or good enough–**The shadow of the Mother.**

- Giving away our money, power, and decisions about money to other people–**The shadow of the Maiden.**

- Being uncomfortable with wealth and excess and feeling the need to make yourself small or diminish your success in front of friends and family–**The shadow of the Maiden.**

- Surrounding yourself with people who have a poverty mindset–**The shadow of the Mother.**

- Overindulging and overspending until all your coffers are empty–**The shadow of the Queen.**

- Feeling inadequate in your abilities and struggling to commit to your career or way of making money because of what others may think–**The shadow of the Maiden.**

- Selling ourselves short and hustling for our worth by bartering with others because we feel that what we have to offer is not good enough for people to pay *real money* for–**The shadow of the Mother.**

Much like healing our stories about the self-sacrificing mother, we have the opportunity to shine some loving, Witness energy on our money stories and heal them as they come up for us.

She AWAKES: Unpacking Your Money Blocks

In your journal use the following prompts to uncover and remove your money blocks.

- **What did you learn about what it means to have money from your family?**

- **What did you learn about money from your culture?**

- **What stories have you told yourself about making money because of this?**

- **What are the unconscious rewards you are getting from living in your old stories about money?**

- **What would it mean to your life if you could give up these old stories about money?**

- **What new stories could you create about money instead?**

Affirmation: *I serve, I deserve.*

if I could go back and speak to my younger self
and to all those that would come after me
I would say

love the body that you are in

time and time again I regret not loving myself
not appreciating myself when I was younger
for years I lived disconnected from who I was
afraid to be me
not owning my presence in the universe
time and again I failed to appreciate my strength
my flexibility
my youth
I think back to the first time I looked in the mirror and decided that I was fat
(I was a size eight at the time)
I wish that I had been more grateful and less critical

> *don't waste time senselessly criticising yourself and hating your body*
> *making your body the enemy*

don't wait around for someone else to see the light in you
instead learn to love the person in the mirror
be grateful for her
be kind to that person
speak to her like she is someone that you love
believe in her
and treat her like the precious being that she is
never let anyone tell you that you are not enough
including yourself

youth and beauty fades
bodies change shape
don't obsess about the opinions of others
living for their approval
enjoy your youth
be you
have fun
wear the short skirts—the bikini
but know that it is okay to have days

where you just want to wear pyjamas
and cry into your ice cream

however remember that your body is but a container
to hold your beautiful spirit
and the vehicle to experience all the amazing adventures of life
think of all that you will do
the places it will take you
and embrace a life well lived
– letter to my daughters

Energy

When it comes unhooking ourselves from the collective dream of society, nothing has the power to fill us with absolute, ice cold, nauseating dread as disclosing this version of ourselves to a parent, a close family member, or friend. We are so deeply imprinted to seek approval from our parents during our time as the nameless Maiden in order to survive in this world that it becomes second nature to conceal our true selves from them.

I know grown ass women and men in their thirties, forties, fifties, and even sixties who would rather die a million deaths than admit to their mothers or fathers that they are smokers, are in a queer relationship, or have put aside the family religious faith. It is ridiculous that we allow the continued hold that our early relationships had on us to still control us. So much damage is caused by these relationships while we are just figuring out the intricacies of what it means to be *human*. Many years later, the menacing shadows of these familial bonds are still ever-present long after these relationships have outgrown their purpose. In the blink of an eye, we can be transported back to these hurtful moments, and we are once again those scared, shy, awkward little girls who are desperately trying to blend in, please, and hustle for our worth.

It is funny how the things which cause us the most pain are often the hardest things to let go of. Part of our transformation is letting go of some people along the way. Friends, family, or lovers, whom we once felt that life was meaningless without now just form part of our back story. In the end, we are all looking for friendship, a belonging, love. To be accepted as we are and to feel as if we matter.

Occasionally, you will come across a person in your life who will not understand the changes they see in you and you might be at the receiving end of their anger, hostility, judgment, or disgust. Past me has taken these reactions to heart and made this all about what a flawed human being I am and that I am doing it all wrong. But present me uses these as information as to how much I have grown. In the past, I may have felt rejection, shame, or anger, however, now I chose to give myself compassion and remind myself that everyone is doing the best they can with what they have. As the American writer, Augusten Burroughs writes, *"I, myself, am made entirely of flaws, stitched together with good intentions."*

Please remember that you have been showing up as the person you were for many years and the people in your life would have become accustomed to the woman you were. You have spent a lifetime schooling them in the past version of you, so there may be some resistance to this *new* you. Gift them time and patience as they adjust but stay strong and confident in who you are.

I have never met a person who isn't trying their best. I find that the best practice is to accept what this person has to teach you about yourself as a shadow teacher, then bless and block. For many of us, our Wild Woman is still in her infancy. Tender shoots of her new life energy are germinating and growing in our soul garden. It is important to be a good gardener while these seedlings take root and grow. One way to protect your new energy is to surround yourself with like-minded people who are on the same journey as you. You may explore a woman's circle in your local community or an online group. Another way is making space for in your life is to continue with the practices you have embraced in this book. Spending time in nature, meditating, praying, or reflecting in your journal. Daily repetition of affirmations which feed you positivity and love.

Imperative to protecting your energy, you must tune into your *Knowing Self* and to practice discernment over the things that drain you of your energy and the things which energise. You may want to take stock of these things by using your "Yes" and "No" knowing, remove practices, people, and things from your life that do not bring life to the person you are becoming. If you cannot remove them, then you may want to lovingly create boundaries around yourself to support the unfolding of the best most generous version of you.

Please remember that if you feel you have no choice but to remove it, you may need to go back and refer to the chapter on grief. Just because something is toxic to us does not mean that letting go will not hurt. So please prepare yourself for this.

She AWAKES: Protecting Your Energy

Reflect on your life and everything that you have learnt so far about yourself on this quest. Tuning into the knowing of your Wise Woman intuition, in your journal list:

- **What are the practices, people, or things which energise you and allow you to be the best version of yourself?**

- **What are the practices, people, and things that make it difficult for you to be this person?**

- What practices, people, or things do you need to remove or let go of?

- What practices, people, or things do you need to place boundaries around?

- What practices, people, or things do you need to make more room for in your life?

Affirmation: *I am a Queen who knows her own worth. I lovingly protect and nurture my energy with healthy boundaries.*

Manifesting New Abundance

Newton's Third Law of Motion states: *"For every action, there is an equal and opposite reaction."* Which means that the energy we put out into the world comes back to us whether we realise it or not.

One of the positive things about removing or creating boundaries around the things that zap or reduce our energy is that we can remove blockages and allow the flow of new energy to flow into our lives.

You may be at the stage of your journey where you want to naturally raise the frequency of the energy in your life, and you would like to invite new energy, new abundance, new adventures or joy into your life. So, in the below exercise, I will talk you through the steps of how you can do this:

She AWAKES: Manifesting Abundance

Revisit your dream from an earlier exercise in the book. Vividly visualise what it looks like.

- **Where are you?**

- **What are you doing?**

- **What are you wearing?**

- **What are you saying?**

- **How do you feel knowing that your dream is a reality?**

In your journal write or draw about this new reality. Then, I invite you to use the steps below to support you in manifesting this new reality into your life:

- Decluttering.

- Become ultra-specific about what you would like to manifest in your life. In other words, *what*, *why*, and *when*. State your goal in the affirmative as if this has already happened.

- Creating positive energy about what you would like to manifest. Place affirmations and pictorial reminders around your home and office to remind you of what is coming.

- Get super excited about your new reality.

- Taking inspired action that moves you in the direction of your reality.

- Being open to receiving abundance into your life in all its many different forms. As well as noticing, celebrating, and practicing gratitude for all the ways, big or small, in which you have been blessed.

Affirmation: *I am manifesting a new reality into existence.*

Resetting Your Energy

When we live in the ordinary world, we live in the *real* world. We all know that the real world is full of upsets, disappointments, mistakes, and false starts. One of the most important lessons that all Queens need to learn is how to get back up, dust themselves off, straighten their crowns, and carry on. *"Carry on you're the Queen."*

How do we do this?

How do we learn to rise when we fall?

One of my favourite Brené Brown quotes is, *"When we have the courage to walk into our own story and own it, we get to write the ending."* This gives us vital clues on how to proceed. When we fall, and we will, it is important for us to have the courage to walk ourselves back into the cave of our own story and come face to face with our Wild Women. We need to learn to unpack the story of our fall, take ownership for our mistakes and short fallings, and with courageous humility, make amends. However, we also get to claim ownership of our lessons which we can use to make us a better Queen. And then to *practice, practice, practice.*

I also find that a regular, energy resetting ritual helps my inner Huntress stay healthy and keenly mission-focused. In the lesson below I have outlined the process I use.

She AWAKES: Resetting Ritual

At the beginning of each new moon cycle—the day where no moon is present—I perform the following ritual to reset my energy. I also perform this ritual if I have suffered an upset and need a reset.

- **I write down all the things that I want to invite into my life.**

- **Second, I write down all the things that I would like to let go of.**

- **Then, I burn the list.**

- **I open all my doors and windows, and I light a smudging stick.**

- **I walk around my house with the smudging stick, and I cleanse all the areas in my house that I would like to reset.**

- **As I do this, I repeat to myself *'I release the energy of [things I would like to let go of] and invite into my life [things I would like to invite into my life.]'***

- **Once I have done this, I say, *'And so it is'.***

- **I follow this with burning essential oils which represent the new energy I would like to embrace, such as lavender for a calming effect).**

- **I conclude with vacuuming or sweeping away the remnants of the old energy that might still be hanging around, and I tell myself, *'I am cleaning away old energies which no longer serve me.'***

Affirmation: *I release the old energy and I invite new energy into my life.*

feed yourself

all the hopes and dreams
the kindness
that you needed

when you were young

Enjoyment and Exploration

WHEN MY CHILDREN WERE BABIES, I subconsciously told myself that if my husband was out slaving away to support us then it meant that my time at home with my children had to be work too. And so, when I was playing with my children and having fun, I told myself to stop and to do chores instead. If a friend asked me to visit her house for coffee or suggested we meet at the beach for a picnic, I made an excuse and prioritised grocery shopping instead. The funny thing was that no-one ever sat me down and said, 'While you are at home with the kids, it needs to be all work and no play', or 'There will be consequences for getting out and having fun'. I created this story all on my own and I unintentionally robbed myself and my children from precious experiences, connections, and the basic human right of enjoyment.

There are other ways we can deny ourselves joy. We may feel we are not deserving, or that it is up to other people or things to make us happy. Another common version of this is delaying joy. The "when I …, then I will be happy" trap.

- No one is coming to give you permission to be happy…*It can only come from you!*

- The thing you are waiting for to happen so you can finally be happy… *It doesn't exist!*

- You have wasted too many of your precious years waiting for this to happen… *Start living already!*

Happiness is not a place. It is not a magical destination to which we can arrive, pitch a tent, unpack our bags, and stay forever nor are we able to find it from a source outside of ourselves. Happiness is borne from inside us and in many ways, it is the most fragile and vulnerable emotion a human can have as it opens us up to loss. There is always only one degree of separation between the laughter and tears. A moment of intense joy often is felt so deeply in the soul that it results in a watershed moment. Yet, happiness can be found in the most normal of tasks, like washing dishes and taking the time to notice the fragrance of your dish soap, the warmth of the water as it touches your hands, and the feeling of bubbles as they gently pop against your skin. You can find joy in any moment where you take the time to simply notice and open your heart to feeling into the joy.

If you are like me and spent many of your years abdicating your joy for the sake of others you may be so out of touch with your ability to enjoy life and receive pleasure.

One of the ways you can invite more joy and pleasure in your life is by healing the unnamed Maiden and the wounds of the Mother evoking the curiosity of the mature Maiden, the pleasure-seeking energy of the Lover, and open yourself up to exploration and experimentation to notice the reaction in your body, heart, or spirit. Another way is by creating a gratitude practice.

She AWAKES: Practicing Gratitude

One of the most profound ways of opening your life up to joy is by taking the time to notice the amazing things that already have a place in your life. There is a lot of research into the benefits of gratitude in our lives, especially for our mental health. This practice has the best results when completed consistently as a daily practice, and all you need is your pen, your journal, and a grateful heart.

- **Each day before you start your day or before you go to bed at night, think of and write down three things in your life that you are grateful for.**

- **Take a moment to sit with your feelings of joy and appreciation.**

For a deeper practice, learn to see the mundane everyday tasks, or even things that you take for granted or complain about, in a new profound light by choosing one thing you are grateful for and *go deep* using the *seven layers of why* I outlined in Knowing Yourself on page 235.

For example: *I am grateful for my computer.*

- I complete most of my work on my computer, so I am grateful it allows me to make the money I need to support my family.

- I am a writer who enjoys creating with words. I am grateful for my computer because it allows me to record my thoughts so easily. (I remember how frustrating using a typewriter was before computers–UGH!)

- My computer allows me to work from home and access opportunities from around the world, I am grateful for this technology that allows me to be safe in a pandemic.

- My computer allows me to keep in touch with family and friends from around the world. I am grateful to be able to stay connected even though we live far away.

- I am grateful for my computer as I can relax and be entertained by watching movies, binging on series, and reading books all in one place.

- I am grateful for my computer as I can access knowledge about *anything*. I can educate myself and learn new skills at the touch of a button.

- I am grateful for my computer as it allows me to build a community, make friends, and support women from all over the world.

As you can see there are so many things to be grateful for with just one thing in your life. The opportunities for some thankfulness in your life are endless.

Affirmation: *I already have so much in my life to be grateful for when I take the time to notice it.*

it is time to
unearth all the parts of yourself
you left behind to gather dust
and to find the places they now fit

time to grow into those god damned gifts

Evidence

Our brains are funny in that we will only truly believe in the things we see evidence for. As I explained in the chapter, *Authentic Self,* where I described our decisions of destiny. Something happens, we make up a story or a meaning about what happened, we do something based on our new meaning and then we go out and find the evidence to reinforce this new thinking. It isn't until we collect the evidence that we accumulate new knowledge into strong, new brain connections.

As I have previously said, *"trust is built in the doing",* and so I would like to share with you a way you can do this.

She AWAKES: Finding New Evidence

In this exercise, I would like to help you to find some evidence to reinforce the work that you have been doing during this journey of self-discovery.

- **Take out the snapshot letter that you wrote to yourself at the beginning of the book and read it.**

- **Look inward and see for ways you have created change in yourself and your life.**

- **What were these changes?**

- **What has been the impact of these changes—positive and negative?**

- **How have these changes made you feel?**

- **What lessons have you learnt about yourself?**

- **What wisdoms and tools can you take with you into the next part of your journey?**

Affirmation: *I am a magnificent work of art in progress.*

nothing is more magnificent
more beautiful
more potent
more desirable

than a woman
in full flow
living into the fullness of her power

Elevate -
Behold Your Exciting Life

WE ARE NOW WALKING THE FINAL STEPS OF OUR JOURNEY TOGETHER, and I hope you have enjoyed our time together as much as I have. But before I leave you to your exciting life ahead of you, I have one more crown jewel to give you. I would like you to elevate your expectations and imagine what else is possible.

A few years ago, before I went on my own **awaken**ing quest, the life I am leading now lived only in the back of my dreams and imagination.

I knew I wanted to leave the constant survival mode of the city and move to the wide-open spaces of the country.

I knew I wanted to have more time to spend with my children and family.

I knew I wanted to travel more and meet new people.

I knew I wanted to leave my soul-crushing nine-to five-job, live out my childhood dream of being an author, and contributing to my community through literary work.

I knew I wanted to make enough money through my work to elevate my dreams into reality and support my family.

I knew this is what I wanted from my life and that it was simply a reality waiting to be accessed. Once it existed in my imagination, the rest was simply an issue of alignment of my mind, heart, and soul so I could create consistent, courageous, and inspired actions.

I now reside in a house in the country surrounded by mountains, twenty acres of rolling pastures, and cute free range farm friends. I have published several books and have created a thriving business doing what I love to do: supporting other Queens to rise. I know the life I want for my future self already exists too. *How did I access this?* I did it through the power of my imagination, and you can too. As Anais Nin said, *"Had I not created my whole world, I would certainly have died in other people's".*

You, my dear one, are a magical creature, inspiring you to access the life that already exists in your imagination; therefore, your reality is my dream for you so you do not feel as if you will die someone else's.

She AWAKES: Visualising Your Exciting Life into Existence

For this exercise you will need some post-it notes, or a page cut into smaller pieces, a pen, and a jar.

- I invite you to close your eyes and breathe until a state of calm flows through your body.

- Using the imagination prompts I provided you in the exercise on manifesting, fast forward to a time in the not-too-distant future. It could be six months, a year or even eighteen months.

- Allow your imagination to run free and your dreams to dance through the fields of the cortex of your brain.

- Now ask yourself, *'If anything was possible and there were no limits to what you could achieve, what might be possible?'*

- Allow yourself to write down as many of your dreams onto the paper.

- Place your dreams inside the jar.

- Take time to decorate your jar—*take inspiration from how you would like to feel once your dreams have come true. You may want to place a label on your jar that says, "Whatever is inside this jar is..."*

- You may want to anchor this intention with a scent or an aromatherapy oil in your jar.

- Take time every day to visit the dreams in your jar. Pick a dream from your jar and spend a few minutes vividly visualising what it will feel like once this dream has become a reality in your life.

- Then, thank God or the Universe as if it has already happened to you.

Affirmation: *I am an empowered Queen, ready to live my life on my terms.*

it must have been lonely in the darkness

I watched the from shadows
holding my breath
hoping that you would emerge

and you did
slowly
your steps measured
and caution filled

wings in
head down

and when the sun caught the colours on your wing tips
I gasped
as you unfolded your pinions
and took flight

tears of joy pricked my eyes
as I marvelled at
how amazing it is to see you soar

Endings and Celebrations

Dear Wild Heart,

YOU HAVE MADE IT TO THE END. From the bottom of my soul… thank you.

Thank you for bringing me into your inner circle and trusting me to be your guide. But most importantly, thank you for trusting yourself and allowing me to witness the crowning of a brand-new Queen.

Like a proud Queen-mother, I am sitting on the side-lines cheering you on, as I watch you rise and soar.

Take a moment here to hold yourself,
to congratulate yourself
to love yourself
to take in the magnificent **wild authentic knowing empowered** Queen that is *you*.

She AWAKES: Time to Celebrate

In the medieval times, all great quests ended in a celebratory feast. This was a time to tell stories, and to celebrate the joys of being alive.

And I invite you to prepare yourself a feast to mark the end of our quest together. You may want to create this feast for yourself, or you may want to invite other Queens in your life to celebrate with you.

- **Set yourself a beautiful table with your best table linen, candles, flowers and the "good" china and flatware–fit for the Queen that you are.**

- **Create a feast fit for a Queen.**

- **Dine. Relax, savour your meal and the company that you have surrounded yourself with.**

Life is *good!*

there once was a girl who woke up

and discovered that although she still cared about what others thought
she cared more about what she thought

she decided to stop wasting her life
      waiting
            waiting
                  waiting

                        on the side lines

and to rather show up

she lived happily ever after

Into The Treasure Cave

Books to Continue Your Quest With

1.   Doyle, G. (2020). *Untamed.* The Dial Press.

2.   Gilbert, E. (2015). *Big Magic: How to Live a Creative Life and Let Go of Your Fear.* Riverhead Books.

3.   Wambach, A. (2019). *WOLFPACK: How to Come Together, Unleash Our Power, and Change the Game.* Celadon Books N.Y.

4.   Brackett, M. (2020). *Permission to Feel: The Power of Emotional Intelligence to Achieve Well-Being and Success.* Celadon Books N.Y.

5.   Peppernell, C. (2018). *Pillow Thoughts II: Healing the Heart.* Andrews McMeel Publishing.

6.   Katie, B; Mitchell, S. (2002). *Loving What Is: How Four Questions Can Change Your Life.* Random House.

7.   Weaver, L. (2019). *The Invisible Load: A Guide to Overcoming Stress & Overwhelm.* Little Green Frog Publishing Ltd.

8.   Brown, B. (2018). *Dare to Lead: Brave Work. Tough Conversations. Whole Hearts.* Vermilion London.

9.   Ruiz, D.M. (1997). *The Four Agreements: Wisdom Book.* Amber-Allen Publishing California.

10. Clear, J. (2018). *Atomic Habits: An Easy & Proven Way to Build Good Habits & Break Bad Ones.* Random House Business Books.

11. Kessler, D. (2019). *Finding Meaning: The Sixth Stage of Grief.* Random House.

12. Covey, S.R. (1989). *The 7 Habits of Highly Effective People.* Free Press

13. Gottman, J. (2011). *Rising An Emotionally Intelligent Child.* Simon and Schuster.

14. Hoffman, K. Cooper, G. *Powell, B. Raising a Secure Child How Circle of Security Parenting Can Help You Nurture Your Child's Attachment, Emotional Resilience, and Freedom to Explore.* Guilford Publications.

15. Campbell, J. (1990). *The Hero's Journey.* Harper Collins.

16. Collins, J.C. (2001) *Good to Great: Why Some Companies Make the Leap...and Others Don't.* Harper Collins.

17. Lerner, H. (2017). *Why Won't You Apologise? Healing Big Betrayals and Everyday Hurts.* Simon and Schuster.

18. Covey, S.M.R. (2006). *The Speed of Trust: The One Thing That Changes Everything.* New York. Free Press.

19. Green, C. (2017). *She Means Business: Turn Your Ideas into Reality and Become a Wildly Successful Entrepreneur.* Hay House.

20. Kinney, K. Ratzlaff, C. (2010). *Queen of Your Life: The Grown-up Woman's Guide to Claiming Happiness and Getting the Life You Deserve.* Harlequin.

21. Pinkola Estés, C. (1992). *Women Who Run with The Wolves: Contacting the Power of The Wild Woman.* United Kingdom. Rider Books.

22. Brown Taylor, B. (2014). *Learning to Walk in The Dark.* Canterbury Press.

23. Shinola Bolen, J. (2004). *Goddesses in Everywoman: Powerful Archetypes in Women's Lives.* HarperCollins

24. Greenspan, M. (2004). Healing Through the Dark Emotions. Shambhala.

25. Sincero, J. (2013). *You Are a Badass: How to Stop Doubting Your Greatness and Start Living an Awesome Life.* John Murray Learning.

26. Thomashauser, R. (2016). *Pussy: A Reclamation.* Hay House.

27. Duffield-Thomas, D. (2018). *Get Rich, Lucky Bitch! Release Your Money Blocks and Live a First Class Life.* Hay House.

28. Gray, M. (2009). *Red Moon. Understanding and Using the Creative, Sexual and Spiritual Gifts of the Menstrual Cycle.* Dancing Eve.

About the Author

TANYA VALENTIN is a teacher, women's midlife mentor, poet, podcaster and a published author. She is the founder of the **AWAKEN™** mentoring framework and **The Feminine School of Unlearning, an online community for midlife women who are on an awakening journey.**

Tanya supports midlife women who are on an awakening journey to unlearn beliefs and behaviours that no longer serve them so that they can reconnect with and love the woman behind the roles, responsibilities and the weight of other people's expectations.

She lives in beautiful Northland, New Zealand with her husband, three teenage daughters, her dog, three cats, and a collection of happy, cute free-range farm animals. Tanya is committed to co-creating magic in the lives of women so they can discover their purpose, reclaim their joy, find their voice, and live the next half of their lives in a way that feels true to who they authentically are as the magnificent Queen of their own lives.

To work with Tanya or to **Join The Feminine School of Unlearning** go to **https://members.thefeminineschoolofunlearning.com**

Acknowledgements

I would like to say thank you to ALL THE WOMEN WHO INSPIRED ME AND CONTINUE TO INSPIRE ME with the courageous sharing of their stories. Thank you to all the amazing authors and artists that I continue to learn from.

I would like to express my gratitude to LEESA ELLIS for her support and encouragement and for holding my hand and guiding me through the process of getting this book published and out into the world. Thank you to ELIZABETH ANN VAN RIE for polishing my book till it gleamed with her editing.

Thank you to my mentor DEBORAH JOHNSTON for helping me to step into my inner-Queen, and my friend and photographer STACEY MILICH SMITH for capturing my energy so beautifully for the cover of this book.

My deep gratitude to my sisters and dear friends HEIDI ARMISTEAD, NIKKI HAMILTON and TONYA RUSSELL. For your tireless cheerleading, thank you from the bottom of my heart.

Finally, to my husband and partner in life, WAYNE. Thank you for believing in me when I didn't and pushing me when I wanted to give up. Thank you for fussing about me, making me endless cups of tea, and reminding me to eat something when I got lost in my writing.